Writing the Welsh borderlands in Anglo-Saxon England

Manchester University Press

artes liberales

Series Editors

Carrie E. Beneš, T. J. H. McCarthy, Stephen Mossman and Jochen Schenk

Artes Liberales aims to promote the study of the Middle Ages – broadly defined in geography and chronology – from a perspective that transcends modern disciplinary divisions. It seeks to publish scholarship of the highest quality that is interdisciplinary in topic or approach, integrating elements such as history, art history, musicology, literature, religion, political thought, philosophy and science. The series particularly seeks to support research based on the study of original manuscripts and archival sources, and to provide a recognised venue for increased exposure for scholars at all career stages around the world.

Writing the Welsh borderlands in Anglo-Saxon England

Lindy Brady

Manchester University Press

Copyright © Lindy Brady 2017

The right of Lindy Brady to be identified as the author of this work has been asserted by her in accordance with the Copyright, Designs and Patents Act 1988.

Published by Manchester University Press
Altrincham Street, Manchester M1 7JA

www.manchesteruniversitypress.co.uk

British Library Cataloguing-in-Publication Data
A catalogue record for this book is available from the British Library

ISBN   978 1 7849 9419 8   hardback

First published 2017

ISBN   978 1 5261 3932 0   paperback

First published 2019

The publisher has no responsibility for the persistence or accuracy of URLs for any external or third-party internet websites referred to in this book, and does not guarantee that any content on such websites is, or will remain, accurate or appropriate.

Typeset in 10/12 Cormorant by
Servis Filmsetting Ltd, Stockport, Cheshire

To my parents, Ken and Sue Alender

Contents

List of maps	*page* viii
Acknowledgements	ix

1	Introduction: the *Dunsæte Agreement* and daily life in the Welsh borderlands	1
2	Penda of Mercia and the Welsh borderlands in Bede's *Historia Ecclesiastica*	23
3	The Welsh borderlands in the *Lives* of St Guthlac	53
4	The 'dark Welsh' as slaves and slave raiders in Exeter Book riddles 52 and 72	82
5	The Welsh borderlands in the *Anglo-Saxon Chronicle*	109
6	The transformation of the borderlands outlaw in the eleventh century	138
7	Conclusion: Harold Godwinson, the last Anglo-Saxon in the Welsh borderlands	159

Bibliography	171
Index	194

Maps

1 The region of the Welsh borderlands *page* 9
2 Significant battles in Bede's *Historia Ecclesiastica* 25
3 Southern Wales in the tenth century 113

Acknowledgements

This book would not have been possible without the support of so many friends and colleagues over the years. I had no intention of becoming an academic, and I would not be in this profession without the support and encouragement of my undergraduate and MA professors at Brown University, particularly Elizabeth J. Bryan, Ravit Reichman, and Geoffrey R. Russom, whose mentorship continues to this day. I am thankful for the good friends I made during my MA at Brown, especially Corey McEleney and Jay Zysk. The convivial yet rigorous intellectual environment of the University of Connecticut's Medieval Studies Program is the best place I can imagine to write a dissertation, and I am grateful for the ongoing support of all my UConn friends and colleagues, particularly Brandon W. Hawk and Andrew Pfrenger.

I thank UConn's Humanities Institute for awarding me a fellowship in 2011–12 that allowed me to finish writing my dissertation free of teaching obligations, and I thank my fellow UCHI fellows that year for their input and friendship. C. David Benson, Mary Burke, Robert Hasenfratz, and Clare Costley King'oo offered invaluable guidance during my PhD and while I was on the job market. I remain grateful to Brendan Kane for his friendship at UConn and beyond, and for reading, commenting, and thoughtfully discussing many drafts of this book project.

I have been lucky to have written this book in the supportive environment of the University of Mississippi's Department of English, and I am grateful to the many friends and colleagues here — especially Magalí Armillas-Tiseyra, Erin Drew, Cristin Ellis, Melissa Ginsburg, Derrick A. Harriell, Gregory Heyworth, Steven Justice, Chris Offutt, Daniel O'Sullivan, Peter Reed, Daniel Stout, Ian Whittington, and Caroline Wigginton — who have made living and working in Oxford such a pleasure.

Acknowledgements

The A. W. Mellon Postdoctoral Fellowship in Medieval Studies at the University of Notre Dame's Medieval Institute generously provided funding that allowed me to finish writing this book in 2015–16. I am grateful to the Andrew W. Mellon Foundation, the National Endowment for the Humanities, the University of Notre Dame, and the Medieval Institute for this opportunity, as well as to my department chair, Ivo Kamps, and to the College of Liberal Arts at the University of Mississippi for supporting this research leave. At Notre Dame, this project benefitted enormously from the friendship and collegiality of everyone in the Medieval Institute, especially Chris Abram, Kathryn Kerby-Fulton, Tim Machan, Amy Mulligan, and John Van Engen, and all the current and former MI graduate students who became my good friends over the year.

Both my work and life have been enriched in so many ways by fantastic friends in the fields of Anglo-Saxon and Celtic studies. I am particularly grateful to Lori Garner, Shannon Godlove, Ben Guy, Georgia Henley, David F. Johnson, Johanna Kramer, Vicky McAlister, Joey McMullen, M. J. Toswell, Patrick Wadden, and Eric Weiskott; and to Thomas A. Bredehoft and Charles Insley for reading and commenting on drafts of this project. This book would be much poorer without the years-long friendship and mentorship of Elaine Treharne and of Paul Russell, and I am grateful to them and to Andrew Rabin for their incredibly detailed and thoughtful comments on the penultimate draft of this book at the Mellon Colloquium at the University of Notre Dame's Medieval Institute in January 2016.

I could not have finished writing this book without the friendship and encouragement of Joshua Byron Smith and our writing group that came at just the right time. I am so grateful to Josh for his continued support, advice and collaboration. My greatest intellectual debt is to my dissertation director and continued mentor, Fred Biggs. I am so lucky to have worked with him and to have him as a continued supporter and sounding board. He is responsible for every best part of the scholar I am today (and for none of the mistakes!). Finally, this book would not exist without the continued support of my family. I am so grateful to my wonderfully patient husband Tom Brady, who has lived with this project for its entirety, and to Murphy Brady, for unflagging support and encouragement. My sister Sarah Alender and my parents, Ken and Sue Alender, are the ones who encouraged a life-long love of reading and learning. This book would not exist without them, and it is dedicated to them in thanks and love.

Lindy Brady
Oxford, Mississippi
August 2016

1

Introduction: the *Dunsæte Agreement* and daily life in the Welsh borderlands

Sometime in late Anglo-Saxon England, a territory called the Dunsæte was having problems with cattle theft. Men skilled at law from within this community sat down together and drew up a document outlining an agreement that addressed the situation. They thought about what ought to happen in a variety of circumstances. If a man sees the tracks of his stolen cattle leave his own property and cross into his neighbour's land, who is responsible for following the trail and trying to recover the animals at that point? What type of oath is sufficient to prove someone's innocence? What is the monetary value of the stolen cattle, or of other commonly pilfered animals such as horses, pigs, sheep or goats? Who in the community should arbitrate between the parties involved in these disputes? (The *Dunsæte Agreement* refers to *man/mon* and *men*, and it seems almost certain that those who wrote it down *were* men. However, *mon* can also mean 'anyone' and it is clear that the agreement applied to the whole community. If I write about a man tracking down his cattle, that is because it almost always *was* a man, but women too might have owned cattle and made use of the agreement.)

The types of problem faced by the men who wrote the *Dunsæte Agreement* were not unusual in early medieval Britain,[1] and neither were most of the solutions they decided upon.[2] What sets the *Dunsæte Agreement* apart from other Anglo-Saxon law codes grappling with cattle theft is that the men who created this document, and the community that it concerns, included both Anglo-Saxons and Welsh. The text's prologue states that 'Þis is seo gerædnes, þe Angelcynnes witan and Wealhþeode rædboran betweox Dunsetan gesetton' (this is the agreement which the advisers of the English and the counsellors of the Welsh put in place among the Dunsæte).[3]

We know nothing about this community apart from the information in the *Dunsæte Agreement* itself, but the details it reveals are intriguing. The territory of the Dunsæte was centred on a river,[4] which cattle thieves seem to have been using to their advantage, to judge from the text's outlining of the proper procedure 'Gif mon trode bedrifð forstolenes yrfes of stæðe on oðer' (if a man follows the track of stolen cattle from one riverbank to the other).[5] We know that the community's Welsh and Anglo-Saxon inhabitants lived on opposite banks of the river from the proviso that 'Nah naðer to farenne ne Wyliscman on Ænglisclund ne Ænglisc on Wylisc þe ma, butan gesettan landmen, se hine sceal æt stæðe underfon, and eft þær butan facne gebringan' (a Welshman is not allowed to travel into English territory, nor an Englishman into Welsh territory either, unless men who live in that territory are put in place who will receive him at the bank and bring him back without deceit).[6] Men living in these English and Welsh districts appear to have had few reservations about colluding with one another in cattle theft, as the document outlines the penalty for 'ælc þe gewita oððe gewryhta si, þær utlendisc man inlendiscan derie' (anyone who knows or engages when a stranger harms a native).[7] Finally, we can narrow down the approximate location of the Dunsæte territory (see Map 1) to the River Wye between Monmouth and Hereford,[8] from the *Agreement*'s final clause stating that 'Hwilon Wentsæte hyrdon into Dunsætan, ac hit gebyreð rihtor into Westsexan' (at one point the people of Gwent belonged to the Dunsæte, but that territory belongs more rightly to the West Saxons).[9]

The *Dunsæte Agreement* raises intriguing questions. When so few historical documents from Anglo-Saxon England survive, how can we tell whether the circumstances of this mixed Welsh and Anglo-Saxon community were typical or extraordinary? What was everyday life like in the Dunsæte territory? What language did the 'Angelcynnes witan and Wealhþeode rædboran' use to communicate – Old English, Welsh, Latin or a *lingua franca*? For that matter, what language did they use to draft this document? The *Dunsæte Agreement* is preserved in one copy in Cambridge, Corpus Christi College MS, 383, an important early twelfth-century compilation of Anglo-Saxon legal material, and it later became one of the many Old English legal documents translated into Latin as part of the *Quadripartitus*.[10] Could there have been an original Latin copy of the *Dunsæte Agreement*, or perhaps a Welsh version parallel to the Old English? The *Agreement* describes how 'XII lahmen scylon riht tæcean Wealan and Ænglan, VI Engliscne and VI Wylisce' (twelve lawmen shall proclaim what is just for Welsh and English: six Englishmen and six Welshmen).[11] Who were these *lahmen*? The word is a Scandinavian borrowing known only from this text, although its Latin equivalent, *lagemanni*, appears in a few legal documents written after 1066.[12]

2

Introduction: the Dunsæte Agreement

Were they the same people as the 'Angelcynnes witan and Wealhþeode rædboran' who drafted the *Dunsæte Agreement*? It is unclear if the text implies any practical difference between the *witan* and *rædboran* – both terms were used throughout the Old English corpus to indicate counsellors, often legal ones, with *rædbora* glossing *jurisperitus*.[13] Could anyone living within the Dunsæte territory be a *lahmann*, or did these men hold permanent positions as legal advisers to their community?

These fascinating questions lead to deeper observations that challenge modern critical assumptions about the relationship between the Anglo-Saxon and Welsh peoples in early medieval Britain, which has been understood as one of warfare and mutual hostility. The community that we can glimpse through the *Dunsæte Agreement* is, of course, not a multicultural utopia – cattle theft appears rampant, there is distrust between neighbours, and provisions for the amount of *wergild* due 'Gif Wealh Engliscne man ofslea' (if a Welshman were to slay an Englishman) or vice versa hint at violence far darker than cattle rustling.[14] Yet at the same time, the *Dunsæte Agreement* reveals a community that worked together to solve its problems, had a system of legal rights and responsibilities for all its members, and possessed a functional level of both linguistic and legal comprehension between its Anglo-Saxon and Welsh inhabitants. Most significantly, even though the surviving text is written in Old English from the perspective of the Anglo-Saxon inhabitants of this region, the *Dunsæte Agreement* reflects complete Anglo-Welsh equality at every turn – its penultimate clause, after laying out the procedure for warranty, takes care to emphasise that 'Gelice þam Ænglisc sceal Wyliscan rihte wyrcean' (likewise must an Englishman undertake what is right for a Welshman).[15] The Dunsæte territory was a community where Anglo-Saxons and Welsh lived together, treated one another as equals, and worked together to sustain peace.

This book explores communities in early medieval Britain like the territory of the Dunsæte that were part of a broader region where Anglo-Saxons and Welsh lived in close proximity for hundreds of years. This region has a different story to tell about the relationship between these peoples than most historical narratives from the Anglo-Saxon period, which were in large part written by educated elites, at a geographical and temporal remove from the events they described and with the benefit of hindsight. The arrival of the Anglo-Saxons in Britain looks like a military conquest when viewed from the perspective of ninth-century Wessex, where the *Anglo-Saxon Chronicle* was likely begun, or eighth-century Northumbria, where Bede wrote his *Historia Ecclesiastica Gentis Anglorum*. But for those in the region inhabited by both Welsh and Anglo-Saxons for several centuries

– the western territories of the Anglo-Saxon kingdom of Mercia and the eastern portions of the northern Welsh kingdoms of Gwynedd and Powys – warfare was not a daily reality. Even in those texts that have been understood to exhibit Anglo/Welsh conflict on a broad scale, this region – the Welsh borderlands – can be seen functioning differently.[16]

The *Dunsæte Agreement* illustrates how the Welsh borderlands were different from other Anglo-Saxon and Welsh kingdoms in more ways than their reflection of Anglo-Welsh equality. As Michael Fordham and George Molyneaux have independently argued, this document places a high value on compromise and peacekeeping.[17] In so doing, the *Dunsæte Agreement* distinguishes itself from contemporary Anglo-Saxon and Welsh law codes, lacking many of their common features. Another strikingly unique feature of this text is its fusion of Anglo-Saxon and Welsh legal customs. In its legal singularity, the *Dunsæte Agreement* appears most analogous to the post-Conquest Law of the March of Wales, a hybrid system of frontier law. Within the *Dunsæte Agreement*, we can see some of the qualities that made the Welsh borderlands region distinctive during the Anglo-Saxon period.

The *Dunsæte Agreement* is an unofficial memorandum of understanding drawn up within a community, not an official royal law code. Nonetheless, its careful emphasis on Anglo-Welsh equality sets this text apart from other contemporary Anglo-Saxon legal practices.[18] We do not know precisely when the *Dunsæte Agreement* was written. It has traditionally been dated to the first quarter of the tenth century by Felix Liebermann and most subsequent scholars, but George Molyneaux has recently made a convincing argument for a late tenth- or eleventh-century date instead.[19] Yet despite its origins in the late Anglo-Saxon period, the *Dunsæte Agreement* shows no evidence of influence by Ine's laws, even though they were still valid in the tenth century via their preservation in Alfred's *domboc* and the *Norðleoda laga*.[20] Ine's laws are notorious for an ethnically tiered system of *wergilds*, in which Britons appear to be valued significantly less than their Anglo-Saxon counterparts in social rank. They are most often interpreted as casting the Britons in an 'inferior social position', creating a 'sense of ethnic superiority on the part of the Saxons' in which 'the "otherness" of the Britons' is emphasised 'in order to manufacture a more unified West Saxon society'.[21] The *Dunsæte Agreement* is unlike contemporary Anglo-Saxon law codes influenced by Ine's laws in reflecting Anglo-Welsh equality, rather than disparate *wergilds* based on ethnicity. Indeed, the same holds true from a Welsh perspective, since the legal status of an *alltud* (alien or foreigner, literally 'someone of another people') was likewise distinguished from that of a native.[22] The distinctions between 'foreigners' and 'natives' in other

Introduction: the Dunsæte Agreement

Welsh and Anglo-Saxon law codes and the lack of such differentiation in the *Dunsæte Agreement* set it outside evident contemporary legal norms.

The Anglo-Welsh equality in the *Dunsæte Agreement* is also one of several indications that this community placed a higher value on peaceful resolution of conflicts than on reaffirming social status. While it is easy to see how codified inequality like that of Ine's laws could lead to Anglo/Welsh resentment and conflict, the impartiality of the *Dunsæte Agreement* underscores the structure of this community as one of equitable coexistence. Further indication that the Dunsæte territory prioritised peacekeeping comes from the *Agreement*'s 'deliberately modest'[23] penalties, which are significantly less than those in contemporary Anglo-Saxon and Welsh legal codes. Clause 4 of this document lays out a penalty for a failed defence that by its own admission is lighter than normal: 'Þeah æt stæltyhtlan lad teorie, Ængliscan oððe Wiliscan, gylde angyldes þæt he mid beled wæs. Þæs oðres gyldes nan þing, ne þæs wites þe ma' (Even when a defence against a charge of theft should fail, for an Englishman or for a Welshman, let him pay a single compensation for what he was charged with; there should be no additional payment at all, nor a penalty either).[24] The penalty for killing someone is also lighter than usual, regardless of the victim's social rank. The *Dunsæte Agreement* explains that, 'Gif Wealh Engliscne man ofslea, ne þearf he hine hidenofer buton be healfan were gyldan, ne Ænglisc Wyliscne geonofer þe ma, sy he þegenboren sy he ceorlboren; healf wer þær ætfealð' (If a Welshman were to slay an Englishman, there is no obligation on him to give hither [this bank] any more than half a *wergild*, nor an Englishman any more thither [opposite bank] for a Welshman; if he is born a thegn or if he is born a ceorl, half the *wergild* falls away).[25]

As Michael Fordham has argued, these provisos suggest that the *Dunsæte Agreement* was intended to facilitate the rapid resolution of disputes, because lighter penalties 'would have allowed for faster settlement, in that a lower wergeld price would be easier to raise'.[26] These equitably reduced penalties again distinguish the *Dunsæte Agreement* from contemporary Anglo-Saxon and Welsh legal traditions, in which social rank was what determined a person's *wergild* in Anglo-Saxon England or *galanas* in Wales.[27] Such unusually modest penalties driven by practical considerations reflect a community that prioritised peace over social status.

Those features of the *Dunsæte Agreement* which underscore its prioritisation of peacekeeping are legally distinctive. So too is what seems to be its mixture of Welsh and Anglo-Saxon legal customs. Molyneaux has recently noted a likely 'degree of fusion between English and Welsh legal practices' in the *Dunsæte Agreement*'s nine-day time limits,[28] a period of time which is unusual in Anglo-Saxon laws but very common in Welsh ones.[29] T.M. Charles-Edwards has also pointed to the *Dunsæte Agreement* as a 'context in which English law might influence Welsh law'.[30] In blending Anglo-Saxon and Welsh legal practices, the *Dunsæte Agreement* is analogous to the post-1066 law of the March of Wales. The most important defining feature of this region was its recognised status as legally exceptional[31] – even in Anglo-Norman literature, as Ralph Hanna has recently noted, the March is depicted as 'cowboy country' not because of lawlessness per se, but because of its 'specific unique legal status'.[32] The law of the March was defined by its distinction from the laws of England and Wales, and in practice its singularity stemmed from its amalgamation of Welsh and English law.[33] The more that the legal anomalies in the *Dunsæte Agreement* are explored, the more they resemble our understanding of how known frontier laws worked. As Rees Davies – the foremost historian of the March of Wales in the Anglo-Norman period – writes, 'marcher law provided a series of local, working solutions to the problems of a frontier society … where two peoples met and overlapped'.[34] The *Dunsæte Agreement* reflects a parallel structure of compromise, flexibility and blending of Anglo-Saxon and Welsh legal customs in the Welsh borderlands during the Anglo-Saxon period. The glimpse of daily life in this region illuminated by the *Dunsæte Agreement* helps us to understand its representation as culturally discrete in contemporary Anglo-Saxon and Welsh texts.

Writing the Welsh borderlands in Anglo-Saxon England

Two deceptively simple questions stand at the heart of this book: what were interactions between the Anglo-Saxon and Welsh peoples in early medieval Britain like, and how are they depicted in the surviving textual record? There is no doubt that the answer to both questions often involved a great deal of violence. The *Anglo-Saxon Chronicle* entry for 473, 'Her Hengest 7 Æsc gefuhton wiþ Walas 7 genamon unarimedlico herereaf, 7 þa Walas flugon þa Englan swa [þer] fyr'[35] (here Hengest and Æsc fought the Welsh and took innumerable spoil, and the Welsh fled the English like fire) and a line from the Middle Welsh prophetic poem *Armes Prydein*, 'Saesson rac Brython gwae a genyn' (the Saxons will sing their lamentation before the Britons)[36] are good illustrations of why the traditional critical narrative has been that 'when they recorded their past, the Anglo-Saxons and the Britons presented themselves as races apart'.[37] Anglo-Saxon literature in particular has been seen to present an 'unremittingly bellicose narrative' of Anglo/Welsh relations.[38]

Introduction: the Dunsæte Agreement

Yet recent work by historians and archaeologists has underscored the disparity between written records of a violent Anglo-Saxon 'invasion' or 'conquest' and the likely reality of a gradual, piecemeal migration, with fairly amicable Anglo/Welsh relations, in this early period;[39] and, in later Anglo-Saxon England, alliances between individual Welsh and Anglo-Saxon rulers have been long acknowledged.[40] This book brings these practical perspectives on quotidian relations between Anglo-Saxons and Welsh in early medieval Britain to bear on the textual record and discovers that moments like the *Dunsæte Agreement* of mixed Anglo-Welsh community are more widespread than has been recognised and significantly alter our current picture of Anglo/Welsh relations before the Norman Conquest. *Writing the Welsh Borderlands in Anglo-Saxon England* overturns the long-standing critical belief that Anglo/Welsh relations in the Anglo-Saxon period were predominantly contentious. The Welsh borderlands were a mixture of Anglo-Saxons and Welsh, and contemporary texts depicted the region as a highly distinctive place.

One of the reasons why this has not been previously elucidated is the lingering impact of a critical moment in which postcolonial theory was applied to medieval literature in very narrow ways.[41] While it is valuable to interrogate the inequalities potentially embedded within cultural difference, most postcolonial studies of Anglo/Welsh relations to date have begun from the premise that the Edwardian conquest of Wales in the late thirteenth century was a foregone conclusion. When Old English texts are seen to reflect the 'formulation of Anglo-Saxon unity constructed against a British inferiority', the Anglo-Saxons become singleminded conquerors while the Welsh are hopelessly subjugated, and both peoples are understood to have defined themselves antagonistically, through a very modern conceptualisation of ethnic difference.[42] Another problem for postcolonial readings of the early Anglo-Saxon period has been that the Welsh are cast as subaltern without an accompanying analysis of Welsh-language material,[43] meaning Anglo-Welsh relations are viewed solely from the perspective of Old English and Anglo-Latin texts.[44] A central premise of this book is that defining identity oppositionally within an Anglo/Welsh binary system results in an incomplete picture not only of Anglo-Welsh interactions in early medieval Britain, but also of the ways in which Anglo-Saxon texts depicted them. The Welsh are not always characterised as an enemy 'other' – or, at least, no more so than are those Anglo-Saxons with whom they shared a common culture in the borderlands.

This book is about textual depictions of the Welsh borderlands, not the Welsh themselves, and so it does not catalogue every appearance of the

Welsh in Anglo-Saxon literary or historical records. Its focus is the Welsh borderlands alone and not frontiers between other Anglo-Saxon kingdoms or between England and Scotland. Although the Welsh and Scottish frontiers after 1066 shared some cultural similarities, as most frontier societies do, their histories were also very different because there was never a Norman military conquest of Scotland in the same way as was the case in Wales, and so the Scottish frontier did not experience the same type of violence as did Wales during this period. A comparison of the Welsh and Scottish borderlands in the Anglo-Saxon period would be a valuable study but a difficult undertaking because so little Anglo-Saxon material about the Scottish frontier survives, and it is unfortunately beyond the scope of the present book.[45]

Rather, this book's focus is the region in western Anglo-Saxon England and eastern Wales, at the feet of the Cambrian mountains, where the peoples who comprised the Anglo-Saxon kingdom of Mercia and the northern Welsh kingdoms of Gwynedd and Powys lived in close proximity to one another for centuries. This region encompassed some of the same geographical space as the March of Wales in the Anglo-Norman period[46] but, unlike that territory, it was not formally recognised as an entity by any Anglo-Saxon or Welsh kingdoms. While the post-1066 March of Wales was itself in many ways geographically nebulous, it was nonetheless a region defined by specific geographical, temporal and political conditions related to the Norman presence in England – Max Lieberman, for example, defines a march as 'a territory under the command of a select group of border lords'.[47] To avoid anachronism, I will not describe the region discussed in this book as a march. While the name of the Anglo-Saxon kingdom of Mercia means 'the border/boundary people' and is the etymon of the later Anglo-Norman *marche*, there is also an important distinction to be drawn between this kingdom – a territory which at one point spanned the whole of the Midlands – and its western portion which shared cultural contact with the Welsh. For these reasons, I will use the phrase 'the Welsh borderlands' to refer to this amorphous territory at the foot of the Cambrian mountains where the Anglo-Saxons of western Mercia and the Welsh of eastern Gwynedd and Powys came together.

The concept of the 'borderlands', drawing on Gloria Anzaldúa's foundational work *Borderlands/La Frontera: The New Mestiza*,[48] aptly characterises this region in ways that other terminology cannot. Words like 'border' or 'boundary' imply lines on a map that did not exist in early medieval Britain, where kingdoms were centred around tribes and where territories shifted often. As many excellent recent studies have made clear, medieval frontiers

Introduction: the Dunsæte Agreement

Map 1 The region of the Welsh borderlands[49]

were often places where cultures were not separated, but blended together in various ways.[50] In the introduction to his significant collection of essays, *Borders, Barriers, and Ethnogenesis: Frontiers in Late Antiquity and the Middle Ages*, Florin Curta notes the crucial shift in recent decades of frontier scholarship away from the 'frontier-as-barrier' concept and towards an understanding of frontiers as important zones of cultural exchange.[51] The role of medieval frontiers in creating rather than dividing cultures underlies Robert Bartlett's argument for the importance of hundreds of individual frontier zones in the eventual coalescence of western Europe.[52]

However, the word 'frontier' itself is an inadequate characterisation of the situation in the Anglo-Welsh borderlands prior to 1066. Medieval frontier societies could of course vary widely, as David Abulafia has usefully outlined in the introduction to his and Nora Berend's collection, *Medieval Frontiers: Concepts and Practices*.[53] Yet, as Daniel Power explains in the introduction to his and Naomi Standen's important volume *Frontiers in Question: Eurasian Borderlands, 700-1700*, the term 'frontier' holds two distinct meanings in British and North American English. In British English, a frontier has been a 'political barrier between states or peoples, often militarised' while in North America the concept has come to mean 'not a barrier but a zone of passage and a land of opportunity, involving conflict with the natural environment rather than neighbours'.[54] Power helpfully relabels these concepts as 'political frontiers' and 'frontiers of settlement'.

The Welsh borderlands during the Anglo-Saxon period were closer to the North American concept of a 'frontier of settlement' than a political frontier in that the region was defined by no official military or political border. Yet it is important to bear in mind that the concept of a 'frontier of settlement' encompasses to some degree the myth that early American settlers moved west into an area that was largely wilderness, largely glossing over the Native Americans whose lands were consumed in the process. In early Britain, those Anglo-Saxons who came to inhabit the Welsh borderlands encountered not wilderness but another people. While indebted to a group of recent studies examining the ways in which medieval identities were often constructed in relationship to the landscapes people inhabited,[55] this book's focus is on both land and people. It explores the ways in which the particular region of the borderlands, where Anglo-Saxons and Welsh came together, produced a culture different from those around them.

The Welsh borderlands were not based on a kingdom or a tribe; they were a zone of mutual influence in which Anglo-Saxon and Welsh peoples both lived. This territory was neither a military frontier nor an economic hinterland to the rest of Anglo-Saxon England or medieval Wales – both of which, it must be remembered, did not yet exist as concepts. Rather, this was a region that looked both ways: it formed the borderlands between Anglo-Saxon and Welsh kingdoms, and between Welsh and Anglo-Saxon ones. The borderlands are the region that emerges when following Michiel Baud and Willem van Schendel's argument for 'a view from the periphery' rather than the centre(s).[56] The Welsh borderlands were a nebulous, undefined territory whose geography shifted over time, yet the region retained its identity as a concept – a cultural zone where two peoples came together – for several hundred years over the course of the Anglo-Saxon period.

In this book, I define the Welsh borderlands as a cultural nexus. By this, I mean a region where two peoples and two cultures came together relatively equitably for a long period of time, and out of that region's role as a nexus between Welsh and Mercian cultures something new and distinctive emerged. Some terminological clarification is in order. In order to avoid anachronism, I am deliberately avoiding the use of words with modern political connotations, like 'diverse', 'multicultural' or 'melting pot', to describe the cultural qualities of this region. Neither would it be accurate to characterise the Welsh borderlands as a place of cultural syncretism or pluralism, as these terms imply a power imbalance between dominant and subordinate cultures which did not exist at this time. The postcolonial concept of hybridity developed by Homi K. Bhabha is an important one in understanding multicultural societies.[57] However, because the word 'hybrid' was used to signify monstrosity – either literally or for racist purposes – in medieval (and modern) writings, I will not be using it here. More importantly, Bhabha's reclaiming of this term is predicated upon the power imbalance of a society divided into coloniser and colonised, and requires a sense of self-awareness and agency on the part of the hybrid subaltern that did not exist in the Welsh borderlands. The region that this book describes was not formed as the result of a military conquest, and so the cultural hierarchy upon which Bhabha's concept of hybridity rests was not present at this time.

The Welsh borderlands during the Anglo-Saxon period were simply a place where two peoples came together. It can perhaps be best envisioned as a distinctive cultural estuary where Welsh influence flowed in from the west and Mercian from the east. As the balance of saltwater and freshwater in an estuary at any given moment ebbs and flows with the tide, so too did the degree of Welsh or Mercian influence in the region of the Welsh borderlands fluctuate over time with the rise and fall of individual tribes, families or rulers. Yet, like an estuary, some degree of cultural mixing was always at work in this region. Simon Meecham-Jones has coined the apt phrase 'the Welsh penumbra' to describe the similar zone of 'profound cultural contact' between English and Welsh that existed without any official designation in Anglo-Norman and later medieval England.[58] Crucially, Meecham-Jones's concept of the 'Welsh penumbra' both distinguishes a zone of cultural influence from one of military aggression and recognises that those inside this zone were in some ways distinct from the rest of late medieval England. In early medieval Britain, the Welsh borderlands were uniquely a place where two peoples lived together relatively peacefully for a very long period of time. In its varying yet consistent drawing together of Welsh and Mercian influences, the region of the Welsh borderlands formed a singular nexus of Anglo-Welsh culture.

This book is a study of how the Welsh borderlands before 1066 were depicted in literary and historical texts from early medieval Britain. Its chapters draw together, in chronological order, the corpus of those Anglo-Saxon narrative works that contain the most sustained discussions of this region. By narrative texts as opposed to documentary material, I mean a category of writing which was in some way undertaken to tell a story intended for a broader audience rather than record a business transaction between two parties. Included in this definition are works of poetry, history and hagiography, whereas charters, wills and letters are omitted from this study, with the exception of the *Dunsæte Agreement* discussed in this introduction as framework.

This distinction between narrative and documentary texts is admittedly somewhat artificial. Many narrative chronicles of monastic foundation consider documentary material such as charters and letters to be central to their stories, for instance, while charters and legal documents can encapsulate quite lively narratives indeed. Still, this book as a whole focuses on narrative rather than documentary texts for a few reasons. The first is that – while no other monograph focused on the region of the Anglo-Welsh borderlands has yet been written – individual studies by historians and archaeologists have reviewed the documentary material well enough to make clear the historical reality that this region was not a site of sustained warfare throughout the Anglo-Saxon period.[59] My interest in narrative texts is driven by the critical consensus among historians that there is nonetheless a significant disparity between the reality of Anglo/Welsh relations 'on the ground' in the border areas and the ways in which Anglo-Saxon texts depict those relations. A sustained focus on narrative texts from Anglo-Saxon England reveals that, when it comes to their depiction of the Welsh borderlands, these texts present a more accurate picture of the region than they have been given credit for.

The works studied in these chapters represent a range of genres – saints' lives, historical chronicles, popular poetry – and each was created for a different purpose. However, these texts have some important characteristics in common. They were written and set in Anglo-Saxon England, have some sustained focus on Wales and have traditionally been interpreted as reflecting a clear, and adversarial, Anglo/Welsh divide. From this diverse

Introduction: the Dunsæte Agreement

corpus emerges a picture of the Welsh borderlands as a nexus of Anglo-Welsh culture. These texts depict the borderlands differently from the rest of Wales: not as the site of Anglo/Welsh strife, but as a distinct region. Contemporary Welsh material represents this territory with the same singularity looking east as Anglo-Saxon works do looking west. I present this material in chronological order to show the region's persistence as a distinct cultural entity throughout the Anglo-Saxon period.

I begin with one of the earliest and most historically significant surviving Anglo-Saxon texts, Bede's *Historia Ecclesiastica Gentis Anglorum*. Chapter Two argues that Bede's narrative of Anglo-Saxon religious and ethnic cohesion also depicts a distinct culture in the borderlands in the seventh century, shared between the Anglo-Saxon kingdom of Mercia and the Welsh kingdoms of Gwynedd and Powys, a cohesion formed in opposition to cultural changes brought about by the conversion of surrounding Anglo-Saxon kingdoms to Roman Christianity. Bede has long been understood as highly critical of both the heretical Britons and the heathen Mercians, but in his hostility he preserves important details about the life of King Penda of Mercia which provide a window into the culture of the borderlands as a region that stands apart from Bede's narrative of ethnic division between Anglo-Saxons and Britons. Several early Welsh poems reflect the same perspective from the west: the borderlands not as a site of strife, but as a nexus of Anglo-Welsh culture.

The book's third chapter moves forward in time to an eighth-century setting and shifts from history to hagiography, focusing on a corpus of Old English and Latin works about the popular Anglo-Saxon saint Guthlac of Crowland (673–714) whose Mercian youth and later career as a hermit in the Fens of eastern England link him indelibly to two of Britain's most nebulous geographical spaces. I argue first that the various *Lives* of Guthlac depict the borderlands as a locus of military advancement for Mercian and Welsh elites. As in Bede's *Historia Ecclesiastica*, this region is a place where a young Mercian warrior can advance his career by living among the British and leading a multi-ethnic war band, features of military life in the borderlands that are also evident in contemporary Welsh and Cambro-Latin texts. The geographically fluid nature of this region is also evident in this chapter's second significant argument: that, even within this Anglo-Saxon saint's life, the politics of land control are much less clear-cut than has been assumed. While St Guthlac's battles with demons have been understood to reflect Anglo/Welsh ethnic division, this chapter argues that the Old English poem *Guthlac A* is far more conflicted towards land ownership, reflecting the fluid boundaries of Mercia itself.

Chapter Four examines some depictions of the Welsh borderlands in anonymous, popular literary tradition, arguing that a group of Old English riddles located on the *mearc* (march or boundary) between Anglo-Saxon England and Wales reflect a common regional culture by depicting shared values of a warrior elite across the ostensible Anglo-Welsh divide. These riddles, which link the 'dark Welsh' to agricultural labour, have long been understood to depict the Welsh as slaves and thus reflect Anglo-Saxon awareness of both ethnic and social division. Drawing upon understudied Welsh legal material, this chapter argues that these riddles have a multilayered solution in which the Welsh are both slaves and slave traders, complicating readings of negative Anglo/Welsh relations. This polysemic solution reveals that the Welsh, like the Anglo-Saxons, were stratified by class into the enslaved and a warrior elite, with less distance between the two elites than has been understood. The location of these riddles on the *mearc* further characterises the Welsh borderlands in the early period as a distinctive region, which – like the later March of Wales – was notorious for cattle raiding. Coupled with archaeological evidence of drove roads, these riddles counter the common perception that the Welsh borderlands in Anglo-Saxon England were defined by Offa's Dyke, suggesting that this region is better understood as a space that both Anglo-Saxons and Welsh permeated in raiding or trading.

The last two main chapters of the book return to historical chronicles and explore the Welsh borderlands as a distinct region in the later Anglo-Saxon period. Chapter Five argues for a significant pattern of political alliance in the Welsh borderlands during this time, beginning in the tenth century, when half a dozen raids were carried out jointly by Mercian earls and northern Welsh rulers have gone unnoticed because they are recorded largely in Welsh sources. This pattern of political cohesion within the Welsh borderlands continues in the *Anglo-Saxon Chronicle* throughout the eleventh century, both before and after the impact of 1066. The *Anglo-Saxon Chronicle* represents the Welsh borderlands as a region which acted as an independent political force throughout the eleventh century.

Chapter Five also argues that the *Anglo-Saxon Chronicle* represents the military culture of the Welsh borderlands in a distinctive way which aligns its inhabitants with outlaws. By the end of the eleventh century, this region had undergone a significant shift in representation from a distinct territory with a singular style of fighting to a place linked particularly with outlawry. Chapter Six explores the transitional moment between these conceptualisations of the borderlands through an extended study of the *Peterborough Chronicle*, the recension of the *Anglo-Saxon Chronicle* continued

Introduction: the Dunsæte Agreement

for the longest period after the Norman Conquest. This text marks the beginning of an important conceptual shift in which a culture of outlawry moved from the mixed Anglo-Welsh inhabitants of the borderlands to the Welsh alone by the end of the eleventh century, underscoring the impact of the Norman presence on the culture of this region.

I conclude with the Latin *Life of Harold Godwinson*, an understudied text set during the transition from Anglo-Saxon to Anglo-Norman England. The *Vita Haroldi* continues to depict the Welsh borderlands as a distinctive territory where two peoples came together across the temporal divide of the Norman Conquest. This work claims that Harold was not killed at the Battle of Hastings, but survived and lived for many years afterwards disguised as a hermit in the Welsh borderlands, a place of obscurity. Harold's curious *Vita* is a fitting microcosm of this book. The Welsh borderlands serve as the cultural intersection between Anglo-Saxon and Anglo-Norman England, the last place where English identity is preserved after the Norman arrival. Yet Harold, the last Anglo-Saxon, can survive only in the borderlands, a cultural nexus of Anglo-Saxon and Welsh. The *Vita Haroldi* underscores the reputation of the Welsh borderlands as a distinct region where two peoples came together, even from a perspective of longing for a lost English past after the Norman Conquest.

This book alters our understanding of how the Anglo-Saxons and Welsh interacted with one another in the centuries before the Normans arrived. Its conclusions also suggest that some of the singular characteristics of the region that would later become the March of Wales began to take shape during the Anglo-Saxon period. The March has traditionally been understood as a product of 'the character and chronology of the Anglo-Norman penetration and conquest of Wales',[60] created when necessity compelled the new rulers of England to grant a greater degree of legal and political autonomy to those lords living along its tumultuous western border.[61] A good deal of surviving documentary material from the Anglo-Norman period[62] makes clear that the March of Wales, 'a land which lay between Wales and England, attached to each of them but separate from both',[63] was a distinct territory, 'indeterminate in its status, laws, and governance', with 'its own recognizable and recognized habits and institutions'.[64] I am not suggesting that the 'March of Wales' as a legal entity existed before its designation by the Normans. However, I do think that both our comfort with 1066 as a historical, linguistic and disciplinary boundary and the comparative wealth of surviving texts from the Anglo-Norman period have obscured cultural commonalities between the Welsh borderlands in the Anglo-Saxon period and the later March of Wales.[65] A number of

Anglo-Saxon and Welsh texts written before the Norman arrival represent a similar geographical area in similar ways – as a region with both Anglo-Saxon and Welsh inhabitants which was somehow different from other Anglo-Saxon and Welsh kingdoms. The culture of the Welsh borderlands in the Anglo-Saxon period appears to have paved the way for some of the later cultural singularity of the March of Wales.

At the same time, the March of Wales in the Anglo-Norman period was no multicultural utopia either. It was formed as the direct result of a royal policy intended to encourage military aggression towards Wales which 'had decisively altered the military balance of strength; after this a new intensification of the process of cultural invasion began'.[66] As Simon Meecham-Jones has argued, the story of Welsh conquest has been written as a foregone conclusion in both medieval and modern times: 'the process of absorbing the land of Wales into an English political superstructure seems to have represented so obvious a conclusion, for English medieval writers, and for later historians and literary critics commenting on their work, that the lack of any reflection by medieval authors on the process of subjugation and colonization being undertaken in Wales has gone unremarked'.[67] Lost too in this silence of historical commentary on the Norman and Edwardian conquest of Wales is a sense of how much else vanished with the Norman arrival.

The existence of the Welsh borderlands in the Anglo-Saxon period evinces the full impact of the Norman Conquest and what else was erased in its wake apart from Englishness. The region of the Welsh borderlands was much more culturally coherent, and the impact of the Norman Conquest on it much greater, than has been realised. This background sharpens the contrast between England's violence towards Wales in the later medieval period and the mixed culture that had been there before. Much scholarship on the Norman Conquest has focused on its destruction or suppression of English culture. This book articulates a discernible culture in the Welsh borderlands prior to 1066, revealing a new facet of the Norman impact on England. It was not just Englishness that was affected by the Norman arrival, but also a mixed Anglo-Welsh culture in the borderlands, suggesting that the damage done by the Conquest resulted in sharper divisions between English and Welsh after 1066 than had existed before.

Notes

1 The text of the *Dunsæte Agreement* is printed in Felix Liebermann, *Die Gesetze der Angelsachsen*, 3 vols. (Halle: Niemeyer, 1903–16), I, 358–63, and all quota-

tions are from this edition by clause and line number (except for the prologue), cited as *Dunsæte*. This document is usually referred to as the *Dunsæte Ordinance* or *Ordinance concerning the Dunsæte*, but I am calling it the *Dunsæte Agreement* because 'Ordinance' gives the impression of an official law code when this was actually a memorandum of understanding drawn up within a community. The text is translated with facing-page facsimile in Frank Noble, *Offa's Dyke Reviewed*, ed. Margaret Gelling, BAR, Brit. Ser. 114 (Oxford: BAR, 1983), 105–9, and translated and discussed by T. M. Charles-Edwards, 'The three columns of law: a comparative perspective', in *Tair Colofn Cyfraith: The Three Columns of Law in Medieval Wales: Homicide, Theft and Fire*, ed. T. M. Charles-Edwards and Paul Russell, Cymdeithas Hanes Cyfraith Cymru 5 (Bangor: Cymdeithas Hanes Cyfraith Cymru, 2005): 26–59 at 53–9.

2   See Carole Hough, 'Cattle-tracking in the Fonthill letter', *English Historical Review* 115 (2000): 864–92, for more on cattle rustling in Anglo-Saxon England. As she discusses, procedures for cattle-tracking are also outlined in the Anglo-Saxon law codes II Edward 4, V Æthelstan 2, III Edmund 6 and VI Æthelstan 8,4, with further continental parallels.

3   *Dunsæte* Prologue. George Molyneaux, 'The Ordinance concerning the Dunsæte and the Welsh frontier in the late tenth and eleventh centuries', *Anglo-Saxon England* 40 (2012): 249–72 at 268 notes that the word *gerædnes* 'was used to refer to the London peace regulations of Æthelstan's reign, the *Hundred Ordinance*, *Edward and Guthrum* and several legal texts in the names of Edgar, Æthelred and Cnut; by contrast, *Alfred and Guthrum* and *II Æthelred*, which were both agreed in response to conflicts, call themselves *frið* ('peace') and *friðmal* ('agreement of peace') respectively'.

4   As Max Lieberman, *The Medieval March of Wales: The Creation and Perception of a Frontier, 1066–1283* (Cambridge: Cambridge University Press, 2010), 26, notes of the post-Conquest March, 'the importance of waterways in the medieval period meant that river drainage systems contributed towards providing communications within, and thereby unifying, regions', citing R. R. Hilton, *A Medieval Society: The West Midlands at the End of the Thirteenth Century* (New York: John Wiley & Sons, 1966), 10–13. See also Fiona Edmonds, 'Barrier or unifying feature? Defining the nature of early medieval water transport in the North-West', 21–36 and Della Hooke, 'Uses of waterways in Anglo-Saxon England', 37–54, in John Blair, ed., *Waterways and Canal-Building in Medieval England* (Oxford: Oxford University Press, 2007).

5   *Dunsæte* 1,1.

6   Ibid. 6,1.

7   Ibid. 6,3.

8   Charles-Edwards, 'Comparative perspective', 53.

9   *Dunsæte* 9,1. There is a good discussion of the geography of this territory in Margaret Gelling, *The West Midlands in the Early Middle Ages* (Leicester: Leicester University Press, 1992), 112–19. She concludes (118): 'The district, place, or

natural feature called *Dun*, from which the Dunsæte took their name, has defeated all attempts at identification. It is not likely to be the Welsh word meaning 'fort', as that would have given **Din*. It is most probably the Old English word *dun*, modern down, perhaps used in the sense 'mountain'; but it would be very difficult to identify a suitable mountain'.

10 Patrick Wormald, *The Making of English Law: King Alfred to the Twelfth Century* (Oxford: Blackwell, 1999), 228–44.
11 *Dunsæte* 3,3.
12 See George Molyneaux, '*The Ordinance concerning the Dunsæte* and the Welsh frontier in the late tenth and eleventh centuries', *Anglo-Saxon England* 40 (2012): 249–72 at 262–5.
13 See the entries for *wita* and *rædbora* in *An Anglo-Saxon Dictionary, Based on the Manuscript Collections of the Late Joseph Bosworth*, ed. T. Northcote Toller (Oxford: Clarendon Press, 1898) and T. Northcote Toller, *An Anglo-Saxon Dictionary Supplement* (Oxford: Clarendon Press, 1921).
14 *Dunsæte* 5,1.
15 Ibid. 8,4.
16 For an analogous situation in a different time and place, see Jukka Kokkonen, 'Border peace agreements: local attempts to regulate early modern border conflicts', in *Imagined, Negotiated, Remembered: Constructing European Borders and Borderlands*, ed. Kimmo Katajala and Maria Lähteenmäki (Münster: LIT Verlag, 2012), 47–66.
17 Michael Fordham, 'Peacekeeping and order on the Anglo-Welsh frontier in the early tenth century', *Midland History* 32 (2007): 1–18 and Molyneaux, '*The Ordinance concerning the Dunsæte*'.
18 On the disparities between written law codes and law as it was practised in Anglo-Saxon England, see Patrick Wormald, 'A handlist of Anglo-Saxon lawsuits', *Anglo-Saxon England* 17 (1988): 247–81 and Elaine M. Treharne, 'A unique Old English formula for excommunication from Cambridge, Corpus Christi College 303', *Anglo-Saxon England* 24 (1995): 185–211.
19 See Wormald, *The Making of English Law*, 232–3, 381–2 and 388; Sarah Foot, *Æthelstan: The First King of England* (New Haven CT: Yale University Press, 2011), 163–4; and Molyneaux, '*The Ordinance concerning the Dunsæte*'.
20 Charles-Edwards, 'Comparative perspective', 54.
21 Martin Grimmer, 'Britons in Early Wessex: the evidence of the law code of Ine', in N. J. Higham, ed., *Britons in Anglo-Saxon England*, Publications of the Manchester Centre for Anglo-Saxon Studies 7 (Woodbridge, Suffolk: Boydell, 2007), 102–14 at 104, 106 and 114. See further L. F. Rushbrook Williams, 'The status of the Welsh in the laws of Ine', *English Historical Review*, 30 (1915): 271–7; Margaret Lindsay Faull, 'The semantic development of Old English *Wealh*', Leeds Studies in English 8 (1975): 20–44; and Louis M. Alexander, 'The legal status of the native Britons in late seventh-century Wessex as reflected by the law code of Ine', *Haskins Society Journal* 7 (1995): 31–8.

Introduction: the Dunsæte Agreement

22 'The status of an *alltud* varied according to that of his lord, so that a king's *alltud* was worth twice an *uchelwr's alltud* ... an *alltud*, therefore, was assumed to have a lord and belonged among the broader category of persons of dependent status'; Charles-Edwards and Russell, *Tair Colofn Cyfraith*, 308; referencing *Llyfr Iorwerth*, ed. A. Rh. Wiliam (Cardiff: University of Wales Press, 1960); E 110/9–9a and B 110/14–15.
23 Charles-Edwards, 'Comparative perspective', 47.
24 *Dunsæte* 4,1–2.
25 *Ibid.* 5,1.
26 Fordham, 'Peacekeeping and order', 10.
27 For the Anglo-Saxon side of things, see Lisi Oliver, *The Body Legal in Barbarian Law* (Toronto: University of Toronto Press, 2011), 203–26, and for the Welsh, see Dafydd Jenkins (trans. Charles-Edwards), 'Crime and tort and the three columns of law', in *Tair Colofn Cyfraith*, ed. Charles-Edwards and Russell, 1–25 at 15–22.
28 *Dunsæte* 2,1.
29 Molyneaux, 'The Ordinance concerning the Dunsæte', 270.
30 Charles-Edwards, 'Comparative perspective', 45.
31 Rees Davies, *Conquest, Coexistence, and Change: Wales, 1063–1415* (Oxford: Clarendon Press, 1987), 285; and see also Rees Davies, 'The Law of the March', *Welsh History Review* 5 (1970): 1–30.
32 Ralph Hanna, 'The matter of Fulk: romance and history in the Marches', *Journal of English and Germanic Philology* 110 (2011): 337–58 at 338.
33 Davies, 'The Law of the March'.
34 *Ibid.*, 23.
35 Janet M. Bately, *The Anglo-Saxon Chronicle: A Collaborative Edition*, Volume 3, MS A (Cambridge: D. S. Brewer, 1986), 18.
36 Sir Ifor Williams, ed. and ann., and Rachel Bromwich, English trans., *Armes Prydein: The Prophecy of Britain*, Mediaeval and Modern Welsh Series, vol. 6 (Dublin: Dublin Institute for Advanced Studies, School of Celtic Studies, 2006), l. 90, pp. 8–9.
37 Bryan Ward-Perkins, 'Why did the Anglo-Saxons not become more British?', *English Historical Review* 115 (2000): 513–33 at 515.
38 Grimmer, 'Britons in early Wessex', 102.
39 See Patrick Sims-Williams, 'The settlement of England in Bede and the *Chronicle*', *Anglo-Saxon England* 12 (1983): 1–41; Steven Bassett, ed., *The Origins of Anglo-Saxon Kingdoms* (London: Leicester University Press, 1989); Barbara Yorke, *Kings and Kingdoms of Early Anglo-Saxon England* (London: Routledge 1990, repr. 1997); Steven Fanning, 'Bede, *Imperium*, and the Bretwaldas', *Speculum* 66 (1991): 1–26; Barbara Yorke, 'Fact or fiction? The written evidence for the fifth and sixth centuries AD', *Anglo-Saxon Studies in Archaeology and History* 6 (1993): 45–50; Higham, ed., *Britons in Anglo-Saxon England*; N. J. Higham, *The English Conquest: Gildas and Britain in the Fifth Century* (Manchester:

Manchester University Press, 1994); Steven Bassett, 'How the West was won: the Anglo-Saxon takeover of the West Midlands', *Anglo-Saxon Studies in Archaeology and History* 11 (2000): 107–18.

40 Damian J. Tyler, 'Early Mercia and the Britons', in *Britons in Anglo-Saxon England*, ed. Higham, 91–101 at 92. See further Damian J. Tyler, 'An early Mercian hegemony: Penda and overkingship in the seventh century', *Midland History* 30 (2005): 1–19; H. P. R. Finberg, 'Mercians and Welsh', in *Lucerna – Studies of Some Problems in the Early History of England* (London, 1964): 66–82; and Nicholas Brooks, 'The formation of the Mercian kingdom', in *The Origins of Anglo-Saxon Kingdoms*, ed. Bassett, 159–70.

41 For overviews of postcolonial approaches to the Middle Ages, see Gabrielle M. Spiegel, 'Épater les médiévistes', *History and Theory* 39 (2000): 243–50, Margreta de Grazia, 'The modern divide: from either side', *Journal of Medieval and Early Modern Studies* 37 (2007): 453–67, Lisa Lampert-Weissig, *Medieval Literature and Postcolonial Studies* (Edinburgh: Edinburgh University Press, 2010), and Simon Gaunt, 'Can the Middle Ages be postcolonial?' *Comparative Literature* 61 (2009): 160–76.

42 Jeffrey Jerome Cohen, *Medieval Identity Machines*, Medieval Cultures 35 (Minneapolis: University of Minnesota Press, 2003), 117. See also, for example, Jeffrey Jerome Cohen, ed., *The Postcolonial Middle Ages* (New York: Palgrave Macmillan, 2000); Michelle R. Warren, *History on the Edge: Excalibur and the Borders of Britain, 1100–1300*, Medieval Cultures 22 (Minneapolis: University of Minnesota Press, 2000); Patricia Clare Ingham, *Sovereign Fantasies: Arthurian Romance and the Making of Britain* (Philadelphia: University of Pennsylvania Press, 2001); Alfred K. Siewers, 'Landscapes of conversion: Guthlac's mound and Grendel's mere as expressions of Anglo-Saxon nation building', *Viator* 34 (2003): 1–39; Jeffrey Jerome Cohen, *Hybridity, Identity and Monstrosity in Medieval Britain* (New York: Palgrave Macmillan, 2006).

43 See Gayatri Chakravorty Spivak, 'Can the subaltern speak?' in *Marxism and the Interpretation of Culture*, ed. Cary Nelson and Lawrence Grossberg (Urbana: University of Illinois Press, 1988), 271–313.

44 As Gaunt, 'Can the Middle Ages be postcolonial?', 164, notes, such studies have created 'the unfortunate impression that the main thing a medievalist can learn about by adopting a postcolonial perspective is Englishness'.

45 On the Scottish frontier see Geoffrey Barrow, 'Frontier and settlement: which influenced which? England and Scotland, 1100–1300', 3–21 and Anthony Goodman, 'Religion and warfare in the Anglo-Scottish marches', 245–66 in *Medieval Frontier Societies*, ed. Robert Bartlett and Angus MacKay (Oxford: Clarendon Press, 1989); and John Gillingham, 'The beginnings of English imperialism', 71–88 and Michael Brown, 'Lords and communities: political society in the thirteenth century', 123–47 in James Muldoon, ed., *The North Atlantic Frontier of Medieval Europe* (Farnham: Ashgate, 2009).

46 For maps of the post-1066 March of Wales, see Max Lieberman, *The March of*

Introduction: the Dunsæte *Agreement*

    Wales, 1067–1300: A Borderland of Medieval Britain (Cardiff: University of Wales Press, 2008), 129–37.
47 Lieberman, *Medieval March of Wales*, 56.
48 Gloria Anzaldúa, *Borderlands/La Frontera: The New Mestiza* (San Francisco: Aunt Lutte Books, 1987).
49 See also maps in Rees Davies, *The Age of Conquest: Wales, 1063–1415* (Oxford: Oxford University Press, 1991), 5; David Hill, *An Atlas of Anglo-Saxon England* (Toronto: University of Toronto Press, 1981); p. 4 map 5, 'simplified soil geology'; p. 6 map 8, 'relief'; and p. 7 map 9, 'land quality'; and David Hill, 'Mercians: the dwellers on the boundary', in *Mercia: An Anglo-Saxon Kingdom in Europe*, ed. Michelle P. Brown and Carol A. Farr. Studies in the Early History of Europe (London: Continuum, 2001), 173–82 at 174.
50 Some notable examples include Bartlett and MacKay, eds, *Medieval Frontier Societies*; Daniel Power and Naomi Standen, eds, *Frontiers in Question: Eurasian Borderlands, 700–1700* (Basingstoke: Macmillan, 1999); David Abulafia and Nora Berend, eds, *Medieval Frontiers: Concepts and Practices* (Aldershot: Ashgate, 2002); Daniel Power, *The Norman Frontier in the Twelfth and Early Thirteenth Centuries* (Cambridge: Cambridge University Press, 2004); Florin Curta, ed., *Borders, Barriers, and Ethnogenesis: Frontiers in Late Antiquity and the Middle Ages* (Turnhout: Brepols, 2005); Lud'a Klusáková and Steven G. Ellis, eds, *Frontiers and Identities: Exploring the Research Area* (Pisa: Edizioni Plus/Pisa University Press, 2006); Muldoon, ed., *The North Atlantic Frontier of Medieval Europe*; and Kimmo Katajala and Maria Lähteenmäki, eds, *Imagined, Negotiated, Remembered: Constructing European Borders and Borderlands* (Münster: LIT Verlag, 2012).
51 Florin Curta, 'Introduction', in *Borders, Barriers, and Ethnogenesis*, 1–9. Another good survey of the historiography of frontier studies is Nora Berend, 'Preface', in *Medieval Frontiers: Concepts and Practices*, ed. David Abulafia and Nora Berend (Aldershot: Ashgate, 2002), pp. x–xv.
52 Robert Bartlett, *The Making of Europe: Conquest, Colonization and Cultural Change, 950–1350* (Princeton NJ: Princeton University Press, 1993).
53 David Abulafia, 'Introduction: seven types of ambiguity, c. 1100–c. 1500', in *Medieval Frontiers: Concepts and Practices*, ed. Abulafia and Berend, 1–34.
54 Daniel Power, 'Introduction: frontiers: terms, concepts, and the historians of medieval and early modern Europe', in *Frontiers in Question*, ed. Power and Standen, 1–12 at 2–3. There is another useful discussion of terminology in Lud'a Klusáková and Steven Ellis, 'Terms and concepts: "frontier" and "identity" in academic and popular usage', in *Frontiers and Identities*, ed. Klusáková and Ellis, 1–15.
55 Catherine A. M. Clarke, *Literary Landscapes and the Idea of England, 700–1400* (Cambridge: Boydell & Brewer, 2006); Clare A. Lees and Gillian R. Overing, eds, *A Place to Believe In: Locating Medieval Landscapes* (University Park PA: Pennsylvania State University Press, 2006); Fabienne L. Michelet, *Creation, Migration, and Conquest: Imaginary Geography and Sense of Space in Old English*

Literature (Oxford: Oxford University Press, 2006); and Nicholas Howe, *Writing the Map of Anglo-Saxon England: Essays in Cultural Geography* (New Haven: Yale University Press, 2008), to which the title of this book is indebted.
56   Michiel Baud and Willem van Schendel, 'Toward a comparative history of borderlands', *Journal of World History* 8 (1997): 211–42 at 211.
57   Homi K. Bhabha, *The Location of Culture* (London: Routledge, 1994).
58   Simon Meecham-Jones, 'Where was Wales? The erasure of Wales in medieval English culture', in *Authority and Subjugation in Writing of Medieval Wales*, ed. Ruth Kennedy and Simon Meecham-Jones (New York: Palgrave Macmillan, 2008), 27–55 at 32.
59   For previous studies, see the works listed in nn. 39 and 40 above, and also T. M. Charles-Edwards, *Wales and the Britons, 350–1064* (Oxford: Oxford University Press, 2013).
60   Rees Davies, 'Frontier arrangements in fragmented societies: Ireland and Wales', in *Medieval Frontier Societies*, ed. Bartlett and MacKay, 77–100 at 81.
61   For example, Lieberman, *Medieval March of Wales*, 56, defines a march as 'a territory under the command of a select group of border lords'.
62   H. C. Darby, 'The March of Wales in 1086', *Transactions of the Institute of British Geographers* 11 (1986): 259–78 at 259, notes the presence of the phrase *Marcha de Wales* in the Domesday Book; and Lieberman, *Medieval March of Wales*, 6, charts its increasing prevalence during the 1160s.
63   Rees Davies, *Conquest, Coexistence, and Change*, 284–5.
64   Davies, 'Fragmented societies', 81.
65   Recent studies have found more cultural, textual and legal continuity across the 1066 divide than has traditionally been assumed. See in particular Wormald, *The Making of English Law*; John Hudson, *The Formation of the English Common Law: Law and Society in England from the Norman Conquest to Magna Carta* (New York: Longman Press, 1996); Bruce O'Brien, *God's Peace and the King's Peace: The Laws of Edward the Confessor* (Philadelphia: University of Pennsylvania Press, 1999); Mary Swan and Elaine M. Treharne, eds, *Rewriting Old English in the Twelfth Century* (Cambridge: Cambridge University Press, 2000); Elaine M. Treharne, *Living Through Conquest: The Politics of Early English, 1020–1220* (Oxford: Oxford University Press, 2012); and Martin Brett and David A. Woodman, eds, *The Long Twelfth Century View of the Anglo-Saxon Past* (Farnham: Ashgate, 2015).
66   Meecham-Jones, 'Where was Wales?', 27–8.
67   *Ibid.*, 28.

2

Penda of Mercia and the Welsh borderlands in Bede's *Historia Ecclesiastica*

Bede's eighth-century *Historia Ecclesiastica Gentis Anglorum*, one of the earliest and most historically significant surviving texts of the Anglo-Saxon period, narrates the conversion of the Anglo-Saxons to Christianity and the nascent formation of what might be called an 'English' identity. The *Historia Ecclesiastica* has long been interpreted as a narrative of Anglo/British strife, because Bede is so critical of the Britons, who are in his perspective heretical. Yet because of Bede's equal rancour towards the pagan Mercians, the *Historia Ecclesiastica* inadvertently preserves a substantial amount of information about the life of Penda of Mercia, whose entire reign over this borderlands kingdom was defined by consistent political and military unity with the Welsh rulers of Gwynedd and Powys against other Anglo-Saxon kingdoms. Penda's life provides a window into the mixed Anglo-Welsh culture of the borderlands as a region which stands apart from Bede's narrative of ethnic division between Anglo-Saxons and Britons.

This chapter follows recent scholarship on the *Historia Ecclesiastica* in understanding it as a carefully constructed narrative with a political agenda, in which Bede shapes a story of the Anglo-Saxons as a people united by ethnicity and religion to become God's chosen inhabitants of Britain.[1] Bede wrote a *Historia Ecclesiastica Gentis Anglorum*, not a *Historia Britanniae* or even a *Historia Gentis Anglorum* – to him, it was the embrace of (Roman) Christianity that made the Anglo-Saxons a people. Yet because Christianity brought such significant political and cultural changes to Anglo-Saxon England, the Welsh borderlands in the early Anglo-Saxon period were a region both united by rejection of Anglo-Saxon Christianity and its ensuing cultural shifts and increasingly defined in opposition to it. Bede's *Historia Ecclesiastica*, while written from the external perspective of

Christian Northumbria, is our earliest surviving source for the history of the Welsh borderlands. Like the *Dunsæte Agreement*, the *Historia Ecclesiastica* provides an important window into life in this region during one moment in the Anglo-Saxon period, and the picture that it reveals is also of a mixed Anglo-Welsh culture in the borderlands. A small group of surviving early Welsh annals and poems reflects the same perspective from the west. In the life of Penda of Mercia, we see the seventh-century borderlands as a region distinct from other Anglo-Saxon and Welsh kingdoms.

The Battle of Hatfield Chase

The *Historia Ecclesiastica* first mentions Penda as a participant in the 633 Battle of Hatfield Chase, in which an army led by Cadwallon of Gwynedd with Penda's support decisively defeated the forces of the Christian Northumbrian king Edwin.[2] This battle is one of several moments throughout Penda's life when the *Historia Ecclesiastica* characterises the borderlands as an identifiably distinct region, set apart by its mixed Anglo-Welsh culture from other Anglo-Saxon and Welsh kingdoms.

The Battle of Hatfield Chase was fought at a location between the northernmost territory of Mercia and southernmost territory of Northumbria, near Doncaster in modern Yorkshire. The battle took place when

> At uero Eduini cum X et VII annis genti Anglorum simul et Brettonum gloriosissime praeesset, e quibus sex etiam ipse, ut diximus, Christi regno militauit, rebellauit aduersus eum Caedualla rex Brettonum, auxilium praebente illi Penda uiro strenuissimo de regio genere Merciorum, qui et ipse ex eo tempore gentis eiusdem regno annis XX et duobus uaria sorte praefuit: et conserto graui proelio in campo qui uocatur Haethfelth occisus est Eduini die quarto iduum Octobrium, anno dominicae incarnationis DCXXXIII, cum esset annorum XL et VIII, eiusque totus uel interemtus uel dispersus exercitus. In quo etiam bello ante illum unus filius eius Osfrid iuuenis bellicosus cecidit; alter Eadfrid necessitate cogente ad Pendam regem transfugit, et ab eo postmodum, regnante Osualdo, contra fidem iurisiurandi peremtus est.[3]

> (Edwin had reigned most gloriously over the English and the British race for seventeen years, for six of which, as we have said, he was also a soldier in the kingdom of Christ, when Cædwalla, king of the Britons, rebelled against him. He was supported by Penda, a man exceptionally gifted as a warrior, a member of the royal house of Mercia, who from that date ruled over that nation for twenty-two years with varying success. A fierce battle was fought on the plain called *Hæthfelth* [Hatfield Chase] and Edwin was killed on 12

Penda in Bede's Historia Ecclesiastica

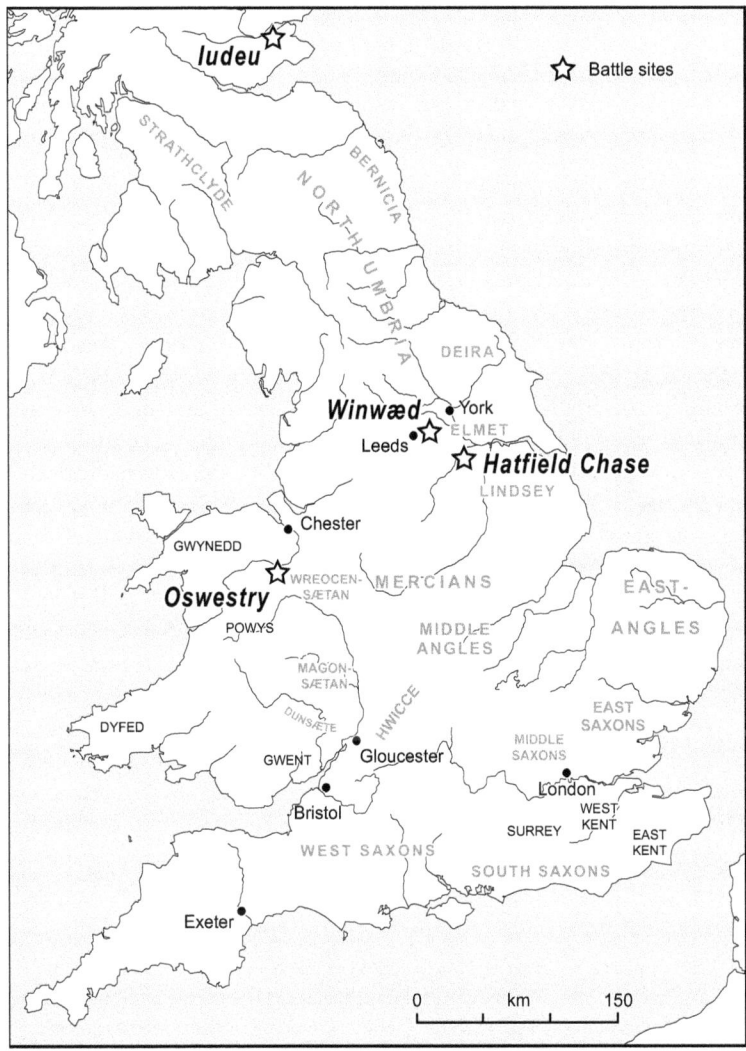

Map 2 Significant battles in Bede's *Historia Ecclesiastica*, following David Hill, *An Atlas of Anglo-Saxon England*: Hatfield Chase, the Battle of Maserfelth at Oswestry, the Battle of the Winwæd near Leeds, and the northern fortress of Iudeu

October in the year of our Lord 633, in his forty-eighth year. The whole of his army was either slain or scattered. In this war too, one of his sons, Osfrith, a warlike youth, fell before him while the other, Eadfrith, was compelled to desert to King Penda; the latter, in spite of an oath, afterwards murdered him, during the reign of Oswald.)[5]

This battle is also recorded by both the *Annales Cambriae* and the *Historia Brittonum*, the sole extant Welsh chronicles for this period, testifying to its importance in Welsh history.[6] The *Annales Cambriae* records 'Gueith Meicen; et ibi interfectus est Etguin cum duobus filiis suis; Catguollaun autem victor fuit' (the Battle of Meigen; and there Edwin was killed with his two sons, but Cadwallon was the victor).[7] The *Historia Brittonum* likewise narrates that 'duo filii Edguin erant, et cum ipso corruerunt in bello Meicen, et de origine illius numquam iteratum est regnum, quia non evasit unus de genere illius de isto bello, sed interfecti omnes sunt cum illo ab exercitu Catguollauni, regis Guendotae regionis' (Osfrid and Eadfrid were the two sons of Edwin, and they fell with him at the Battle of Meicen, and the kingdom was never revived from their stock, for none of their line survived that battle, but they were all killed with him by the army of Catwallaun, king of the country of Gwynedd).[8] The records of this battle reveal that cultural changes brought by Christianity to other Anglo-Saxon kingdoms did not affect the Welsh borderlands, making the region increasingly distinctive for its mixed Anglo-Welsh culture.

Edwin's conversion and reign were admirable in hindsight to Bede as a Christian Northumbrian, but they placed the kingdom in conflict with Mercia and Gwynedd, the territories to its south and west.[9] The Battle of Hatfield Chase took place only after Edwin's conversion, and the *Historia Ecclesiastica* underscores the differences between Christian Northumbria and the borderlands. Bede comments on the singularity of Edwin's expansionist kingship:

> Quo tempore etiam gens Nordanhymbrorum, hoc est ea natio Anglorum quae ad aquilonalem Humbrae fluminis plagam habitabat, cum rege suo Eduino uerbum fidei praedicante Paulino, cuius supra meminimus, suscepit. Cui uidelicet regi, in auspicium suscipiendae fidei et regni caelestis, potestas etiam terreni creuerat imperii, ita ut quod nemo Anglorum ante eum, omnes Brittaniae fines, qua uel ipsorum uel Brettonum prouinciae habitabant, sub dicione acciperet. Quin et Meuanias insulas, sicut et supra docuimus, imperio subiugauit Anglorum; quarum prior, quae ad austrum est, et situ amplior et frugum prouentu atque ubertate felicior, nongentarum sexaginta familiarum mensuram iuxta aestimationem Anglorum, secunda trecentarum et ultra spatium tenet.[10]

(At this time the Northumbrian race, that is the English race which dwelt north of the River Humber, together with their king, Edwin, also accepted the word of faith through the preaching of Paulinus already mentioned. The king's earthly power had increased as an augury that he was to become a believer and have a share in the heavenly kingdom. So, like no other English king before him, he held under his sway the whole realm of Britain, not only English kingdoms but those ruled over by the Britons as well. He even brought the islands of Anglesey and Man under his power as we have said before. The former of these, which is to the south, is larger in size and more fruitful, containing 960 hides according to the English way of reckoning, while the latter has more than 300.)[11]

The discussion of the hidages and fruitfulness of these islands emphasises that they were acquired to increase Northumbria's size, and significantly, Bede draws rhetorical links between this territorial expansion and Edwin's conversion in his connection of the king's earthly power to his future share in the heavenly kingdom. It is worth recalling, as D. P. Kirby has noted, just how exceptional Edwin's conversion was, at a time when 'there was no Christian king anywhere in England outside Kent'.[12] The rarity of Christian Anglo-Saxon rulers at this time means that Edwin's new status as 'a soldier in the kingdom of Christ' stood out already, the more so for being linked by Bede to his aggressive territorial expansion. In Bede's description of the Battle of Hatfield Chase, we begin to see Christian Anglo-Saxon kingdoms characterised differently from the Welsh borderlands.

Welsh texts preserve some traditions about Edwin's youth that open another window into the mixed Anglo-Welsh culture of the borderlands. Edwin was exiled during his youth, and according to Welsh sources he spent this time in Wales, where he was raised with Cadwallon at the court of his father Cadfan in Gwynedd and baptised by Rhun ap Urien of Rheged.[13] The story that Edwin was fostered by Cadwallon's father Cadfan is recorded in Reginald of Durham's *Life of St Oswald* and Geoffrey of Monmouth's *Historia Regum Britanniae*, and Rachel Bromwich has argued for echoes of this tradition in early Welsh verse as well.[14] These narratives depict a comfortably mixed Anglo-Welsh culture in the borderlands, a culture to which Edwin belonged until his later conversion to Anglo-Saxon Christianity.[15]

A separate British tradition preserved in the *Annales Cambriae* and *Historia Brittonum* also reflects a mixed Anglo-Welsh culture in the borderlands by recording – in contrast to Bede's famous narrative of Edwin's conversion, which takes up a large part of Book II of the *Historia Ecclesiastica* – Edwin's earlier baptism by Rhun ap Urien of Rheged. The

Annales Cambriae records that 'Etguin baptizatus est, et Run filius Urbgen baptizavit eum' (Edwin is baptised, and Rhun son of Urien baptised him).[16] The *Historia Brittonum* preserves a slightly longer narrative: 'Eadguin vero in sequenti Pasca baptismum suscepit et duodecim milia hominum baptizati sunt cum eo. Si quis scire voluerit quis eos baptizavit, Rum map Urbgen baptizavit eos, et per quadraginta dies non cessavit baptizare omne genus ambronum et per praedicationem illius multi crediderunt in Christo' (Edwin was baptised at the Easter following, and twelve thousand men were baptised with him. If anyone wants to know who baptised them, Rhun son of Urien baptised them, and for forty days on end he went on baptising the whole nation of the thugs, and through his teaching many of them believed in Christ).[17] While their ultimate historicity is impossible to determine, these traditions are quite plausible, and these narratives reflect both the mixed Anglo-Welsh culture of the borderlands and the fact that Edwin was remembered as having strong ties to this region in his youth, indicating the extent of the cultural shift caused by his later conversion.

The *Historia Ecclesiastica* also preserves a tradition connecting Edwin to the borderlands in his youth, when Bede mentions that two of Edwin's sons, Osfrith and Eadfrith, were born to Cwenburh, daughter of the Mercian king, Ceorl, during the time that Edwin was in exile: 'in quibus erant Osfrid et Eadfrid filii regis Eduini, qui ambo ei exuli nati sunt de Quoenburga filia Cearli regis Merciorum'[18] (among whom were Osfrith and Eadfrith, sons of King Edwin, their mother being Cwenburh, daughter of Ceorl, king of the Mercians; they were born while he was in exile).[19] Bede glosses over these births, but Edwin must have been on very good terms with the Mercian royal family during his exile in order to marry the king's daughter.[20] Yet after his return to Northumbria and conversion to Roman Christianity, these relationships crumbled,[21] underscoring the shift caused by his conversion and kingship.

This shift is also evidenced in the language Bede uses to describe ethnic identities, in which the pagan Mercians and 'heretical' Britons are perceived as closer to one another than to Christian Anglo-Saxon kingdoms. As Stephen Harris has demonstrated, Bede shapes a history of ethnogenesis in which the identity and unity of the *natio* or *gens Anglorum* is equated with Anglo-Saxon Christianity.[22] Writing from a Christian Northumbrian perspective, Bede claims Edwin for the *gens Anglorum*, distinct from both Cadwallon as *Brettonum* and Penda as part of the *gens Merciorum*. Significantly, Cadwallon also distinguishes the Mercians from the *gens Anglorum*. Bede reports that Cadwallon was 'ac totum genus Anglorum Brittaniae finibus erasurum se esse deliberans'[23] (meaning to wipe out the whole English nation from the land of Britain), indicating that (Bede thought) Cadwallon did not see his permanent allies as part of the whole English nation.[24] The same ethnic distinction between Mercians and 'English' on the part of the Welsh underlies Bede's statement that 'Sed nec religioni Christianae, quae apud eos exorta erat, aliquid impendebat honoris, quippe cum usque hodie moris sit Brettonum fidem religionemque Anglorum pro nihili habere, neque in aliquo eis magis communicare quam paganis'[25] (Nor did he pay any respect to the Christian religion which had sprung up amongst them. Indeed to this very day it is the habit of the Britons to despise the faith and religion of the English and not to cooperate with them in anything more than with the heathen).[26] These passages depict 'the English' (Christian Anglo-Saxon kingdoms) as a distinct people from 'the heathen' Mercians from the perspectives of both Bede and the Welsh.

Identity is usually understood as shared on the basis of a common ethnicity, language or religion. Yet, as Christianity brought political and cultural changes to those Anglo-Saxon kingdoms that first converted, the Mercian and Welsh kingdoms in the borderlands drew closer together despite these apparent differences. After Hatfield Chase, the Welsh borderlands were perceived as not simply a temporary enemy in battle, but a region that stood apart in its very nature from Christian Northumbria.

A cultural nexus

The borderlands were set apart from Christian Anglo-Saxon kingdoms by their mixed Anglo-Welsh culture. One facet of this cultural singularity is the distinctive naming patterns of the Mercian noble family, which incorporate British elements. Penda's name reflects a clear British influence through its incorporation of Welsh *penn*, chief/head. Similarly mixed Anglo-Welsh names appear throughout the Mercian royal line. The name of Penda's son Merewalh (the first known ruler of the Magonsætan) likely incorporates the Old English word for Welshman, *wealh*, as do the names of Penda's brother-in-law Cenwealh and his son Cundwalh, as well as the later father of Saint Guthlac, Penwalh, discussed further in Chapter Three.[27]

As Patrick Sims-Williams has cautiously noted, 'some British alliance or intermarriage may be implied' by these names, but 'this argument cannot be pressed'.[28] Sims-Williams is right to be wary of automatically equating names with ethnic identity, yet the significance of so many names in the Mercian royal genealogy with British components cannot be overlooked.[29] These British elements reflect several possibilities, each of which indicates a different level of mixed Anglo-Welsh culture in the borderlands. Some

Mercian rulers could indeed have been ethnically British, while another possibility is that these names signal intermarriage. Finally, the Mercian nobility could simply have chosen to adopt British names for themselves. While this last scenario need not imply that any of the Mercian nobility was ethnically British, it is perhaps the most interesting cultural possibility, demonstrating a significant Welsh influence on Mercian society.[30] An interesting contrast is reflected by the Durham *Liber Vitae*, in which 'names for which a Celtic origin of one sort or another can be established do not form a single distinguishable group in *LVD*; they are rather scattered mainly through the lists of clerics, priests, and monks, with the occasional royal figure to raise the tone'.[31] In contrast, the British-influenced names of the members of the early Mercian royal line form a noticeable pattern. No matter the reason for these British name elements, they reflect the mixed Anglo-Welsh culture of the borderlands.

The distinctive naming practices within this region reveal another feature of the borderlands which set it apart from surrounding Christian Anglo-Saxon kingdoms – an older, more flexible system of determining succession in which a wider pool of noble individuals could be eligible for kingship, which stood in contrast to the system approaching primogeniture encouraged by the Roman Christian Church. Penda is not a king's son, but 'uiro strenuissimo de regio genere Merciorum, qui et ipse ex eo tempore gentis eiusdem regno annis XX et duobus uaria sorte praefuit'[32] (a man exceptionally gifted as a warrior, a member of the royal house of Mercia, who from that date ruled over that nation for twenty-two years with varying success).[33] His name alliterates with that of his father, Pybba, but not with the previous Mercian king, Ceorl, indicating that they come from separate branches of the Mercian royal family. The description of Penda's rise to power identifies him as part of the broader periphery of Mercian nobility, but his ascent was not predetermined by inheritance; it was gained through success in battle.

As Frederick M. Biggs has demonstrated in his work on *Beowulf*, the introduction of Christianity to Anglo-Saxon England brought with it a shift from the traditional horizontal model of succession 'in which the next king is chosen from among a relatively broadly defined kin group' to a vertical Christian system 'in which the pool of eligible candidates is restricted primarily to sons'.[34] The *Historia Ecclesiastica* itself appears to illustrate the opposition between this older system of succession and the newer Christian model through the events that took place in Northumbria after Edwin's death: his successors simultaneously apostatised and returned to an older model of joint kingship, reverting Northumbria into its constituent kingdoms of Deira and Bernicia.[35]

The Welsh borderlands appear to have adhered to this older model of succession in which a broad pool of nobles was eligible and a warrior could become king through victory on the battlefield. As we will see in Chapter Three, these conditions still seem to have held true during the youth of the late-seventh to early-eighth century Mercian warrior-turned-saint Guthlac. Mercia appears to participate in this horizontal model at several points in the *Historia Ecclesiastica*. Penda had an unusually long reign, but there is some evidence that an older system of joint kingship was in place even during his rule. He deprived Cenwealh of his kingdom for his repudiation of Penda's sister, indicating that Cenwealh was ruling jointly or as a sub-king with Penda's approval. Likewise, Penda installed his son Peada as king of the Middle Angles while he was still living.[36] This horizontal model of succession aligns with what is known of the practice in early Ireland and Wales, where kings also appear to have been drawn from a broader pool of possible contenders.[37] As Christian Anglo-Saxon kingdoms shifted to a new model of succession approaching that of primogeniture, Mercia's adherence to an older system seems to have aligned it more closely with the Welsh tribes to its west than the Anglo-Saxon ones to its east, resulting in a shared political structure in the Welsh borderlands.

A mixed Anglo-Welsh culture in this region is further reflected by Penda's tolerance of Christianity, which shows Germanic paganism, British Christianity and Anglo-Saxon Christianity co-existing peacefully in the borderlands. Penda's son Peada converted to Christianity as a condition of his marriage to Oswiu's daughter Alhflæd. (He is further persuaded by his friend and brother-in-law Alhfrith son of Oswiu, who has married Penda's daughter Cyneburh).[38] Describing Peada's conversion, Bede writes:

> Nec prohibuit Penda rex, quin etiam in sua, hoc est Merciorum, natione uerbum, siqui uellent audire, praedicaretur. Quin potius odio habebat et despiciebat eos, quos fide Christi imbutos opera fidei non habere deprehendit, dicens contemnendos esse eos et miseros, qui Deo suo, in quem crederent, oboedire contemnerent.[39]

> (Now King Penda did not forbid the preaching of the Word, even in his own Mercian kingdom, if any wished to hear it. But he hated and despised those who, after they had accepted the Christian faith, were clearly lacking in the works of faith. He said that they were despicable and wretched creatures who scorned to obey the God in whom they believed.)[40]

Penda's support of Peada's conversion illustrates both its political motivations and the mix of cultures that co-existed within the borderlands. As N. J. Higham has argued, 'rulers treated religious policy as an integral part of the strategies available to them by which to pursue their own interests'.[41] Peada seems to have had a good sense of which way the winds of change were blowing,[42] and Penda – whatever his actual religious beliefs may have been – clearly supported his son's shrewd decision to convert. Bede's uncharacteristic praise of Penda's religious tolerance is undoubtedly meant to underscore the hypocrisy of inconstant Christians. Yet at the same time, it is a comment on the mixed culture within the borderlands, where three religions co-existed, seemingly unproblematically.

The *Historia Ecclesiastica* depicts the continued unity of the Welsh borderlands after the Battle of Hatfield Chase, as the region was increasingly set apart from other Anglo-Saxon kingdoms. The borderlands army was not formed by a temporary alliance for this battle alone, but continued to attack Northumbria afterwards. Bede describes how,

> Quo tempore maxima est facta strages in ecclesia uel gente Nordanhymbrorum, maxime quod unus ex ducibus, a quibus acta est, paganus, alter quia barbarus erat pagano saeuior. Siquidem Penda cum omni Merciorum gente idolis deditus et Christiani erat nominis ignarus; at uero Caedualla, quamuis nomen et professionem haberet Christiani, adeo tamen erat animo ac moribus barbarus, ut ne sexui quidem muliebri uel innocuae paruulorum parceret aetati.[43]

> (At this time there was a great slaughter both of the Church and of the people of Northumbria, one of the perpetrators being a heathen and the other a barbarian who was even more cruel than the heathen. Now Penda and the whole Mercian race were idolaters and ignorant of the name of Christ; but Cædwalla, although a Christian by name and profession, was nevertheless a barbarian in heart and disposition and spared neither women nor innocent children.)[44]

Bede's critical portraits of Cadwallon and Penda draw the two closer together while at the same time distancing them further from Christian Northumbria. Further, Cadwallon 'dein cum anno integro prouincias Nordanhymbrorum non ut rex uictor possideret, sed quasi tyrannus saeuiens disperderet ac tragica caede dilaceraret'[45] (after this he occupied the Northumbrian kingdoms for a whole year, not ruling them like a victorious king but ravaging them like a savage tyrant, tearing them to pieces with fearful bloodshed).[46] Bede equates the two rulers as violent barbarians – Cadwallon is a 'barbarian in heart and disposition' while Penda's paganism makes him an actual barbarian. It is shared behaviours that unify the Welsh borderlands from Bede's perspective.[47] Conversion created more than religious distance between Northumbria and this region; in Bede's eyes, the barbarism of their warfare sets the borderlands apart.

Bede's definition of a barbarian as someone so violent that he does not spare noncombatants is significant because this style of warfare – raids undertaken by warbands, as opposed to pitched battles by standing armies – was practised generally among the Celtic and Germanic tribes of early Britain before the conversion of the Anglo-Saxons.[48] That such warfare involved a high level of violence to noncombatants[49] is evident from an incident related earlier in the *Historia Ecclesiastica* which demonstrates that Penda's and Cadwallon's codes of acceptable behaviour in war mirror those of pre-conversion Northumbria. Bede dispassionately describes the Battle of Chester (615/16), in which the (pagan) Northumbrian king, Æthelfrith massacred twelve hundred unarmed monks from the British monastery of Bangor Iscoed.[50] Only after Northumbria's conversion was violence against noncombatants understood as a mark of barbarity. Increasingly, the Welsh borderlands were defined by their common values, which were no longer shared by newly Christian Anglo-Saxon kingdoms.

Throughout Book III of the *Historia Ecclesiastica* Bede consistently describes Penda's army as containing both Mercian and British fighters and he emphasises its perceived cultural distance from Christian Northumbria. Bede writes that 'quo completo annorum curriculo occisus est, commisso graui proelio, ab eadem pagana gente paganoque rege Merciorum, a quo et prodecessor eius Eduini peremtus fuerat'[51] (at the end of this period, [Oswald] was killed in a great battle by the same heathen people and the same heathen Mercian king as his predecessor Edwin).[52] Penda's army at this battle included Welsh troops, meaning that Bede dismisses all of the borderlands under the umbrella of 'heathen people'. This characterisation of Penda's army as heathen, violent and set apart from Christian Anglo-Saxon kingdoms continues throughout Book III. After Oswald's death, his brother Oswiu succeeded to the kingdom of Bernicia, and 'impugnatus uidelicet et ab ea, quae fratrem eius occiderat, pagana gentes Merciorum et a filio quoque suo Alhfrido necnon et a fratruo, id est fratris sui qui ante eum regnauit filio, Oidilualdo'[53] (he was attacked by the heathen people, the Mercians, who had slain his brother, and in addition, by his own son Alhfrith and his nephew Oethelwald, the son of his brother and predecessor).[54]

While Aidan is bishop, 'nam tempore episcopatus eius hostilis Merciorum exercitus Penda duce Nordanhymbrorum regiones impia clade longe lateque deuastans peruenit ad urbem usque regiam, quae ex Bebbae quondam reginae uocabulo cognominatur'[55] (during the time of his episcopate a hostile Mercian army, under the leadership of Penda, which had been cruelly devastating the kingdom of Northumbria far and wide, reached the royal city called after a former queen Bebbe [Bamburgh]).[56] Some years later, when Finan succeeded Aidan as bishop, 'contigit autem post aliquot annos, ut Penda Merciorum rex, cum hostili exercitu haec in loca perueniens, cum cuncta quae poterat ferro flammaque perderet, uicus quoque ille, in quo antistes obiit, una cum ecclesia memorata flammis absumeretur'[57] (now it happened a few years afterwards that Penda, king of Mercia, came with a hostile army to these parts destroying everything he could with fire and sword; and the village in which the bishop had died, together with the church just mentioned, was burnt down).[58]

An earlier moment in Book II describes how 'attamen in Campodono, ubi tunc etiam uilla regia erat, fecit basilicam, quam postmodum pagani, a quibus Eduini rex occisus est, cum tota eadem uilla succenderunt'[59] (nevertheless in *Campodonum*, where there was also a royal dwelling, he built a church which was afterwards burnt down, together with the whole of the buildings, by the heathen who slew King Edwin).[60] Bede uses the same rhetoric to describe Penda's defeat of the East Angles: the former East Anglian king, Sigeberht, 'occisusque est una cum rege Ecgrico, et cunctus eorum insistentibus paganis caesus siue dispersus exercitus'[61] (he was killed together with King Ecgric, and the whole army was either slain or scattered by the heathen attacks),[62] and Anna, successor of Sigeberht and Ecgric, was 'qui et ipse postea ab eodem pagano Merciorum duce, a quo et prodecessores eius, occisus est'[63] (he also was slain later on, like his predecessors, by the heathen Mercian leader).[64] From the Battle of Hatfield Chase onwards, throughout Book III of the *Historia Ecclesiastica*, Bede characterises Penda's army in the same way. The borderlands are dismissed as violent and heathen, distinguishing this region from Christian Anglo-Saxon kingdoms.

Because Welsh sources for this time period are so limited, it is worth discussing a group of poems set in the seventh century, though preserved in much later manuscripts. Three Welsh poems in praise of Cadwallon and Cynan, the kings of Gwynedd and Powys who were allied with Penda throughout the seventh century, record litanies of battles with other Welsh kingdoms and Northumbria, but never with Mercia. Although each of these poems has its own difficulties of dating and interpretation, taken together, they present a picture of aggression radiating outward from the Welsh borderlands – north and east against Northumbria, and west and south against other Welsh kingdoms – which suggests that there may have been a similar sense of distance between other Welsh kingdoms and the borderlands as there was between other Anglo-Saxon kingdoms and this region.

Two poems in praise of Cadwallon laud his victories over other Welsh kingdoms and Edwin, but hold no mention of strife with Mercia. The poem *Moliant Cadwallon* ('In Praise of Cadwallon') is narrated as if it was written before Cadwallon's death.[65] While most medieval Welsh poems are at least preserved in medieval manuscripts, the dating of *Moliant Cadwallon* is made very difficult by the fact that no medieval manuscript of the poem has survived, and it is known only from copies made by early modern antiquarians. While its date of composition is contested, its two most recent editors, Geraint Gruffydd and John T. Koch, largely agree that the poem's narrative is consistent with seventh-century history, in that it introduces no obvious anachronisms.[66] The poem praises Cadwallon's extensive victories over other Welsh kingdoms and Northumbria, remarking specifically (ll. 23–6) that it is a lie to say Cadwallon ever negotiated with the Bernicians or with Edwin.

A similar litany of aggression directed against other Welsh kingdoms is recorded in the poem known as *Englynion Cadwallon* ('The Stanzas of Cadwallon', as Jenny Rowland titles it) or *Marwnad Cadwallon* ('The Elegy of Cadwallon', in Geraint Gruffydd's edition).[67] While this poem is preserved in medieval manuscripts – the fourteenth-century Red Book of Hergest and White Book of Rhydderch – it is regarded as a late poem more concerned with Cadwallon's legendary than historical career.[68] Still, as Jenny Rowland has noted, 'the dramatized saga *englynion* arose out of history' – 'even when the saga tale is closer to pseudo-history, the stories themselves are plausible, not fabulous'.[69] *Englynion/Marwnad Cadwallon* is written in such a historically plausible voice, from the perspective of posthumous praise of Cadwallon's victories. The poem notably lists his campaigns against other Welsh kingdoms and Northumbria, but never Mercia. Geraint Gruffydd has demonstrated that these campaigns are presented in a clockwise circuit around Wales,[70] which Rowland has argued might indicate Cadwallon's symbolic conquest or overlordship.[71] She has also demonstrated that this poem is part of a group which together provides important 'evidence of a Powys-Gwynedd-Mercia alliance against Northumbria',[72] drawing the distinction between its consistent reflection of contemporary historical circumstances and the anti-English perspectives found throughout the rest of the non-historical *Canu Heledd* cycle, which was written centuries later after the collapse of Powys.[73] Regardless of precisely when these poems were composed, *Moliant Cadwallon* and *Englynion/ Marwnad Cadwallon* reflect either a Welsh perspective of unity within the borderlands during the seventh century – or the memory of that unity in later centuries – in their litanies of Cadwallon's battles against southern Wales and Northumbria alone.

Finally, the poem *Trawsganu Kynan Garwyn mab Brochfael* ('In praise of Cynan Garwyn son of Brochfael'), a praise-poem for a sixth-century king of Powys, also preserves a long list of battles between Cynan and other Welsh kingdoms but no conflict with Mercia.[74] Cynan Garwyn was the father of Selyf ap Cynan, who died at the Battle of Chester in 616.[75] This poem is preserved in the fourteenth-century Book of Taliesin, a manuscript which is understood by many to preserve material far older than the date at which it was copied. The dating of *Trawsganu Kynan Garwyn mab Brochfael* has been hotly debated – Ifor Williams and John Koch have argued that the work is plausibly contemporary with Cynan Garwyn, while Graham R. Isaac has dated the work as a tenth-century piece of political propaganda. Yet regardless of its moment of composition, the work itself preserves no memory of conflict with Mercia in this poem about a sixth-century king of Powys. Like the poems on Cadwallon, *Trawsganu Kynan Garwyn mab Brochfael* recounts Cynan's triumphant victories over other Welsh kingdoms alone.[76] Taken together, these poems preserve a Welsh point of view which did not remember strife between Gwynedd or Powys and Mercia. Early Welsh kings were remembered for their victories over other Welsh kingdoms, but the Welsh borderlands itself was not understood to be a site of strife.

Another characteristic of warfare in the borderlands that set the region apart from Christian Anglo-Saxon kingdoms in the *Historia Ecclesiastica* was the prominent decapitation of defeated enemies. While archaeological records indicate that decapitation did occur frequently throughout early Britain,[77] such high-status decapitations as those performed upon Kings Edwin, Oswald and Eanfrith by the armies of the Welsh borderlands are rare in the textual record. These decapitations stand out within the *Historia Ecclesiastica* as political statements of the borderlands, distinguishing warfare within this region from that of other Anglo-Saxon kingdoms in Bede's text.

Three Christian Anglo-Saxon kings were beheaded after their defeat by a Welsh borderlands army. We know that Edwin was decapitated after he was killed at Hatfield Chase because Bede records that 'allatum est autem caput Eduini regis Eburacum, et illatum postea in ecclesiam beati apostoli Petri'[78] (the head of King Edwin was brought to York and afterwards placed in the church of the apostle St Peter).[79] Interestingly, a competing Welsh tradition has Edwin's head taken to Aberffraw, in Anglesey. The poem, *Gofara Braint*, is fragmentary and undatable,[80] so it is different to determine the validity of this tradition. Regardless, *Gofara Braint* indicates that Edwin's decapitation was well-remembered in Welsh tradition as well as in English.

Likewise, when Oswald is killed at the later Battle of Maserfelth (Welsh *Maes Cogwy*) at Oswestry in Shropshire (see Map 2) in 642,[81] Bede describes how 'porro caput et manus cum brachiis a corpore praecisas iussit rex, qui occiderat, in stipitibus suspendi'[82] (the king who slew him [Penda] ordered his head and his hands to be severed from his body and hung on stakes).[83] Oswald's head, like Edwin's, is later buried separately from the rest of his remains: 'Quo post annum deueniens cum exercitu successor regni eius Osuiu abstultit ea, et caput quidem in cymiterio Lindisfarnensis ecclesiae, in regia uero ciuitate manus cum brachiis condidit'[84] (A year afterwards, his successor Oswiu came thither with an army and took them away. He buried the head in a burial place in the church at Lindisfarne, but the hands and arms he buried in the royal city of Bamburgh).[85] Finally, though it has not previously been connected to the deaths of Edwin and Oswald, Cadwallon's killing of Eanfrith is described as a beheading in the Irish *Annals of Tigernach*, identifying it as part of the same pattern. The *Annals of Tigernach* record 'Cath la Cathlon 7 Anfraith qui decollatus est, in quo Osualt mac Etalfraith uictor erat et Catlon, rex Britonum, cecidit' (a battle by Cadwallon and Eanfrith who was beheaded, in which Oswald son of Æthelfrith was the victor and Cadwallon, king of the Britons, fell).[86] While this entry conflates Cadwallon's killing of Eanfrith with Oswald's killing of Cadwallon,[87] Eanfrith's decapitation is unambiguous. A pattern emerges from the evidence of politically symbolic decapitations in the Welsh borderlands.

It is important to note that while Bede does not mention Welsh participation in the Battle of Maserfelth where Oswald was killed, Welsh sources make clear that this was a mixed Anglo-Welsh army, even though Cadwallon had been earlier slain by Oswald.[88] The *Annales Cambriae* record 'bellum Cocboy in quo Oswald rex Nordorum et Eoba rex Merciorum corruerunt' (the Battle of Cogfry in which Oswald king of the Northmen and Eawa king of the Mercians fell)[89] and the *Historia Brittonum* says that 'ipse fecit bellum Cocboy, in quo cecidit Eoua, filius Pippa, frater ejus, rex Merciorum, et Oswald, rex Nordorum' ([Penda] fought the Battle of Cogwy, in which fell his brother, Eobba, son of Pybba, and Oswald, king of the Northerners).[90] Moreover, the battle is also mentioned in a Welsh *englyn* which may date to the ninth century[91] that names Cynddylan, king of Powys, as a participant. The verse reads, 'Gwelais ar lawr maes Cogwy

/ byddinawr a gawr gymwy / Cynddylan oedd kynhorthwy' (I saw on the ground of the field of Cogwy / armies and battle affliction. / Cynddylan was an ally).[92] A twelfth-century poem known as *Canu Tyssilyaw* (a praise-poem to the seventh-century Welsh saint Tysilio) by Cynddelw of Powys also recalls the participation of warriors from Powys in this battle,[93] which as Ifor Williams has noted 'shows that there was a tradition in Powys in the twelfth century that the battle in which Oswald fell, was fought between the Cymry of that region and the Northumbrians'.[94] All three decapitations, then, are linked to the armies of the borderlands.

Because Bede places so much emphasis on Penda's paganism, these beheadings have often been interpreted in the context of pagan Germanic cult practices, with arguments ranging from actual human sacrifice to a visible homage to the efficacy of any non-Christian powers that Penda may have aligned himself with.[95] Head cults do appear to have played a prominent role in both pagan Germanic and Celtic cultures, perhaps making the act of symbolic decapitation a familiar one.[96] But it is a questionable exercise to extrapolate Penda's genuine religious beliefs from the hostile testimony of the *Historia Ecclesiastica*, and the recent work of Andrew Reynolds makes clear that decapitation also occurred in Christian Anglo-Saxon kingdoms and for many reasons other than human sacrifice.[97] What we can see in the *Historia Ecclesiastica* is the clear political symbolism of decapitating a king. For Bede, Oswald's decapitation by the pagan Penda transforms him from defeated king to Christian martyr, in the tradition of the British saint Alban whose execution by Romans is related earlier in the *Historia Ecclesiastica*[98] or the later example of the ninth-century East Anglian King Edmund, whose purported beheading by an invading Viking army bolstered his cult in the tenth century.[99] Bede calls attention to the anomaly of these decapitations, and in so doing distances the Welsh borderlands further from the Christian Anglo-Saxon kingdoms where his sympathies lie.[100]

That the borderlands appear to have been particularly associated with decapitation is further suggested by the manner of Penda's own death. After his loss at the Battle of the Winwæd, he was himself decapitated by Oswiu, presumably in revenge for the decapitations he himself had carried out over the course of his life. Bede distances Penda's decapitation from his account of the battle itself, mentioning just briefly, in the course of his account of the conversion of the Mercians after Penda's death, that Oswiu 'desecto capite perfido'[101] (severed his treacherous head). Colgrave and Mynors translate this as 'having destroyed their heathen ruler'[102] but, as J. M. Wallace-Hadrill noted in his *Historical Commentary*, 'Penda was not "destroyed" by Oswiu: his head was cut off and doubtless displayed as a sign of vengeance taken'.[103] Oswiu's decapitation of Penda is unusual and speaks to the strong associations of this type of desecration of the body of a defeated enemy with the region of the borderlands in the seventh century.

The Battle of the Winwæd

Penda's fatal last battle in 655 at the Winwæd, a river most commonly identified as the River Went, which lies between modern Leeds and Doncaster (see Map 2), shows the continued mixed culture of the borderlands and its distinction from other Anglo-Saxon kingdoms. At this battle, Penda commanded a coalition of thirty Anglo-Saxon and British kings and their troops, and his army's distinctive composition and structure sets the borderlands apart. The *Historia Ecclesiastica* reports that in Penda's army 'siquidem ipsi XXX legiones ducibus nobilissimis instructas in bello habuere'[104] (they had thirty legions of soldiers experienced in war and commanded by the most famous ealdormen),[105] who are also described as 'duces regii xxx'[106] (thirty royal ealdormen).[107]

Bede names only a few of the Anglo-Saxon kings who were part of Penda's forces. One of Oswiu's sons is left a hostage: 'nam alius filius eius Ecgfrid eo tempore in prouincia Merciorum apud reginam Cynuise obses tenebatur'[108] (Oswiu's other son Ecgfrith was at the time a hostage in the Mercian kingdom with Queen Cynewise).[109] Oswald's son takes Penda's side but does not fight: 'filius autem Osualdi regis Oidiluald, qui eis auxilio esse debuerat, in parte erat aduersariorum, eisdemque contra patriam et patruum suum pugnaturis ductor extiterat, quamuis ipso tempore pugnandi sese pugnae subtraxerat, euentumque discriminis tuto in loco exspectabat'[110] (But Oethelwald, King Oswald's son, who ought to have helped them, was on the side of his foes and was leading the enemies of his own uncle and of his native land; he withdrew, however, in the hour of battle and awaited the outcome in a place of safety).[111] The East Anglian king, Æthelhere, is killed: 'Inito ergo certamine fugati sunt et caesi pagani, duces regii XXX, qui ad auxilium uenerant, paene omnes interfecti; in quibus Aedilheri, frater Anna regis Orientalium Anglorum'[112] (The battle was joined and the heathens were put to flight or destroyed; of the thirty royal ealdormen who had come to Penda's help nearly all were killed. Among them was Æthelhere, brother and successor to Anna, king of the East Angles).[113] Interestingly, Bede again dismisses Penda's whole army as made up of pagans – 'denique fertur quia tricies maiorem pagani habuerint exercitum'[114] (indeed it is said that the heathens had an army which was thirty times as great)[115] – despite the presence of Christian British kings, indicating that from his perspective the whole of the borderlands could be written off together as Northumbria's enemy.

The account of this battle in the *Historia Brittonum* makes clear that many of those kings whom Bede does not identify were Welsh,[116] though the only British king among Penda's allies that it names is Cadafael of Gwynedd.[117] However, the *Historia Brittonum* states at several points that British kings were involved, for example 'et ipse occidit Pantha in campo Gai, et nunc facta est strages Gai campi, et reges Brittonum interfecti sunt, qui exierant cum rege Pantha in expeditione usque ad urbem quae vocatur Iudeu' (Oswiu killed Penda, at Gaius' Field, and now was the slaughter at Gaius' Field, and the kings of the British, who had gone forth with King Penda in his campaign to the city called Iudeu, were killed).[118] The mixed composition of Penda's army indicates the military continuity of the borderlands.

Bede's narrative of this battle conflates two distinct encounters between the armies of Oswiu and Penda. As described in the *Historia Brittonum*, the first is a successful campaign at a city known as 'Iudeu' (most often identified as Stirling; see Map 2), at which 'tunc reddidit Osguid omnes divitias quae errant cum eo in urbe usque in manu Pendae, et Penda distribuit ea regibus Brittonum, id est Atbret Iudeu' (Oswiu delivered all the riches that he had in the city into the hand of Penda, and Penda distributed them to the kings of the British, that is the 'Distribution [or Restitution] of Iudeu').[119] In the *Historia Ecclesiastica*, this event is conflated with the Battle at the Winwæd as an offer of tribute which Penda rejects: 'ad ultimum necessitate cogente promisit se ei innumera et maiora quam credi potest ornamenta regia uel donaria in pretium pacis largiturum, dummodo ille domum rediret et prouincias regni eius usque ad internicionem uastare desineret. Cumque rex perfidus nullatenus precibus illius assensum praeberet, qui totam eius gentem a paruo usque ad magnum delere atque exterminare decreuerat'[120] (Oswiu was at last forced to promise him an incalculable and incredible store of royal treasures and gifts as the price of peace, on condition that Penda would return home and cease to devastate, or rather utterly destroy, the kingdoms under his rule. But the heathen king would not accept this offer, for he was determined to destroy and exterminate the whole people from the greatest to the least).[121]

As Kenneth Jackson has argued, 'Bede's account is easily reconciled with this if we suppose that the two events have been telescoped in such a way that the offer appears to have been made just before the Battle of the Winwæd and was therefore necessarily taken by Bede or his source to have been refused'.[122] As T. M. Charles-Edwards explains further:

The main difficulty in accepting [Bede's] story as it stands is topographical: Oswiu is said to have been forced to offer the treasure to Penda after he had been driven to a desperate extremity by savage attacks. Yet, the site of the battle was in the south-west of Deira, a kingdom in which one of his enemies, Oethelwald, was king. The people that Penda was supposed to be bent on destroying was hardly the Northumbrians as a whole, again since many of the Deirans were his own allies. Moreover, the site of the battle was about sixty miles south of the Bernician Welsh borderlands, not a plausible location for a desperate attempt to prevent the extermination of the Bernicians. As soon, therefore, as we accept Bede's location of the battle in the district of *Loidis*, his narrative becomes barely credible. If we accept the *Historia Brittonum*, however, in thinking that Oswiu's offer of treasure was accepted, and that the offer was made at the northern extremity of his kingdom, Oswiu's success in defeating Penda becomes intelligible: Penda would have been on his way home; and some of his allies would have left his army, not out of treachery but for straightforward geographical reasons. In this instance, at least, the *Historia Brittonum* emerges as a credible and independent source, offering information most unlikely to be of early ninth-century origin.[123]

The *Historia Brittonum* stands on its own as a historical source for the Battle of the Winwæd, making clear the mixed nature of Penda's army.

Penda's role as the commander of thirty kings and their troops is a military structure particular to the borderlands in the *Historia Ecclesiastica*. The structure of the army at the Winwæd, with Penda in command, mirrors Cadwallon's earlier role at the Battle of Hatfield Chase, where he was the primary leader who revolted against Edwin with Penda's support.[124] The way that Cadwallon's and Penda's rank in these battles is described mirrors other passages in the *Historia Brittonum* which seem to establish this military structure as a familiar one. It is said that 'tunc Arthur pugnabat contra illos in illis diebus cum regibus Brittonum, sed ipse dux erat bellorum' (then Arthur fought against them [the Saxons] in those days, together with the kings of the British; but he was their leader in battle).[125] Likewise, when the Saxons attacked the British, 'et postea pugnabant contra reges nostrae gentis' (and afterwards they used to fight against the kings of one nation).[126] Arthurian mythology aside, this military structure reflects older British and Germanic battle practice, which was based on groupings of warbands with a flexible commander. As Stephen S. Evans has noted, in 'dark ages' warfare, large military forces were formed by 'mustering the warbands' – the basic unit was the *comitatus*, each commanded by its own lord and 'committed to the fray as an integral fighting unit'.[127] The *Historia Ecclesiastica* and *Historia Brittonum* indicate that the borderlands continued to fight with this military structure of mixed

Anglo-Welsh groupings of warbands, distinguishing the region from surrounding Anglo-Saxon kingdoms.

The mixed military culture of the borderlands from a Welsh perspective is further evidenced by an early vernacular poem, *Marwnad Cynddylan* ('A Lament for Cynddylan'),[128] which mourns the death of the Welsh prince Cynddylan of Powys. Cynddylan was one of Penda's allies at the Battle of Maserfelth/Maes Cogwy in Oswestry, which we know from the *englyn* mentioned above: 'Gwelais ar lawr maes Cogwy / byddinawr a gawr gymwy / Cynddylan oedd kynhorthwy' (I saw on the ground of the field of Cogwy / armies and battle affliction. / Cynddylan was an ally).[129] The longer poem *Marwnad Cynddylan* likewise evokes Cynddylan's role as a supporter of Penda, here in the context of a lament for his untimely death: 'pan fynnwys mab pyd mor fu parawd' (when the son of Pyd [i.e. Penda] desired, how ready he was!).[130] *Marwnad Cynddylan*, like the poem *Moliant Cadwallon* discussed above, does not survive in any medieval manuscript – its earliest witness is a seventeenth-century copy made by an early modern antiquarian. Yet despite the fact that no medieval manuscript of this poem survives, *Marwnad Cynddylan* has long been understood as an accurate reflection of its seventh-century historical context, a 'near-contemporary lament for Cynddylan' reflecting the stability of 'a Powys-Mercia alliance extending throughout the seventh century' from a Welsh perspective.[131]

Jenny Rowland has argued convincingly that Cynddylan was one of the British kings who died alongside Penda at the Battle of the Winwæd and that it is this disaster which *Marwnad Cynddylan* laments.[132] Building on her conclusions, John Koch has further suggested that 'the poem is not just a dark lament for Cynddylan and his comrades, but for the Welsh-Mercian alliance in general'.[133] In both Anglo-Saxon and Welsh sources, the Welsh borderlands were remembered as an allied region during the early Anglo-Saxon period.

Conclusions

Bede's *Historia Ecclesiastica* is the earliest significant surviving source for the history of the Welsh borderlands. Through the window of the life of Penda of Mercia, Bede's text shows the gradual consolidation of a mixed Anglo-Welsh culture in this region, which became distinguished from those other Anglo-Saxon kingdoms which had been converted to Roman Christianity. The *Historia Ecclesiastica* depicts no strife between Mercia and any of its Welsh neighbours, and Welsh sources paint the same portrait from the west. In contrast to the frequent violence among other Anglo-Saxon and

Welsh kingdoms, the attacks of the Welsh borderlands are always turned outward. The *Historia Ecclesiastica* reveals that the Welsh borderlands were depicted by one of the earliest and most significant Anglo-Saxon historical texts as a cohesive, identifiable region whose distinctively mixed Anglo-Welsh culture placed it in opposition to newly Christian Anglo-Saxon kingdoms.

Penda's death at the Battle of the Winwæd is often characterised as the moment which 'sounded the death-knell of English paganism as a political ideology and public religion',[134] but it was not the death knell for the distinctive culture of the borderlands which we can see taking shape in the seventh century. Chapter Three turns to our next chronological pieces of significant textual evidence for the culture of this region: several Latin and vernacular hagiographical texts about the popular Anglo-Saxon saint Guthlac. His various *Lives* depict the continuance of a mixed Anglo-Welsh culture in the borderlands into the eighth century, when the region is a locus of elite military advancement. Chapter Three illuminates further facets of the borderlands' role as a culture nexus in early medieval Britain by arguing that even within an Anglo-Saxon saint's life, the politics of land control are much less clear-cut than has been assumed. While Guthlac's battles with demons have been understood to reflect Anglo/Welsh ethnic division, Chapter Three reveals that the Old English poem *Guthlac A* is far more conflicted towards land ownership, reflecting the fluid boundaries of the Welsh borderlands themselves.

Notes

1 See for example Walter Goffart, *The Narrators of Barbarian History (A.D. 550–800): Jordanes, Gregory of Tours, Bede, and Paul the Deacon* (Princeton: Princeton University Press, 1988); N. J. Higham, *The Convert Kings: Power and Religious Affiliation in Early Anglo-Saxon England* (Manchester: Manchester University Press, 1997); Stephen J. Harris, *Race and Ethnicity in Anglo-Saxon Literature*, Studies in Medieval History and Culture 24 (New York: Routledge, 2003); N. J. Higham, *(Re-)Reading Bede: The Ecclesiastical History in Context* (New York: Routledge, 2006).

2 All quotations from the *Historia Ecclesiastica* are cited by book, chapter and page number in the edition by Michael Lapidge, *Beda: Storia Degli Inglesi (Historia ecclesiastica gentis Anglorum)*, with Italian translation by Paolo Chiesa, 2 vols: vol. I [books I–II] and vol. II [books III–V] (Milan: Fondazione Lorenzo Valla, 2008 and 2010). English translations are from Bertram Colgrave and R. A. B. Mynors, ed. and trans., *Bede's Ecclesiastical History of the English People* (Oxford: Clarendon Press, 1969; repr. 2007). Supplementary notes are

from J. M. Wallace-Hadrill, *Bede's Ecclesiastical History of the English People: A Historical Commentary* (Oxford: Clarendon Press, 1988; paperback 1993).
3 Lapidge, *Beda*, vol. I, Book II, Chapter XX, 268–71.
4 David Hill, *An Atlas of Anglo-Saxon England* (Toronto: University of Toronto Press, 1981), p. 30 map 41, 'the England of Bede c.731. Place names from the Ecclesiastical History', with battle sites discussed in this chapter emphasised.
5 Colgrave and Mynors, *Bede*, Book II, Chapter XX, 202–3, with translation emended following Wallace-Hadrill, *Historical Commentary*, 84. On the most likely length of Penda's reign see Nicholas Brooks, 'The formation of the Mercian kingdom', in *The Origins of Anglo-Saxon Kingdoms*, ed. Steven Bassett (London: Leicester University Press, 1989), 159–70, who reconciles the conflicting accounts given by the *Historia Ecclesiastica*, *Historia Brittonum* and *Anglo-Saxon Chronicle*.
6 All quotations from the *Annales Cambriae* (by annal year) and *Historia Brittonum* (by chapter) are cited in the edition by John Morris, ed. and trans., *Nennius: British History and the Welsh Annals* (London: Phillimore, 1980). The *Annales Cambriae* were kept regularly from 790 onwards at St David's in Wales but probably extended backwards using contemporary Easter tables; see Kathleen Hughes, 'The Welsh Latin chronicles: *Annales Cambriae* and related texts' and 'The A-text of *Annales Cambriae*' in her *Celtic Britain in the Early Middle Ages* (Woodbridge, Suffolk: Boydell, 1980) and David N. Dumville, ed. and trans., *Annales Cambriae, A.D. 682–954: Texts A–C in Parallel* (Cambridge: Department of Anglo-Saxon, Norse, and Celtic, 2002), pp. v–xv. *Annales Cambriae* A was edited by E. Phillimore, 'The *Annales Cambriae* and the Old Welsh genealogies from Harleian MS. 3859', *Y Cymmrodor* 9 (1888): 141–83. A composite of versions A, B and C was published by J. Williams ab Ithel, *Annales Cambriae*, Rolls Series (London: Longman, 1860). While it contains serious errors – see review by L. Jones in *Archaeologia Cambrensis* (1861), 331 – it remains the only published edition of the *Annales Cambriae* after 954.
7 *Annales Cambriae* for 630; Morris, *Nennius*, 86 and 46.
8 *Historia Brittonum* ch. 61; Morris, *Nennius*, 78 and 37. The *Historia Brittonum* was likely first compiled in the 820s in North Wales. On its complex textual tradition, see David N. Dumville, 'Some aspects of the chronology of the *Historia Brittonum*', *Bulletin of the Board of Celtic Studies* 25 (1972): 439–45; '"Nennius" and the *Historia Brittonum*', *Studia Celtica* 10/11 (1975–76): 78–95; 'Sub-Roman Britain: history and legend', *History* 62 (1977): 173–92; *The Historia Brittonum, Volume 3: The Vatican Recension* (Cambridge: D. S. Brewer, 1985); and 'The historical value of the *Historia Brittonum*', *Arthurian Literature* 6 (1986): 1–26; also T. M. Charles-Edwards, 'The Arthur of history', in *The Arthur of the Welsh*, ed. Rachel Bromwich, A. O. H. Jarman and Brynley F. Roberts (Cardiff: University of Wales Press, 1991): 15–32.
9 Alex Woolf, 'Caedwalla Rex Brettonum and the passing of the old North', *Northern History* 41 (2004): 5–24 has recently argued that Cadwallon was the

ruler not of Gwynedd but of northern Britain. His arguments have been found unpersuasive on linguistic, historical and geographical grounds – see T. M. Charles-Edwards, *Wales and the Britons, 350–1064* (Oxford: Oxford University Press, 2013), 390 n.55.

10 Lapidge, *Beda*, vol. I, Book II, Chapter IX, 214–15.
11 Colgrave and Mynors, *Bede*, Book II, Chapter IX, 162–3.
12 D. P. Kirby, *The Earliest English Kings*, revised edn (London: Routledge, 2000), 65.
13 See Colgrave and Mynors, *Bede*, 162 n.1 and 202 n.3; Nora K. Chadwick, 'The conversion of Northumbria: a comparison of sources', in *Celt and Saxon: Studies in the Early British Border*, ed. Nora K. Chadwick (Cambridge: Cambridge University Press, 1963): 138–66 and Charles-Edwards, *Wales and the Britons*, 389, n.52.
14 Reginald of Durham, *Life of St Oswald*, c. 9; Thomas Arnold, ed., *Symeonis Monachi Opera Omnia*, 2 vols., Rolls Series (London: Longmans, 1885), i.345; textual problems discussed in Victoria Tudor, 'Reginald's Life of St Oswald', in *Oswald: Northumbrian King to European Saint*, ed. Clare Stancliffe and Eric Cambridge (Stamford: Paul Watkins, 1995), 178–94. Geoffrey of Monmouth, *Historia Regum Britanniae*, c. 190; Michael D. Reeve, ed., and Neil Wright, trans., Geoffrey of Monmouth. *The History of the Kings of Britain: An Edition and Translation of De gestis Britonum (Historia Regum Britanniae)*, Arthurian Studies LXIX (Woodbridge, Suffolk: Boydell, 2007). The Welsh tradition is discussed by Chadwick, 'Conversion of Northumbria', 148 and Rachel Bromwich, *Trioedd Ynys Prydein*, 3rd edn (Cardiff: University of Wales Press, 2006), 339–40.
15 Fosterage, and the kinship ties it created, were very important to both early Germanic and Celtic societies – see T. M. Charles-Edwards, *Early Irish and Welsh Kinship* (Oxford: Clarendon Press, 1993); T. M. Charles-Edwards, 'Anglo-Saxon kinship revisited', in *The Anglo-Saxons from the Migration Period to the Eighth Century*, ed. John Hines (Woodbridge, Suffolk: Boydell, 1997), 171–204; Stephen S. Evans, *The Lords of Battle: Image and Reality of the Comitatus in Dark-Age Britain* (Woodbridge, Suffolk: Boydell, 1997), 117–120; and Hilda Ellis Davidson, 'The training of warriors', in *Weapons and Warfare in Anglo-Saxon England*, ed. Sonia Chadwick Hawkes (Oxford: Oxford University Committee for Archaeology, 1989), 11–23.
16 *Annales Cambriae* for 626, Morris, *Nennius*, 86 and 46.
17 *Historia Brittonum* ch. 63, Morris, *Nennius*, 38 and 79. For discussion, see Chadwick, 'Conversion of Northumbria', 155–66.
18 Lapidge, *Beda*, vol. I, Book II, Chapter XIIII, 248–9.
19 Colgrave and Mynors, *Bede*, Book II, Chapter XIV, 186–7.
20 Chadwick, 'Conversion of Northumbria', 149. On the oddly-named Ceorl, the earliest known Mercian king before Penda, see Wendy Davies, 'Annals and the origin of Mercia', in *Mercian Studies*, ed. Ann Dornier (Leicester: Leicester

University Press, 1977), 17–30 and N. J. Higham, 'King Cearl, the battle of Chester, and the origins of the Mercian "overkingship"', *Midland History* 17 (1992): 1–15.

21 The same pattern might also apply to Oswiu, who is said by the *Historia Brittonum*, ch. 57, to have two wives (one of them British): 'Osguid autem habuit duas uxores, quarum una vocabatur Rieinmelth, filia Royth, filii Rum, et altera vocabatur Eanfled, filia Eadguin, filii Alii' (But Oswy had two wives, one of whom was called Rieinmellt, daughter of Royth, son of Rhun, and the other was called Eanflæd, daughter of Edwin, son of Aelle), Morris, *Nennius*, 77 and 36. A third wife, the Irish princess Fín, was the mother of Aldrith of Northumbria (d. 704/5)

22 Harris, *Race and Ethnicity in Anglo-Saxon Literature*, 45–82.

23 Lapidge, *Beda*, vol. I, Book II, Chapter XX, 270–1.

24 Colgrave and Mynors, *Bede*, Book II, Chapter XX, 204–5. See further John T. Koch, *Cunedda, Cynan, Cadwallon, Cynddylan: Four Welsh Poems and Britain, 383–655* (Aberystwyth: University of Wales Centre for Advanced Welsh and Celtic Studies, 2013), 180.

25 Lapidge, *Beda*, vol. I, Book II, Chapter XX, 270–1.

26 Colgrave and Mynors, *Bede*, Book II, Chapter XX, 204–5.

27 Paul Russell has noted that the *-walh* element in these names could also be derived from Welsh *gwalch*, falcon (personal communication), which I would argue still reflects a degree of British influence.

28 Patrick Sims-Williams, *Religion and Literature in Western England: 600–800*, Cambridge Studies in Anglo-Saxon England 3 (Cambridge: Cambridge University Press, 1990), 26.

29 On Anglo-Saxon names more broadly, see Fran Colman, *The Grammar of Names in Anglo-Saxon England: The Linguistics and Culture of the Old English Onomasticon* (Oxford: Oxford University Press, 2014).

30 Damian J. Tyler, 'Early Mercia and the Britons', in *Britons in Anglo-Saxon England*, ed. N. J. Higham, Publications of the Manchester Centre for Anglo-Saxon Studies 7 (Woodbridge, Suffolk: Boydell, 2007), 91–101 and 'An early Mercian hegemony: Penda and overkingship in the seventh century', *Midland History* 30 (2005): 1–19, has argued for a significant British presence within the upper echelon of Mercian society.

31 Paul Russell, 'Introduction: the names of Celtic origin' and 'Personal names: Celtic names' (with Peter McClure and David Rollason), in *The Durham Liber Vitae: London, British Library, MS Cotton Domitian A.VII, vol. II: Linguistic Commentary*, ed. David and Lynda Rollason (London: British Library, 2007), 5–8 and 35–43 at 7–8.

32 Lapidge, *Beda*, vol. I, Book II, Chapter XX, 268–71.

33 Colgrave and Mynors, *Bede*, Book II, Chapter XX, 202–3, with translation emended following Wallace-Hadrill, *Historical Commentary*, 84.

34 Frederick M. Biggs, 'The politics of succession in Beowulf and Anglo-Saxon

England', *Speculum* 80 (2005): 709–41 at 710. As this article, alongside his 'Edgar's path to the throne', in *Edgar, King of the English, 959–975*, ed. Donald Scragg (Woodbridge, Suffolk: Boydell, 2008), 124–39, demonstrates, awareness of the very real contrast in these two models of succession is reflected in both the literature and history of Anglo-Saxon England.

35 *Historia Ecclesiastica* Book III, Chapter I.
36 *Historia Ecclesiastica* Book III, Chapter VII and Book III, Chapter XXI. These episodes are discussed further below.
37 See Charles-Edwards, *Wales and the Britons*, 314–39; also his *Early Irish and Welsh Kinship* (Oxford: Clarendon Press, 1993).
38 *Historia Ecclesiastica* Book III, Chapter XXI.
39 Lapidge, *Beda*, vol. II, Book III, Chapter XXI, 98–9.
40 Colgrave and Mynors, *Bede*, Book III, Chapter XXI, 280–1.
41 Higham, *Convert Kings*, 1.
42 *Ibid.*, 241 expresses a typical sentiment in writing that Penda's death 'sounded the death-knell of English paganism as a political ideology and public religion'. The Isle of Wight, the last pagan Anglo-Saxon kingdom, was converted in 686.
43 Lapidge, *Beda*, vol. I, Book II, Chapter XX, 270–1.
44 Colgrave and Mynors, *Bede*, Book II, Chapter XX, 202–3.
45 Lapidge, *Beda*, vol. II, Book III, Chapter I, 14–15.
46 Colgrave and Mynors, *Bede*, Book III, Chapter I, 212–15.
47 Two later passages on the apostasies of Edwin's successors may be significant here. Bede records that 'Infaustus ille annus et omnibus bonis exosus usque hodie permanet, tam propter apostasiam regum Anglorum, qua se fidei sacramentis exuerant, quam propter uaesanam Brettonici regis tyrannidem. Vnde cunctis placuit regum tempora computantibus ut, ablata de medio regum perfidorum memoria, idem annus sequentis regis, id est Osualdi uiri Deo dilecti, regno assignaretur', Lapidge, *Beda*, vol. II, Book III, Chapter I, 14–15 (To this day that year is still held to have been ill-omened and hateful to all good men, not only on account of the apostasy of the English kings who cast aside the mysteries of their faith, but also because of the outrageous tyranny of the British king. So all those who compute the dates of kings have decided to abolish the memory of those perfidious kings and to assign this year to their successor Oswald, a man beloved of God), Colgrave and Mynors, *Bede*, Book III, Chapter I, 214–15. This statement is reiterated a little later in Book III, Chapter IX. While Bede's admission that the reigns of base kings should be struck from the historical record is noteworthy (particularly, one wonders how many other deeds of Cadwallon and Penda may have been likewise omitted), it is perhaps even more interesting that, in Bede's mind, British military violence and Anglo-Saxon paganism always seem to travel hand-in-hand.
48 See Evans, *Lords of Battle* (*passim*, but particularly 9–24 and 25–40).
49 See David Wyatt, *Slaves and Warriors in Medieval Britain and Ireland, 800–1200* (Leiden: Brill, 2009).

50 *Historia Ecclesiastica* Book II, Chapter II. The battle is also recorded in *Annales Cambriae* for 613, 'Gueith Cair Legion, et ibi cecidit Selim filii Cinan. Et Jacob filii Beli dormitatio' (the Battle of Caer Legion and there died Selyf son of Cynan. And Iago son of Beli slept), Morris, *Nennius*, 86 and 46. Cynan is the subject of the early Welsh praise poem *Trawsganu Kynan Garwyn mab Brochfael*, discussed further below.
51 Lapidge, *Beda*, vol. II, Book III, Chapter IX, 46–7.
52 Colgrave and Mynors, *Bede*, Book III, Chapter IX, 240–3.
53 Lapidge, *Beda*, vol. II, Book III, Chapter XIIII, 64–5.
54 Colgrave and Mynors, *Bede*, Book III, Chapter XIV, 254–5.
55 Lapidge, *Beda*, vol. II, Book III, Chapter XVI, 74–5.
56 Colgrave and Mynors, *Bede*, Book III, Chapter XVI, 262–3.
57 Lapidge, *Beda*, vol. II, Book III, Chapter XVII, 76–7.
58 Colgrave and Mynors, *Bede*, Book III, Chapter XVII, 264–5.
59 Lapidge, *Beda*, vol. I, Book II, Chapter XIII, 250–1.
60 Colgrave and Mynors, *Bede*, Book II, Chapter XIV, 188–9.
61 Lapidge, *Beda*, vol. II, Book III, Chapter XVIII, 82–3.
62 Colgrave and Mynors, *Bede*, Book III Chapter 18, 268–9.
63 Lapidge, *Beda*, vol. II, Book III, Chapter XVIII, 82–3.
64 Colgrave and Mynors, *Bede*, Book III Chapter 18, 268–9.
65 Edited and translated in R. Geraint Gruffydd, 'Canu Cadwallon ap Cadfan', *Astudiaethau ar yr Hengeredd*, ed. Rachel Bromwich and R. Brinley Jones (Cardiff: University of Wales Press, 1978): 25–43. *Moliant Cadwallon* is also edited and discussed in Koch, *Cunedda, Cynan, Cadwallon, Cynddylan*, 161–229. While Koch's discussions of these poems can be valuable, his editions are very problematic because he reconstructs the texts into earlier forms of medieval Brythonic based on his views that they were written contemporaneously with the events the describe, which took place in the fifth (Cunedda), sixth (Cynan), and seventh (Cadwallon and Cynddylan) centuries. Very few Celticists agree with his dating of these poems – for critiques of his methodology, see Oliver Padel's review of his *The 'Gododdin' of Aneirin: Text and Context from Dark-Age Britain* (Cardiff: University of Wales Press, 1997) in *Cambrian Medieval Celtic Studies* 35 (1998): 45–55 at 53; the review by Graham R. Isaac, *Llên Cymru* 22 (1999): 138–60 and his 'Readings in the history and transmission of the Gododdin', *Cambrian Medieval Celtic Studies* 37 (1999): 55–78; as well as the essays collected in Alex Woolf, ed., *Beyond the Gododdin: Dark Age Scotland in Medieval Wales* (St Andrews: University of St Andrews, 2013), and its review by Patrick Sims-Williams, *Cambrian Medieval Celtic Studies* 66 (2013): 85–8.
66 Gruffydd, 'Canu Cadwallon ap Cadfan', 27–8 and Koch, *Cunedda, Cynan, Cadwallon, Cynddylan*, 186–7.
67 Edited and translated in Jenny Rowland, *Early Welsh Saga Poetry* (Cambridge: D. S. Brewer, 1990): 120–41 and 169–73 (discussion), 446–7 (text), 495–6 (translation) and 613–16 (notes); and in Gruffydd, 'Canu Cadwallon ap Cadfan', 25–43.

68 Rowland, *Early Welsh Saga Poetry*, 169–73.
69 *Ibid.*, 172.
70 Gruffydd, 'Canu Cadwallon ap Cadfan', 34–5.
71 Rowland, *Early Welsh Saga Poetry*, 170.
72 *Ibid.*, 169.
73 *Ibid.*, 120–41 and 169–73.
74 Ifor Williams, ed., and J. E. Caerwyn Williams, trans., *The Poems of Taliesin* (Dublin: Dublin Institute for Advanced Studies, 1968), pp. ix–lxvii (introduction), 1 (text) and 16–28 (notes); Koch, *Cunedda, Cynan, Cadwallon, Cynddylan*, 105–571; and Graham R. Isaac, 'Trawsganu Kynan Garwyn mab Brochuael: a tenth-century political poem', *Zeitschrift für celtische Philologie* 51 (1999): 173–85. See also Charles-Edwards, *Wales and the Britons*, 16 n.77.
75 *Historia Ecclesiastica* Book II, Chapter II; *Annales Cambriae* for 613. For Selyf ap Cynan's genealogy, see Peter Bartrum, *Early Welsh Genealogical Tracts* (Cardiff: University of Wales Press, 1966).
76 Marged Haycock has made the unpublished suggestion that the 'Cernyw' in this poem – usually understood as Cornwall – actually refers to the Cornovii of Shropshire. Regardless of which place is correct, the point remains that, in this poem, Cynan's aggression is directed only against other British kingdoms. Discussed in Charles-Edwards, *Wales and the Britons*, 16.
77 See Evans, *Lords of Battle*, 128 and Andrew Reynolds, *Anglo-Saxon Deviant Burial Customs* (Oxford: Oxford University Press, 2009), 76–81.
78 Lapidge, *Beda*, vol. I, Book II, Chapter XX, 270–1.
79 Colgrave and Mynors, *Bede*, Book II, Chapter XX, 204–5.
80 Gruffydd, 'Canu Cadwallon ap Cadfan', 41–3.
81 On the location of this battle in modern Oswestry, on the Welsh border, see Clare Stancliffe, 'Where was Oswald killed?', in *Oswald: Northumbrian King to European Saint*, 84–96.
82 Lapidge, *Beda*, vol. II, Book III, Chapter XII, 60–1.
83 Colgrave and Mynors, *Bede*, Book III, Chapter XII, 250–3.
84 Lapidge, *Beda*, vol. II, Book III, Chapter XII, 60–1.
85 Colgrave and Mynors, *Bede*, Book III, Chapter XII, 252–3.
86 Whitley Stokes, ed. and trans., 'The Annals of Tigernach: the third fragment, A.D. 489–766', *Revue Celtique* 17 (1896): 119–263 at 182.
87 Koch, *Cunedda, Cynan, Cadwallon, Cynddylan*, 178.
88 Maserfelth might plausibly have been an attempt by Penda to avenge Cadwallon's death. Cadwallon was killed by Oswald at the Battle of the Denisesburn (*Historia Ecclesiastica*, Book III, Chapter I), known in Welsh as the Battle of Cantscaul (*Annales Cambriae* for 631 and *Historia Brittonum*, ch. 64; see Ifor Williams, 'Bellum Cantscaul', *Bulletin of the Board of Celtic Studies* 6 (1933): 351–4). This, Bede states, was Oswald's vengeance for his brother Eanfrith, whom Cadwallon had previously killed. The chronology of events implies that Maserfelth, in turn, is an attempt by Penda to avenge Cadwallon.

89 *Annales Cambriae* for 644; Morris, *Nennius*, 86 and 46.
90 *Historia Brittonum* ch. 65; Morris, *Nennius*, 80 and 39.
91 Discussed in Stancliffe, 'Where was Oswald killed?', 84–5.
92 The *englyn* is appended as stanza 111 to *Canu Heledd*; see Rowland, *Early Welsh Saga Poetry*, 445 (text), 494 (translation), 612 (notes), and 120–41 and 168–73 (discussion). The alliance between Penda and Cynddylan is examined in greater detail below in the discussion of the Battle of the Winwæd.
93 *Gwaith Cynddelw Brydydd Mawr*, vol. I, ed. N. A. Jones and A. P. Owen (Cardiff: University of Wales Press, 1991), no. 3.
94 Ifor Williams, 'A reference to the Nennian Bellum Cocboy', *Bulletin of the Board of Celtic Studies* 3 (1926/27): 59–62 at 60.
95 See Higham, *Convert Kings*, 221–3; William A. Chaney, *The Cult of Kingship in Anglo-Saxon England: The Transition from Paganism to Christianity* (Manchester: Manchester University Press, 1970), 40–1 and 116–20, with detailed discussion of pan-Germanic parallels (though he presses his case more strongly than most would today); and Alan Thacker, 'Membra disjecta: the division of the body and the diffusion of the cult', in *Oswald*, 97–127, with an excellent discussion of the complex entanglement of Germanic and Celtic religious and cultural beliefs that underlie not only Oswald's death but also the subsequent (Christian) cults surrounding his head.
96 On Germanic head-cults see Chaney, *The Cult of Kingship*, 95, 118–19; H. M. and Nora K. Chadwick, *The Growth of Literature* (Cambridge: Cambridge University Press, 1932), I, 93–4; Thacker, 'Membra disjecta', 100; and D. R. Wilson, *Anglo-Saxon Paganism* (London: Routledge, 1992), 92–5. On Celtic head-cults see A. Ross, *Pagan Celtic Britain* (London: Routledge, 1967), 20–33, 61–126; Thacker, 'Membra disjecta', 102–3; Evans, *Lords of Battle*, 129 n.18; and John T. Koch, *Celtic Culture: A Historical Encyclopedia*, 5 vols. (Santa Barbara CA: ABC-CLIO, 2006), entry on 'head cult', 895–8 and accompanying bibliography. On both, see Evans, *Lords of Battle*, 128.
97 Reynolds, *Anglo-Saxon Deviant Burial Customs*, 76–81.
98 *Historia Ecclesiastica*, Book I, Chapter VII.
99 Abbo of Fleury's *Passio Sancti Eadmundi*, in which the legend of Edmund's decapitation is first recorded, was written over a century after Edmund's death in order to bolster his cult. The most recent edition is Michael Winterbottom, *Three Lives of English Saints* (Toronto: PIMS, 1972).
100 Decapitation was also linked to the March of Wales after the Norman Conquest, where it appeared to be acknowledged as a particular risk of the violence of Marcher life, as Frederick C. Suppe and Ordelle G. Hill have demonstrated: Frederick C. Suppe, 'The cultural significance of decapitation in high medieval Wales and the Marches', *Bulletin of the Board of Celtic Studies* 36 (1989): 147–60; and Ordelle G. Hill, *Looking Westward: Poetry, Landscape, and Politics in 'Sir Gawain and the Green Knight'* (Newark: University of Delaware Press, 2009), Ch. 4, 117–41.

Penda in Bede's Historia Ecclesiastica

101 Lapidge, *Beda*, vol. II, Book III, Chapter XXIIII, 114–15.
102 Colgrave and Mynors, *Bede*, Book III, Chapter XXIV, 292–3.
103 Wallace-Hadrill, *Historical Commentary*, 122–3.
104 Lapidge, *Beda*, vol. II, Book III, Chapter XXIIII, 112–13.
105 Colgrave and Mynors, *Bede*, Book III, Chapter XXIV, 290–1.
106 Lapidge, *Beda*, vol. II, Book III, Chapter XXIIII, 112–13.
107 Colgrave and Mynors, *Bede*, Book III, Chapter XXIV, 290–1.
108 Lapidge, *Beda*, vol. II, Book III, Chapter XXIIII, 112–13.
109 Colgrave and Mynors, *Bede*, Book III, Chapter XXIV, 290–1.
110 Lapidge, *Beda*, vol. II, Book III, Chapter XXIIII, 112–13.
111 Colgrave and Mynors, *Bede*, Book III, Chapter XXIV, 290–1.
112 Lapidge, *Beda*, vol. II, Book III, Chapter XXIIII, 112–13.
113 Colgrave and Mynors, *Bede*, Book III, Chapter XXIV, 290–1. On Æthelhere as *auctor*, see J. O. Prestwich, 'King Æthelhere and the battle of the Winwæd', *English Historical Review* 83 (1968): 89–95, who has convincingly argued for a punctuation error in the manuscript and an original reading that Æthelhere was killed at the Winwæd, as was Penda, the *auctor* of the war.
114 Lapidge, *Beda*, vol. II, Book III, Chapter XXIIII, 112–13.
115 Colgrave and Mynors, *Bede*, Book III, Chapter XXIV, 290–1.
116 The battle is also recorded in the *Annales Cambriae*, underscoring its importance to Welsh history, though no further details are given: 656, 'strages Gaii campi' (the slaughter of Campus Gaius); 657, 'Pantha occisio' (Penda killed); 658 'Osguid venit et praedam duxit' (Oswy came and took plunder); in Morris, *Nennius*, 87 and 46.
117 *Historia Brittonum*, ch. 65, discussed further below.
118 Ibid., ch. 64, Morris, *Nennius*, 79 and 38.
119 *Historia Brittonum*, ch. 65, in Morris, *Nennius*, 79 and 38. Charles-Edwards, *Wales and the Britons*, 394, translates as 'Restitution'.
120 Lapidge, *Beda*, vol. II, Book III, Chapter XXIIII, 110–13.
121 Colgrave and Mynors, *Bede*, Book III, Chapter XXIV, 288–91.
122 Kenneth Jackson, 'On the Northern British section in Nennius', in *Celt and Saxon*, ed. Chadwick, 20–62 at 38, arguing further that the word *atbret* is archaic and this tradition is therefore likely to have historical value.
123 Charles-Edwards, *Wales and the Britons*, 395–6.
124 *Historia Ecclesiastica*, Book II, Chapter XX.
125 *Historia Brittonum*, ch. 56, Morris, *Nennius*, 76 and 35.
126 *Historia Brittonum*, ch. 43, Morris, *Nennius*, 72 and 31.
127 Evans, *Lords of Battle*, 34.
128 *Marwnad Cynddylan* has been edited by Ifor Williams, 'Marwnad Cynddylan', *Bulletin of the Board of Celtic Studies* 6 (1932): 134–41 and again in his *Canu Llywarch Hen*, 3ydd argrff (Caerdydd: Gwasg Prifysgol Cymru, 1970), 50–2; R. Geraint Gruffydd, 'Marwnad Cynddylan', in *Bardos: Penodau ar y Traddodiad Barddol Cymreig a Cheltaidd*, ed. R. Geraint Gruffydd (Caerdydd: Gwasg

Prifysgol Cymru, 1982), 10–28; Rowland, *Early Welsh Saga Poetry*, 174–89; and Koch, *Cunedda, Cynan, Cadwallon, Cynddylan*, 231–92 (reconstructed into early medieval Brythonic). See the introductions and notes to these editions for discussion of the poem's manuscript context and textual difficulties. Citations here are of Rowland's edition, given by line and page number.

129 Rowland, *Early Welsh Saga Poetry*, 445 (text), 494 (translation), 612 (notes), and 120–41 and 168–73 (discussion).
130 *Ibid.*, 176–7, l. 28; see 184 n.28 on 'mab pyd'.
131 Rowland, *Early Welsh Saga Poetry*, 122 and 123. See particularly Ifor Williams, *Canu Llywarch Hen*, pp. lxxiii–iv and 244; H. P. R. Finberg, *Lucerna: Studies of Some Problems in the Early History of England* (London: Macmillan, 1964), 66–82; and Rowland, *Early Welsh Saga Poetry*, 120–41. As Rowland's thorough study makes clear, *Marwnadd Cynddylan* must be treated separately from *Canu Heledd*, a later cycle of saga poems purportedly narrated through the voice of Cynddylan's sister, but reflecting the political situation of ninth-century, not seventh-century, Powys. As Rowland, *Early Welsh Saga Poetry*, 141, concludes, 'the historical background given in *Canu Heledd* is not reliable' and 'the picture presented in *Canu Heledd* of Cynddylan's fall has no historical basis, or rather, the picture of the cataclysmic defeat attributed to his reign has its historical basis in another time and place', 138; see further 120–41 (historical background), 141–69 (discussion of the literary traditions to which *Canu Heledd* belongs), 429–47 (text), 483–96 (translation) and 572–616 (notes).
132 Rowland, *Early Welsh Saga Poetry*, 131.
133 Koch, *Cunedda, Cynan, Cadwallon, Cynddylan*, 235. I agree with his overall impression of the poem's political milieu, but hesitate to accept many of his readings of individual cruxes, particularly regarding the Battle of Chester. For a thorough discussion of the poem's several textual and historical cruxes, see Koch, *Cunedda, Cynan, Cadwallon, Cynddylan*, 231–92 and Rowland, *Early Welsh Saga Poetry*, 131–6 and 180–9.
134 Higham, *Convert Kings*, 241.

3

The Welsh borderlands in the *Lives* of St Guthlac[1]

Chapter Two argued that Bede's *Historia Ecclesiastica* depicts a mixed Anglo-Welsh culture in the Welsh borderlands in the seventh century. This chapter extends this argument into the eighth century through an examination of the various Latin and Old English *Lives* of the popular Anglo-Saxon saint, Guthlac of Crowland (d. 715). Guthlac's Mercian youth and later career as a hermit in the Fens link him indelibly to two of Britain's most geographically ambiguous spaces, and I argue that the group of Anglo-Saxon texts that depict his life show his roots in the cultural nexus of the Welsh borderlands, presented as a locus of elite military advancement. Guthlac spent a portion of his youth exiled among the British and as the leader of a multi-ethnic war band, and contemporary Welsh and Cambro-Latin texts also make clear that these were core characteristics of military life in the borderlands. The mixed culture of the Welsh borderlands is also evident in this chapter's second significant argument: that even in this Anglo-Saxon saint's life, the politics of land control are much less clear-cut than has been assumed. While St Guthlac's battles with demons have been understood to reflect Anglo/Welsh ethnic division, I argue in this chapter that the Old English poem *Guthlac A* is far more conflicted towards territoriality, reflecting the fluid boundaries of Mercia, and of the Welsh borderlands, than it is towards the Welsh as a whole.

Multi-ethnic warbands and Guthlac's youth

Guthlac's life is first recorded in the early eighth-century *Vita Sancti Guthlaci* written by a monk named Felix.[2] Guthlac was born into a noble Mercian family in 674 in the reign of Æthelred, and his early life was that of a successful warrior before a change of heart at age 24 prompted him to abandon the heroic lifestyle and enter the monastery at Repton.³ In 699, he left the monastery to live as a hermit in the Fens, where he remained until his death in 715.⁴ Guthlac was venerated in Anglo-Saxon England even during his lifetime, because he was visited in his hermitage by Æthelbald, the future king of Mercia (from 716), and his *Vita* was written by Felix at the request of Ælfwald, king of the East Angles from 713 to 749.⁵

Guthlac's family background and early life contain details which depict the Welsh borderlands in the late seventh and early eighth centuries as a nexus of Anglo-Welsh culture in several key ways. The first of these is the same pattern of British influence on the names of Mercian nobles discussed in Chapter Two. Guthlac was born into an aristocratic Mercian family, and while his own name is Germanic, his father's is half-British. Felix's *Vita* proper begins by introducing Guthlac's father: 'fuit itaque in diebus Æthelredi inlustris Anglorum regis quidam vir de egregia stirpe Merciorum cognomine Penwalh, cuius mansio in Mediterraneorum Anglorum partibus diversarum rerum fluxu praedita constabat' (now there was in the days of Æthelred the illustrious king of the English a certain man of distinguished Mercian stock named Penwalh, whose dwelling, furnished with an abundance of goods of various kinds, was in the district of the Middle Angles).⁶

As I argued in Chapter Two, Penwalh's name, composed as it is of the Welsh word *pen*, 'chief' or 'head', and the Old English word *wealh*,⁷ Welshman, suggestively reflects a mixed Anglo-Welsh cultural influence. Bertram Colgrave argued that there is 'very little foundation' for reading Penwalh as a Celtic name: he objected that *wealh*, 'though it means a foreigner or a Welshman is frequently found as the second element of O.E. names, so frequently in fact as to make it unlikely that the element was used only in the case of foreigners'.⁸ However, he did not address the Welsh element *pen*, and as Frederick C. Suppe has demonstrated, the comparable Welsh name-element *sais*, meaning Englishman, had 'a broader range of social meanings' than just those Welshmen with English wives or mothers: 'someone who could speak English, or who had been to England [perhaps as a hostage], or who had an English parent, or who admired and imitated English ways'.⁹ As was the case with the British-influenced Mercian names in Bede's *Historia Ecclesiastica*, there is no need to argue that Penwalh was himself British in order to understand that his name likely signified that he was someone with British associations.

Colgrave also takes Penwalh's descent from the Mercian royal house, 'huius etiam viri progenies per nobilissima inlustrium regum nomina antiqua ab origine Icles digesto ordine cucurrit' (moreover the descent of this man was traced in set order through the most noble names of famous kings, back to Icel in whom it began in days of old),[10] as evidence against a possible British ethnicity,[11] finding these connections indicative of a purely Anglo-Saxon ancestry. Yet Felix does not say that the famous kings were all Saxons; indeed, as discussed in Chapter Two, the royal Mercian genealogy is full of what seem to be British-influenced names, including several which alliterate with Penwalh. These names suggest a British cultural influence within the ruling family of early Mercia, and Guthlac's father indicates that this pattern continued at least through the late seventh century.[12]

Guthlac's early life was spent leading a warband in the Welsh borderlands. The descriptions of his youth in Felix's *Vita* represent this region as a space, like the post-Conquest March of Wales,[13] where young warriors could advance their social standing by military prowess. Guthlac's *Vita* reflects two other key facets of the society in the borderlands evidenced in Bede's *Historia Ecclesiastica* in Chapter Two: the young saint led a multi-ethnic warband and spent part of his youth living in exile among the British. Felix's *Vita Sancti Guthlaci*, like Bede's *Historia Ecclesiastica*, depicts the Welsh borderlands as a space apart from the Anglo-Saxon and Welsh kingdoms.

The importance of warfare to Guthlac's identity is famously reflected in his name. Felix provides a false etymology meant to heighten the saint's saintly characteristics: 'Nam ut illius gentis gnari perhibent, Anglorum lingua hoc nomen ex duobus integris constare videtur, hoc est "Guth" et "lac", quod Romani sermonis nitore personat "belli munus", quia ille cum vitiis bellando munera aeternae beatitudinis cum triumphali infula perennis vitae percepisset' (as those who are familiar with that race relate, the name in the tongue of the English is shown to consist of two individual words, namely 'Guth' and 'lac', which in the elegant Latin tongue is 'belli munus' [the reward of war], because by warring against vices he was to receive the reward of eternal bliss, together with the victor's diadem of everlasting life).[14] Yet as Colgrave notes, 'it is more probable that *lac* should be interpreted as "play" ... in which case it might be interpreted as "battle-play"'.[15] Guthlac's name thus emphasises his identity as a warrior.

His youth embodies this identity, and his leadership of a warband in the Welsh borderlands exemplifies its nature as a site of social advancement through military success.[16] In the saint's youth, 'igitur cum adolescentiae vires increvissent, et iuvenili in pectore egregius dominandi amor fervesceret, tunc valida pristinorum heroum facta reminiscens, veluti ex sopore evigilatus, mutata mente, adgregatis satellitum turmis, sese in arma convertit' (now when his youthful strength had increased, and a noble desire for command burned in his young breast, he remembered the valiant deeds of heroes of old, and as though awaking from sleep, he changed his disposition and gathering bands of followers took up arms).[17] His early life makes clear the extent to which warfare defined life in the Welsh borderlands, and indeed the very identity of a young noble. Particularly, Guthlac's inspiration, as he 'remembered the valiant deeds of heroes of old', speaks to longstanding traditions of warbands in the borderland, traditions in which he seeks to place himself.

Yet success in warfare comes with casualties, and Felix's description of Guthlac's career as a warrior also makes clear the particular violence of the Welsh borderlands. Such violence was one of the most widely-recognised features of the post-Conquest March of Wales, which was known as 'a land of war where ruthless mercenaries ... could be let loose to learn their savage trade uninhibitedly'.[18] The opportunity for exceptional violence in the borderlands is evident in Guthlac's *Vita*: 'igitur transcursis novem circiter annorum orbibus, quibus persecutorum suorum adversantiumque sibi hostium famosum excidium crebris vastationum fragoribus peregisset, tandem defessis viribus post tot praedas, caedes rapinasque quas arma triverunt, lassi quieverunt' (so when about nine years had passed away, during which he had achieved the glorious overthrow of his persecutors, foes and adversaries by frequent blows and devastations, at last their strength was exhausted after all the pillage, slaughter and rapine which their arms had wrought, and being worn out, they kept the peace).[19] While Guthlac is a saint who gives back one third of his plunder to his victims, 'pillage, slaughter and rapine' indicate serious violence and damage. Felix is careful to emphasise that Guthlac's violence is aimed at his 'persecutors, foes and adversaries', but it is nonetheless clear from his description that the saint captains a mercenary band and is not engaged in warfare under any official auspices. As T. M. Charles-Edwards has noted, 'aspirants to kingship, with their own war bands, rivals of the current kings and thus often out of their control, may have been responsible for much of the violence and instability on the frontier'.[20]

Guthlac's role as the leader of a warband whose members are of mixed ethnicity is a further testament to the mixed Anglo-Welsh culture of the borderlands. Felix relates the nature of this band as he describes the saint's generosity even in war: 'et cum adversantium sibi urbes et villas, vicos et castella igne ferroque vastaret, conrasis undique diversarum gentium sociis, inmensas praedas gregasset, tunc velut ex divino consilio edoctus tertiam partem adgregatae gazae possidentibus remittebat' (but when he had devastated the towns and residences of his foes, their villages and fortresses with fire and sword, and, gathering together companions from various races and from all directions, had amassed immense booty, then as if instructed by divine counsel, he would return to the owners a third part of the treasure collected).[21] Despite his warband being composed of 'companions from various races and all directions', most scholars characterise the early portion of Guthlac's life as one of warfare against – not alongside – the British: he is typically described as having 'spent his youth fighting the Britons of Wales before becoming a monk of Repton'.[22] Colgrave notes that Guthlac's warfare is 'presumably against the Britons, judging by c. xxxiv, though our knowledge of Mercian history in the latter part of the seventh century is so limited that it is not possible to say if he fought elsewhere',[23] but his warband of 'companions from various races and all directions' strongly suggests that Guthlac fought alongside the British, rather than against them.

More evidence for the multi-ethnic character of Guthlac's warband, and thus the multi-ethnic culture of military life along the Welsh borderlands, comes from a famous passage later on in Guthlac's *Vita* which describes his demonic assailants attacking his hermitage in the fens while disguised as a troop of Britons. While this chapter of Felix's text is usually read as evidence for Anglo-British strife in the early eighth century, I argue that careful consideration of the passage in the context of Guthlac's full biography actually indicates the opposite. The demons' British disguise has been a critical red herring, which has overshadowed the evidence in this passage of Guthlac's culturally mixed background. Chapter 34 of the *Vita* details the time he spent welcomed among the Britons as a young exile from Anglo-Saxon England, beginning:

> Contigit itaque in diebus Coenredi Merciorum regis, cum Brittones, infesti hostes Saxonici generis, bellis, praedis, publicisque vastationibus Anglorum gentem deturbarent, quadam nocte, gallicinali tempore, quo more solito vir beatae memoriae Guthlac orationum vigiliis incumberet, extimplo, cum velut imaginato sopore opprimeretur, visum est sibi tumultuantis turbae audisse clamores.
>
> (It happened in the days of Coenred, king of the Mercians, while the Britons the implacable enemies of the Saxon race, were troubling the English with their attacks, their pillaging, and their devastations of the people, on a certain night about the time of cockcrow, when Guthlac of blessed memory was as usual engaged in vigils and prayers, that he was suddenly overcome by a dream-filled sleep, and it seemed to him that he heard the shouts of a tumultuous crowd.)[24]

While this passage has been taken to indicate that Guthlac's encounter with the demons reflects ongoing Anglo/British strife in Mercia, two important and critically-overlooked considerations give pause to such a reading.

First, while this chapter is set 'in the days' when Coenred is king of the Mercians, the Mercians are actually not the people whom the British are said to be attacking. Rather, it is the Saxons or English – *Saxonici/Anglorum* – who are the Britons' enemies. As Chapter Two argued, the separate identities of the Anglo-Saxon kingdoms should not be elided, and so it is important to remember that an attack against other Anglo-Saxon kingdoms is not the same as one against Mercia – particularly given the fact that Guthlac is in East Anglia at the time of this attack. To characterise this passage as taking place 'just as the Welsh are invading Mercia from the west during the reign of King Coenred',[25] as is so often done, is to overstate the information it actually contains. This passage can be used as evidence for British attacks against other Anglo-Saxon kingdoms, but not for violence within the Welsh borderlands.

Moreover, while this chapter is often used as evidence that the fenlands of East Anglia 'may have harbored an as yet unassimilated British population' in Guthlac's day,[26] as Colgrave notes, the passage has been 'taken too literally' in such readings.[27] Guthlac's *Vita* is modelled on the life of the desert father Saint Anthony, in which a key motif is demonic temptation. Guthlac's demons appear as Britons in chapter 34 – just as they are monsters in chapter 31 and beasts in chapter 36. Colgrave points out that 'these Britons are obviously devils in disguise', as 'the story forms one of a series intended to show Guthlac's power over devils'.[28] The Britons are 'clearly demonic illusions', and 'it is therefore clear that no hypothesis as to British survivors in the fens can be based on this passage'.[29] This chapter of Guthlac's *Vita*, then, does not indicate any actual Mercian/Welsh strife during the time of the saint's hermitage.

Yet most significantly, this chapter also does not contain any evidence for Anglo/British strife during Guthlac's youth. In fact, though it is often interpreted in this way, this passage actually indicates the opposite: that the Welsh borderlands during Guthlac's life were a site of mixed Anglo-Welsh culture, not strife. In the key passage, Guthlac hears the tumult of the crowd outside, and:

> Tunc dicto citius levi somno expergefactus, extra cellulam, qua sedebat, egressus est, et arrectis auribus adstans, verba loquentis vulgi Brittannicaque agmina tectis succedere agnoscit; nam ille aliorum temporum praeteritis voluminibus inter illos exulabat, quoadusque eorum strimulentas loquelas intelligere valuit.

(Then, quicker than words, he was aroused from his light sleep and went out of the cell in which he was sitting; standing, with ears alert, he recognised the words that the crowd were saying, and realised that British hosts were approaching his dwelling: for in years gone by he had been an exile among them, so that he was able to understand their sibilant speech).[30]

This passage has been characterised as 'a particularly striking episode' of 'ethnic hatred', in which Guthlac's ability to understand Welsh results from 'the forced learning of a time spent in captivity among the Britons during his days as a warrior'.[31] Yet Felix's *Vita* says nothing of the sort, for Guthlac is neither captured by the British nor forced to learn Welsh. He is simply a young noble in exile who finds safety and sympathy among the British, as Chapter Two demonstrated was the case for many Anglo-Saxon youths in early medieval Britain. Indeed, as Charles-Edwards notes, 'to be driven into exile was a common fate of members of a dynasty contending for the kingship',[32] and the 'refuge across the frontier' that Guthlac found was even 'more striking because his paternal residence was among the Middle Angles, to the east of the Mercian heartland'.[33] Instead of ethnic hatred, then, this chapter of Guthlac's *Vita* demonstrates that a mixed Anglo-Welsh nobility, to which Guthlac comfortably belonged in his youth, moved fluidly across the Welsh borderlands.

Fluid borders in *Guthlac A*

Felix's *Vita Sancti Guthlaci*, then, situates Guthlac's life within a mixed Anglo-Welsh society in the borderlands. In the second half of this chapter, I argue that this same representation of the borderlands as a cultural nexus is evident in the Old English poem known as *Guthlac A*, a loose rendering of the major events of Guthlac's life. A careful reading of this poem reveals that, even in this Anglo-Saxon saint's life, the politics of territorial control are much less clear-cut than has been assumed. Although Guthlac's battles with demons have been understood to reflect Anglo/Welsh ethnic division, *Guthlac A* displays a far more ambivalent attitude, reflecting the fluid boundaries of the Welsh borderlands.

While Felix's text is the earliest work to mention the saint, a significant body of Anglo-Saxon and early medieval material on Guthlac survives, apart from the Latin *Vita*.[34] However, *Guthlac A* is one of only two Old English poems on this saint, both extant in a single manuscript, the tenth-century poetic anthology known as the Exeter Book.[35] While the two poems adjoin one another, *Guthlac A* and *Guthlac B* are very different works in content, tone, structure and style.[36] *Guthlac B* narrates the saint's death, cleaving closely to its source, chapter 50 of Felix's *Vita*; *Guthlac A*,[37] to the contrary, contains little in the way of linear narrative and has long suffered a poor critical reputation as a result. As Daniel G. Calder has noted, 'while *Guthlac B* customarily garners praise for its clarity, humanity, and poetic power', *Guthlac A* 'usually receives blame for being abstract, repetitive, and didactic'.[38] More recent scholarship has reclaimed *Guthlac A*'s artistry, productively focusing on the distinctiveness of this poem as juxtaposed against the more familiar narrative of Guthlac's life from Felix's *Vita*. While the question of whether the *Guthlac A*-poet was familiar with Felix's text remains unanswered,[39] it has been recognised that this poem departs from the core elements of this saint's legend,[40] becoming largely a description of an extended battle for the *beorg*.

Most recently, postcolonial critics have understood Guthlac's legend as reflecting a nascent sense of Anglo-Saxon colonial aspiration, with the Mercian saint a successful embodiment of Anglo-Saxon land conquest over native British resistance. *Guthlac A* has been read as 'suffused with colonial desires',[41] and its landscape interpreted as a site of 'conquest and possession' in the 'formation of cultural identity'.[42] Yet *Guthlac A* does not easily fit this pattern, but rather depicts both the land and its possession in more ambivalent ways. This poem contains no clear political agenda or allegory; certainly, its depiction of a contested landscape whose geography is ambiguous cannot represent the spread of Anglo-Saxon hegemony, which in any case did not yet exist. *Guthlac A*, uniquely among the corpus of Anglo-Saxon Guthlac texts, places conflicting conditions of ownership upon the contested *beorg*, complicating the process of its repossession. Moreover, this space is also depicted as simultaneously forbidding and congenial to both Guthlac and the demons throughout the poem, making the saint's role as an agent of its manifest physical transformation far less clear. In placing unsettled boundary spaces at the centre of its narrative action, *Guthlac A* stands apart from a familiar legend of 'a saintly figure whose actions are motivated by a desire to control a piece of land'.[43] Of all the Guthlac materials, this is by far the most ambivalent in its representation of Anglo-Saxon conquest and colonisation. This ambivalence, like *Guthlac A*'s shifting landscape, better reflects the fluid social geography of the Welsh borderlands than a binary Anglo/Welsh ethnopolitical division.

The contradictory characteristics of the landscape are reflected in the critical debate over the nature of Guthlac's *beorg*.[44] While there has been no disagreement with Laurence K. Shook's conclusion that *Guthlac A*'s 'constant attention to the barrow sharply distinguishes the Anglo-Saxon poet's treatment of the Guthlac legend from that of Felix',[45] precisely what the *beorg* represents has been a matter of some contention, given the word's dual meanings of 'barrow' and 'hill'.[46] Many have argued that the *beorg* is typologically a mountain, in keeping with patristic tradition and the lives of the Desert Fathers;[47] others have countered that the native character of the Guthlac legend makes 'barrow' the likelier interpretation.[48] While the saint clearly inhabits a burial mound (*tumulus*) in Felix's *Vita* – 'erat itaque in praedicta insula tumulus agrestibus glaebis coacervatus, quem olim avari solitudinis frequentatores lucri ergo illic adquirendi defodientes scindebant' (now there was in the said island a mound built of clods of earth which greedy comers to the waste had dug open, in the hope of finding treasure there)[49] – the lack of specific details in *Guthlac A* makes the nature of his dwelling uncertain. Indeed, this ambiguity is crucial to the poem's structure, for while the *beorg*'s bleakness and demonic inhabitants suggest a pagan barrow, Guthlac's spiritual progression supports a typological reading. Manish Sharma has argued that 'although a mountain in the fens of Croyland would stretch the imagination of most audiences, the precise meaning of *beorg* is secondary while it is the theme of the ascent that is of primary significance',[50] while according to Alexandra Hennessey Olsen, 'because "beorg" is meaningful in both heroic and Christian contexts, its use in *Guthlac A* resonates with both implications'.[51] The most prominent geographical feature of the landscape of *Guthlac A*, then, is productively ambiguous.[52]

The ambiguity of the *beorg* is heightened by the competing claims of ownership that appear uniquely in *Guthlac A*. As Katherine O'Brien O'Keeffe has argued, the political implications of Felix's text are relatively clear:

> Felix's *Vita S. Guthlaci* is first and foremost a discourse of contested territory fundamentally altered through acquisition, purgation, and habitation. To make this outcome possible, Felix must first infest the place in question so that Guthlac might purge it. To follow the trail of transgressions and transformations in the *vita*, we must begin where the *vita* leads: with its close interest in the social and political in a narrative representing a Mercian warrior saint to an East Anglian king.[53]

Yet a similar discourse is not as easily legible in *Guthlac A*, which uniquely positions the *beorg* under three simultaneous yet mutually exclusive conditions of ownership. First, the space stands 'far from ancestral rights' (*eþelriehte feor*, l. 216b). Second, God has granted this place to the demons as a space of respite. Third, it nonetheless awaits the claim 'of a better owner' (*betran hyrdes*, l. 217b). None of these conditions is given priority over the others,[54] for all are necessary to the poem's narrative unity. The *beorg*'s location far from ancestral rights makes it open to repossession, and Guthlac has divine authority to seize control, yet the demons also have just cause to resist him. Where Felix's *Vita* never questions Guthlac's right to the *beorg*, *Guthlac A*'s introduction of these conflicting land claims creates a narrative of an unstable landscape rather than one of straightforward Anglo-Saxon conquest and transformation.

The demons' claim to the land is established by the revelation of a legitimate cause for their anger towards the saint: his presence denies their access to the land that was previously granted to them as a place of sanctuary, even if intermittently and temporarily. They confront Guthlac after he enters the *beorg*:

> wæron teonsmiðas tornes fulle,
> cwædon þæt him Guðlac eac Gode sylfum
> earfeþa mæst ana gefremede
> siþþan he for wlence on westenne
> beorgas bræce; þær hy bidinge
> earme ondsacan, æror mostum
> æfter tintergum tidum brucan,
> ðonne hy of waþum werge cwoman
> restan ryneþragum; rowe gefegon:
> wæs him seo gelyfed þurh lytel fæc. (ll. 205–14)

(The evildoers were filled with distress. They said that Guthlac alone, in addition to God himself, had brought about the most suffering, ever since he pridefully forced his way into the *beorg* in the wilderness where the wretched adversaries formerly might enjoy, for a time, a repose after their torments, when they were weary from wandering and came to rest for a moment; they rejoiced in the quietness. That was granted to them for a little time.)

Only God has the power to grant this space to the demons in such a manner,[55] placing this passage in the apocryphal tradition of the 'respite of the damned'[56] and explaining the demons' attachment to the *beorg*. As has been noted, '*Guthlac A* manipulates our sympathies when Guthlac occupies the territory of the devils',[57] for what the demons want from Guthlac 'is not his soul but his land'.[58] The poem's participation in the 'respite of the damned' tradition creates a basis for the demons' complaints that Guthlac has been given 'privileges in what *they consider* their territory'.[59] The demons clearly believe that they have a claim on the land, as the poem makes a point of mentioning that '7 þær ær fela / setla gesæton' (ll. 143b–44a: and there, previously, they had settled many dwelling-places). Certainly, these lines make it clear that the *beorg* has been long welcome to the demons as a space of refuge. Yet more than that, it is significant that the poem introduces these claims in the first place, creating a landscape whose ownership is contested rather than one whose control by the saint is straightforward.

Even as the demons relate the manner in which the *beorg* has been granted to them, the poem introduces in the same clause two more competing identities for this space: it stands outside the claim of any ancestral rights, and yet it also awaits the coming 'of a better keeper':

> Stod seo dygle stow   dryhtne in gemyndum
> idel 7 æmen,   eþelriehte feor,
> bad bisæce   betran hyrdes. (ll. 215–17)

(That secret place stood far from ancestral rights, empty and desolate in the Lord's mind, and awaited the coming of a better guardian.)

The ambiguity of the *beorg*'s legal status appears linked to that of its geography, as the clause *eþelriehte feor* implies that distance from society is a key factor in its lack of proper claimants to ownership.[60] Yet the phrase *betran hyrdes*, emphasising the suitability of the land's eventual guardian, suggests that the *beorg* was in fact allocated to Guthlac. This is reinforced later in the poem:

> ðone foregengan   fæder ælmihtig
> wið onhælum   ealdorgewinnum
> sylfa gesette. (ll. 533–5a)

(Then the Almighty Father himself established him as an advance-guard against hidden deadly enemies.)

While these lines make it clear that Guthlac was appointed directly by God to cleanse the land of the same demons who had previously been granted the space as a respite, his relationship to the *beorg* is questioned by his severance from his native land. The demons describe the dangers that await him 'gif þu gewitest   swa wilde deor / ana from eþele' (ll. 276–7a: if you depart, like a wild animal, alone from your native land). The use of *eþel* (native land) is a striking parallel to the earlier description of the *beorg* as outside *eþelriehte*, implying that Guthlac – cut off from his own *eþel* – can have no legal claim to the *eþelriehte* of this space.

Reading *Guthlac A* as a narrative of conquest finds a 'venture into the wilderness to confront hostile strangers';[61] yet, while such undertones inform Felix's account,[62] *Guthlac A* positions the saint himself as the stranger to this space. The paradoxical conditions attached to this landscape undermine the concept of a boundary as 'a line that protects and differentiates "us" from outsiders on the one hand, and ... where heroic deeds, namely the appropriation of new territories, are performed on the other'.[63] Here, no line is visible – Guthlac and the demons both exist in the same nebulous space, whose three simultaneous yet mutually exclusive conditions are each necessary for the poem's narrative cohesion. Granting the space to the demons provides them with the motivation to oppose Guthlac, while his appointment by the Lord elevates his actions beyond the unjust seizure of another's land, and the *beorg*'s status outside any ancestral rights legitimises the positions of both. These coinciding yet competing claims make the poem's central narrative tension possible, building spatial ambiguity into the heart of *Guthlac A*.

Equally fluid throughout the narrative is the nature of the landscape itself, which is also described in contradictory ways that point towards the multifaceted nature of this nebulous space.[64] The poem first calls to mind the terrors of the wilderness in order to emphasise Guthlac's strength in entering it:

> Sume þa wuniað   on westennum
> secað 7 gesittað   sylfra willum
> hamas on heolstrum,   hy ðæs heofoncundan
> boldes bidað.   Oft him brogan to
> laðne gelædeð,   se þe him lifes ofonn,
> eaweð him egsan,   hwilum idel wuldor,
> brægdwis bona,   – hafað bega cræft –
> eahteð anbuendra. (ll. 81–88a)

(Some who dwell in the wilderness through their own will, who seek out and settle homes in dark places, they await the heavenly dwelling. Often he who seizes their life brings hateful terror to them. He shows them fear, at times empty glory – he has the power of both. The crafty slayer persecutes those who dwell alone.)

In emphasising the dangers that Guthlac will face in the wilderness, these lines are of course intended to demonstrate the saint's fortitude against the demons. As has been well documented, Fitt IX (ll. 722–59) stands in sharp contrast to this bleak landscape. Bartholomew appears and proclaims Guthlac's victory, ending the lengthy contest of wills between saint and demons,[65] and the *beorg* appears to be transformed (as in Catherine A. M. Clarke's words) 'from a site of suffering and conflict to a place of triumph'.[66] The transformation of wilderness as proof of sanctity is a common trope in saints' lives[67] and has, in *Guthlac A*, been commonly interpreted as 'an outstanding passage of vernacular *locus amoenus* description' highlighting 'the central crux of the Guthlac story: the triumphant transformation of his chosen retreat',[68] the 'theme of dominion over the brute creation'[69] and 'a metaphor for paradise attained'.[70]

However, the landscape of *Guthlac A* does not fit into such a linear narrative. Less than fifty lines after describing the *beorg*'s terrors, the poem relates how Guthlac 'leofedan londes wynne, / bold on beorhge' (ll. 139–40a: loved the land's pleasures, the dwelling in the *beorg*), revealing the value of the land itself to the saint. These contradictory descriptions might be read as a shift of the *beorg* from wilderness to *locus amoenus* under the saint's transformative hand were it not for the frequent characterisations of the *beorg* as both pleasant landscape and desolate wasteland throughout the poem. For instance, immediately following Guthlac's enjoyment of the landscape are lines that evoke its dangers yet again: 'oft þær broga cwom, / egeslic 7 uncuð' (ll. 140b–41a: terror often came there, dreadful and strange). Such wildness suits Guthlac well: it is precisely this wilderness quality that makes the landscape fit for a hermitage. Yet this sequence of lines in its entirety emphasises that the land is both dangerous and appealing to the saint from the poem's beginning. This narrative inconsistency has been observed by Fabienne L. Michelet, who notes that 'the ambiguity surrounding the nature of the *beorg* (is it a pleasant or unpleasant dwelling?) continues throughout the poem. It is often described as a miserable place ... but at other times, the *beorg* seems to be an enjoyable location.'[71] However, she argues that despite this occasional ambiguity the *beorg* nonetheless 'changes into an increasingly agreeable place until its final transformation', which 'illustrates the effects of the saint's settlement in the wilderness: the holy presence purifies the land'.[72] Yet no such transformation of the landscape takes place in this poem, for in *Guthlac A* the *beorg* is depicted as simultaneously dangerous and hospitable before and after Bartholomew's appearance.

While the *beorg*'s dangers have been often noted, what has escaped attention is that the land is also characterised positively even before Guthlac's victory over the demons, as when Guthlac 'bad on beorge – wæs him botles neod' (l. 329: remained on the *beorg* – he was desirous of that dwelling). The demons are aware of the pleasure he derives from this place, and at one point arrive with the intention of discovering 'hwæþre him þæs wonges wyn sweðrade' (l. 352: whether his joy in that plain had weakened). The *beorg* is described as 'þam leofestan / earde on eorðan' (ll. 427b–28a: the dearest dwelling on earth) to Guthlac; his return to it a 'leofne sið' (l. 726b: beloved journey) 'to þam onwillan eorðan dæle' (l. 728: to that desired portion of earth); and his experience living there characterised as 'cempa wunade / bliþe on beorge' (ll. 438b–39a: the warrior remained joyfully in the *beorg*).

The space is also depicted in ways that call attention to its suitability as a home for Guthlac, emphasising its value to him: it is a 'beorgseþel' (l. 102a: dwelling in a mountain or hill), twice a 'beorg on bearwe' (ll. 148a and 429a: mound in a grove), and a 'haligne ham' (l. 149: blessed home), which he 'wong bletsade' (l. 178b: he blessed the plain).[73] On the cusp of Guthlac's triumph, the land is again characterised as a 'wonge' (l. 702a: plain) and 'wic' (l. 702b: dwelling-place).[74]

Furthermore, the *beorg* is also characterised as having value to the demons. While they have previously threatened Guthlac with the landscape's dangers, when confronted with the possibility of its loss, the demons cast it as a lovely space with intrinsic pleasures:

>   hleahtor alegdon,
> sorge seofedon   þa hi swiðra oferstag
> weard on wonge;   sceoldon wræcmæcgas
> ofgiefan gnornende   grene beorgas. (ll. 229b–32)

(They gave up laughter, and lamented with sorrow that a stronger one had defeated them as a guardian on that plain. The mourning outcasts must give up the green hills.)

As with Guthlac's relationship to the landscape, a different vocabulary is used to signal the *beorg*'s positive qualities. What is at times dark and dangerous can also be perceived as a *wang*, an open and inviting plain. The demons' grief at being expelled from this space is cast in terms of precisely these enjoyable physical features, the *grene beorgas* again implying qualities of openness, fertility, and thus desirability. As with Guthlac, the value of the land to the demons is evident at multiple points throughout the poem: elsewhere, 'sægde him to sorge   þæt hy sigelease / þone grene wong   ofgiefan sceoldan' (ll. 476–7: he said, to their sorrow, that they would have to give up that green plain, defeated). The *beorg*, then, is described as a landscape with positive physical qualities to both Guthlac and the demons from the outset.

Yet it is precisely such language that has been interpreted as evidence of the plain's transformation in Fitt IX (ll. 722–59) after Guthlac's victory. Ananya Jahanara Kabir has noted the significance of this vocabulary – used to evoke fertility and desirability of landscape throughout the Old English corpus – as a signal of the 'vernacular equivalent of the *locus amoenus*' in describing Guthlac's *beorg* at the beginning of Fitt IX.[75] She argues that in Old English works, the focus of this motif is 'natural expanse rather than cultivated garden' and that 'the attributes that make it appealing have a predominantly visual force', where 'the rejuvenated dwelling-place of

Guthlac is described as a blossoming plain (*folde geblowen*) and the description is bracketed off by the statements *smolt wæs se sigewong* and *stod se grene wong*.[76] Kabir maintains that 'these visual and emotive elements invariably recur in descriptions of desirable landscapes in Old English poetry', with a common pattern in which 'all ideal landscapes in Old English poetry utilize at least one phrase consisting of an adjective of greenness, light or space and a noun denoting an open area of vegetation', the most common of which is '*grene wang*'.[77] Yet this phrase has appeared throughout the poem to characterise the nature of the landscape to Guthlac and the demons both. While the positive imagery that characterises the *beorg* after Guthlac's victory is undoubtedly powerful, the poem, in its repeated use of similar language elsewhere, presents this moment not as a landscape transformed but as one revealed: the *beorg* is simply as valuable to Guthlac as it has been to both him and the demons all along.

These oscillating descriptions of the *beorg* throughout the poem, then, defy a linear transformation from wilderness to *locus amoenus*, in turn complicating the political implications that have been attributed to that alleged transformation. Clarke reads this moment as evidence of 'the dialectic between hostile, wilderness landscape and the ordered, cultivated landscape of the *locus amoenus*' that 'provides the basis for a powerful ideology of English potential', representing a 'localised enactment of this English mythology which conflates cultivation of the land with spiritual cultivation and the triumph of order'.[78] Cohen argues for a deep-seated proto-imperial reading of *Guthlac A* as 'obsessed by the annexation of new land and its conversion into secure possession', where 'a feral landscape ... transformed' represents a 'formulation of Anglo-Saxon unity constructed against a British inferiority' containing 'consolidating and globalizing impulses' with 'both religious and colonialist utility for eighth-century Mercia'.[79] The poem, for Cohen, is 'suffused with colonial desires' and 'enacts a fantasy of manifest destiny', re-enacting 'Mercia's endeavor ... to justify pan-insular ambitions of expansion'.[80] Similarly, Alfred K. Siewers views the Guthlac legend as an 'Anglo-Saxon construction of literary landscape ... supporting the appropriation of nature for nation-building', which particularly reflects 'the political and cultural situation of eighth-century Mercia ... in desperate need of an ethnic identity'.[81] Indeed, in Siewers's view, the battle for the *beorg* is 'a metaphor of the Anglo-Saxon literary construction of the landscape of Britain' and Guthlac's victory is 'the equivalent of the lifting of a curse on the landscape, which seems to become more fertile as a result'.[82]

It is easy to see why such readings of the poem have been so attractive, given that Guthlac's story is tied so closely to the landscape of Anglo-Saxon

England.[83] Yet the crucial features of this saint's legend that allow political interpretations of other texts do not appear in *Guthlac A*. On the most basic level, the key passage in Felix's *Vita* discussed earlier in this chapter – in which the demons who assault Guthlac take the form of Welsh-speaking British aggressors, mirroring (or so Felix claims) the actual Welsh attacks on Anglo-Saxons that were taking place at the same time[84] – is not reproduced, or even alluded to, in *Guthlac A*. Granted, a folio of the poem is missing, and there is a possibility that the missing lines could reference this moment.[85] However, the brevity of the gap, the absence of any indication or apt context in the surrounding lines and uncertainty whether the *Guthlac A* poet knew Felix's text all suggest that the absent lines are unlikely to have contained this key scene. Furthermore, nothing in the poem suggests that any specific ethnicity is attached to the demons – indeed, as Shook noted, it was precisely this stubborn refusal of the *Guthlac A* poet to firmly ground his text in an identifiably Anglo-Saxon climate that tarnished his reputation among earlier commentators on the work.[86] As Colgrave observes, while 'the Fenland seems to have become a frontier region', it was 'a march-land between East Anglia and Mercia', not Wales.[87] Not only are the Britons conspicuously absent from the text of *Guthlac A*, but there is no historical evidence that the fenlands contained a British population during the saint's lifetime,[88] despite the arguments of some nineteenth- and early twentieth-century scholars to the contrary.[89]

The legend of Guthlac has long been closely linked to Mercia, and for good reason. Frank M. Stenton famously described Felix's *Life* as 'the one historical work which has come down from the ancient Mercian kingdom'.[90] However, neither Mercian politics nor *Guthlac A* are unambiguous. As Barbara Yorke has noted, while 'the name *Mierce/Merci* means "the borderers"', 'it is not immediately clear who or what they were most significantly considered as bordering, though the western British is the explanation that has been generally preferred'.[91] Along similar lines, Charles-Edwards has made the important point that 'we should be quite clear at the outset that Bede had no concept of Wales or the Welsh in the modern sense; neither, more importantly, did the Welsh themselves'.[92] Indeed, 'a reasonable case can be made for seeing the Welsh kingdoms as part of the outer zone of the Mercian hegemony'[93] or, as I have been arguing, we can see the Welsh borderlands as a distinct political and cultural entity in their own right. The relationship between Mercia and its neighbouring Welsh kingdoms was vastly complex, and neither Anglo-Saxon, nor indeed Mercian, violence can be read as an allegory for Anglo/British conflict in the absence of supporting evidence. In the case of *Guthlac A*, that evidence has been adduced from the reading that the transformation of the *beorg* from dangerous wilderness to pleasant landscape takes place only after Guthlac has fully achieved victory over the demons; but, as I have argued, no such linear conversion is to be found in this poem. Rather, from the start the complex text constructs Guthlac's place of habitation as simultaneously dark and welcoming, dangerous and desirable, to both Guthlac and its original demon inhabitants.

I suggest that while it does make sense to read *Guthlac A* in light of the saint's Mercian origins, the poem does not give voice to 'Mercia's endeavor … to justify pan-insular ambitions of expansion';[94] rather, some reflection of the kingdom's geographical instability in the seventh and eighth centuries is retained in the landscape of *Guthlac A* and in the poem's ambivalence towards territorial acquisition in comparison with other texts of this saint's legend. As noted above, most scholars agree that *Guthlac A* is an early, likely eighth-century, work.[95] Yet it is important to note that, regardless of the poem's actual date of composition, *Guthlac A* itself is at pains to give the impression of contemporaneity with the saint. In addition to more formulaic expressions of firsthand testimony ('hwæt we hyrdon oft', l. 108a: lo, we have often heard), the poem includes the unambiguous statements that 'he gecostad wearð / in gemyndigra monna tidum' (ll. 153b–54: 'he became tempted during the time of men's remembrance'), that he was active 'ussum tidum' (l. 401b: 'in our time'), and 'hwæt we þissa wundra gewitan sindon; / eall þas geeodon in ussera / tida timan' (ll. 752–54a: 'lo, we are aware of these wonders; all these things happened in the period of our time'). In other words, whether or not *Guthlac A* was actually composed within a generation or two of the saint's death, the poem wishes to convey that impression and thus to be read in an eighth-century milieu.

While Stenton's memorable characterisation of the second half of the eighth century as the age of 'Mercian supremacy' under Offa has had remarkable staying power,[96] more recent scholarship suggests that 'in the seventh and eighth centuries being Mercian seems to have been a more flexible commodity', in which 'people under the authority of the Mercian kings might always be referred to as the Mercians, but they might not always be exactly the same people'.[97] Yorke suggests that the name *Mierce/Merci* itself 'may be of older formation than the kingdom names incorporating a geographical location, and could have originated as the names of mobile *comitatus* groupings rather than of settled peoples',[98] and certainly Mercia was the most geographically fluid of all the Anglo-Saxon kingdoms well into the Viking Age. As Charles-Edwards has elucidated, 'the Mercian hegemony had three zones': 'in the centre was Mercia proper', 'wrapped around this core were satellite peoples, probably mostly with their own rulers, but often colonized by Mercian nobles', and 'beyond this zone lay another, more loosely dependent, indeed sometimes entirely independent, consisting of kingdoms with their own dynasties, quite separate from that of the Mercians'.[99] In the eighth century, then, Guthlac's Mercian identity would have associated him with a kingdom whose physical boundaries were not fixed. I suggest that some reflection of this geographical instability is preserved in the landscape of *Guthlac A*, manifested in the poem's ambivalence towards land acquisition in comparison with other texts of the Guthlac legend. That Guthlac's colonisation of the *beorg* is not the poem's focus is clear from its structure: while Bartholomew appears in chapter 32 of 53 in Felix's *Vita*, leaving the last third of the text focused on the saint's witnessed miracles and growing reputation, *Guthlac A* has Bartholomew restore Guthlac to the demon-cleansed *beorg* less than one hundred lines from the eight-hundred-line poem's end, which concludes abruptly with the saint's death and appearance in Heaven. Thus, despite the narrative focus on Guthlac's battle against the demons, the *beorg* itself is not the point: Guthlac's spiritual, not physical, triumph is what matters in this poem.

This chapter has argued that the fluid treatment of the *beorg* in *Guthlac A* does not support readings of this text that find a hostile Anglo/Welsh divide and Mercian territorial aggression. I would like to end by suggesting that such readings are also undermined by the poem's unique description of Guthlac's temptation to outlawry after he enters the fens. By equating Guthlac's past as a warrior to the career of an outlaw, *Guthlac A* appears to disavow warfare entirely, not encourage it. Of course, a key feature of this saint's legend as a whole is his change of heart from warrior to hermit:

> Hwæt we hyrdon oft   þæt se halga wer
> in þa ærestan   ældu gelufade
> frecnessa fela;   fyrst wæs swa þeana
> in Godes dome   hwonne Guðlace
> on his ondgietan   engel sealde
> þæt him sweðraden   synna lustas. (ll. 108–13)

(Lo, we have often heard that this holy man loved many dangers in his first youth. However, there was thus a space of time in God's will, when he gave an angel to Guthlac [in his mind] so that it would weaken his desire for sin.)

Guthlac A uniquely transfers the motivation to abandon his secular heroic path from Guthlac to the prompting of an angel sent by God. While this curious feature has been criticised as a failing of artistry that nearly eradicates 'one of the best points of the "Antonian" tradition',[100] it also adds a singular level of narrative richness to *Guthlac A*, which alone among the Guthlac material envisions a protecting angel and a tempting devil who contend for Guthlac's soul during his time in the fenlands:

> hine twegen ymb
> weardas wacedon   þa gewin drugon –
> engel dryhtnes   7 se atela gæst. (ll. 114b–16)

(Two guardians, who endured struggle, kept watch around him: an angel of the Lord and the terrible spirit.)

While the angel of course encourages Guthlac to remember God,

> Oþer hyne scyhte   þæt he sceaðena gemot
> nihtes sohte   7 þurh neþinge
> wunne æfter worulde   swa doð wræcmæcgas
> þa þe ne bimurnað   monnes feore
> þæs þe him to honda   huþe gelæded
> butan hy þy reafe   rædan motan. (ll. 127–32)

(The other urged him to seek out the assembly of marauders at night, and through audacity strive for the world, as do outcasts who do not mourn the lives of the men who bring plunder into their hands, as long as they can dispose of the spoils.)

Regardless of whether or not this moment is 'clearly a *psychomachia* which takes place in Guthlac's mind',[101] these passages make it clear that the saint's temptations, at least, are material in nature. As Sarah Semple has noted, 'even in the thirteenth century, the barrow was a place where outcasts could hide',[102] and *Guthlac A* certainly envisages its landscape as a likely refuge for the types of outlaw whom Guthlac might be tempted to seek out.

Thus, whereas other versions of Guthlac's life tempt him solely with despair, this poem uniquely presents the saint's trials in a realistic manner that is intimately entwined with his own past: he is lured, tellingly, not by a return to his former life or companions but to begin again with a darker version of his previous lifestyle in a different place and time. By presenting this idea as genuinely tempting, *Guthlac A* implies a troubling closeness between his earlier life as a warrior and that of an outlaw. The slide from warrior to criminal suggests very little separation between the two: in tempting Guthlac to enter the company of a band of outlaws, the poem suggests that the element of his nature that enjoyed the life of a warrior would be equally attracted to that of a mercenary. Indeed, this correspondence between hero and outlaw brings the matter of their perpetration of violence to the forefront – and this is emphasised by categorising the marauders as those who do not mourn for lives lost in their attacks. This equivalence suggests that *Guthlac A* possesses an awareness that, regardless of its motivation, the end result of aggression would be violence. Set against the backdrop of Mercia's shifting borders, rather than displaying a simple desire for annexation and aggrandisement, this moment appears to acknowledge the damage caused by hostilities, no matter their source. Indeed, the poem's opposition to the violence of warfare is evident in Guthlac's later speech to the demons. He declares:

> No ic eow sweord ongean
> mid gebolgne hond   oðberan þence,
> worulde wæpen,   ne sceal þes wong Gode
> þurh blodgyte   gebuen weorðan
> ac ic minum Criste   cweman þence
> leofran lace   nu ic þis lond gestag. (ll. 302b–7)

(I do not intend to bring a sword – a weapon of the world – against you with an enraged hand, nor shall this place become occupied for God through bloodshed, but I intend to please my Christ with a more beloved gift, now that I have ascended this land.)

This passage could not be a clearer in its indication that spiritual, not martial, warfare is the purpose of Guthlac's struggles in the *beorg* in this poem.

It is evident that 'the legend of Guthlac of Crowland undoubtedly engaged the attention of many audiences throughout the Anglo-Saxon age and beyond'.[103] While we are fortunate that such rich literary material on the life of this saint has survived, we should be cautious of using one text to draw conclusions about another when no direct relationship between the two has yet been demonstrated, as is the case with Felix's *Vita* and *Guthlac A*. It is perfectly reasonable to explore the political implications of a text like Felix's that 'heaps praise on'[104] a Mercian king while characterising the Britons as 'infesti hostes Saxonici generis' (the implacable enemies of the Saxon race).[105] Yet, as this chapter has argued, no such overt political allegory informs *Guthlac A*, which on the contrary depicts the *beorg* – and the process by which the saint gains possession of it – with far more ambivalence. *Guthlac A* does not present a linear narrative of the saint's claiming the land from its demon inhabitants, but rather goes to great pains to place three simultaneous yet conflicting conditions of ownership upon the *beorg* that complicate Guthlac's possession of this space. Moreover, the land itself does not undergo an overt transformation in this poem, but is depicted from the poem's beginning as both appealing and dangerous to Guthlac and to the demons, meaning that the saint cannot be read as a clear-cut instrument of the physical transformation of the landscape. The ambivalence towards the land in this poem means that *Guthlac A* cannot be read as a latent allegory for Anglo-Saxon imperialism, and this argument is supported by the poem's apparent distaste for the violence of Guthlac's past as a warrior. Although I have suggested that *Guthlac A*'s fluid representation of the landscape may reflect the uncertain and continually fluctuating borders of the saint's Mercian homeland in the eighth century, my main point is that this poem displays little concern for the acquisition of any lands in the temporal world. Guthlac's 'ham in heofonun' (l. 98a: 'home in the heavens') is the only space worth gaining.

This chapter has argued that two of the most prominent Anglo-Saxon texts of the life of Saint Guthlac – Felix's *Vita Sancti Guthlaci* and the anonymous Old English poem *Guthlac A* – are evidence for a mixed Anglo-Welsh culture in the borderlands in the eighth century. Some of the defining features of this borderlands culture foreshadow those aspects of the March of Wales that came to set it apart from Wales and England after the Norman Conquest. That the singular culture of the borderlands in the Anglo-Saxon period prefigured some of the most distinctive features of later Marcher society is intriguingly suggested by the Middle English poetic version of Guthlac's life included in the *South English Legendary*.[106] In this poem, Guthlac's family is said to be 'of þe march of Walis'[107] – that is, 'from the March of Wales'. The Middle English author of Guthlac's life in the *South English Legendary* saw such distinctive geographical and cultural features in his biography that this most Anglo-Saxon of saints was ascribed without hesitation to the March of Wales itself, suggesting cultural continuity in the region of the Welsh borderlands as a space apart from the rest of England.

As the *South English Legendary* shows, Guthlac was a very popular saint. Felix's *Vita* nonetheless reflects a perception of the Welsh borderlands among early medieval intellectuals. Chapter Four turns from hagiography in Latin and the vernacular to a more popular literary tradition yet, the anonymous Old English riddles found in the same manuscript as *Guthlac A*. The tenth-century Exeter Book is our next witness to the Welsh borderlands in Anglo-Saxon England. As was the case with Guthlac's life, I argue that a group of Old English riddles situated on the *mearc*, march or boundary, between Anglo-Saxon England and Wales likewise depict a common culture in the borderlands through the representation of the shared values of a warrior elite across an ostensible Anglo/Welsh divide.

Notes

1 Part of this chapter appeared in an earlier form as 'Colonial desire or political disengagement? The contested landscape of *Guthlac A*', *Journal of English and Germanic Philology* 115 (2016): 61–78. It appears here with the permission of the University of Illinois Press.
2 Bertram Colgrave, ed. and trans., *Felix's Life of Saint Guthlac* (Cambridge: Cambridge University Press, 1956; repr. 1985). Colgrave (15–19) dates the composition of the *Vita* to between 730 and 740. All citations of Felix's *Vita* are from this edition, by page number.
3 *Ibid.*, 2–4.
4 *Ibid.*, 3–4 and 18.
5 *Ibid.*, 6 and 15–19.
6 *Ibid.*, 72–3.
7 Or Welsh *gwalch*, see p. 46 n. 27 above.
8 Colgrave, *Felix's Life of Saint Guthlac*, 176 n.
9 Frederick C. Suppe, 'Who was Rhys Sais? Some comments on Anglo-Welsh relations before 1066', *Haskins Society Journal* 7 (1995): 63–73 at 64–5, citing Melville Richards, 'Gwŷr, gwragedd a gwehelyth', *Transactions of the Honourable Society of Cymmrodorion* (1965), 41, and A. D. Carr, *Medieval Anglesey* (Llangefni: Anglesey Antiquarian Society, 1982), 163.
10 Colgrave, *Felix's Life of Saint Guthlac*, 74–5.
11 *Ibid.*, 176 n.
12 The link between this possibly British name and Mercia is even stronger than it first appears. As Colgrave, *Felix's Life of Saint Guthlac*, 176 n., notes, Penwalh appears as Penwald in MSs H and D, a name which is also 'the name of a Mercian moneyer found on a coin of Offa' (C. F. Keary, *Catalogue of English Coins in the British Museum: Anglo-Saxon Series*, I (London: William Clowes & Sons, 1887), 28, but 'no other example of either form of the name seems to be forthcoming'. See also the PASE (Prosopography of Anglo-Saxon England) database: www.pase.ac.uk.
13 See Max Lieberman, *The March of Wales, 1067–1300: A Borderland of Medieval Britain* (Cardiff: University of Wales Press, 2008), 1.
14 Colgrave, *Felix's Life of Saint Guthlac*, 76–9.
15 *Ibid.*, 174 n.
16 T. M. Charles-Edwards, *Wales and the Britons, 350–1064* (Oxford: Oxford University Press, 2013), 412.
17 Colgrave, *Felix's Life of Saint Guthlac*, 80–1.
18 Rees Davies, *Lordship and Society in the March of Wales* (Oxford: Clarendon Press, 1978), 2.
19 Colgrave, *Felix's Life of Saint Guthlac*, 80–1.
20 Charles-Edwards, *Wales and the Britons*, 412.
21 Colgrave, *Felix's Life of Saint Guthlac*, 80–1.

22 Antonia Gransden, *Historical Writing in England I: c. 550 to c. 1307* (New York: Routledge, 1974; repr. 1996, 2000), 70.
23 Colgrave, *Felix's Life of Saint Guthlac*, 178 n.
24 Ibid., 108–11.
25 Jeffrey Jerome Cohen, *Medieval Identity Machines*, Medieval Cultures 35 (Minneapolis: University of Minnesota Press, 2003), 143.
26 Cohen, *Medieval Identity Machines*, 143.
27 Colgrave, *Felix's Life of Saint Guthlac*, 185 n. For instance, Graham Jones, 'Guthlac', in John T. Koch, *Celtic Culture: A Historical Encyclopedia*, 5 vols. (Santa Barbara CA: ABC-CLIO, 2006), 857, writes that 'this anecdote implies that early Welsh or a language closely akin to it continued to be spoken in parts of eastern England c. 700 by a still restive native population, after more than two centuries of English dominance in the area'.
28 Colgrave, *Felix's Life of Saint Guthlac*, 185 n.
29 Ibid., 186 n.
30 Ibid., 110–11.
31 Cohen, *Medieval Identity Machines*, 143 and 144.
32 Charles-Edwards, *Wales and the Britons*, 412 n.8.
33 Ibid., 412.
34 On the extent of Guthlac's cult, see Colgrave, *Felix's Life of Saint Guthlac*, 9–15 and 19–25, Jane Roberts, 'An inventory of early Guthlac materials', *Mediaeval Studies* 32 (1970): 193–233 and 'Hagiography and literature: the case of Guthlac of Crowland', in *Mercia: An Anglo-Saxon Kingdom in Europe*, ed. Michelle P. Brown and Carol A. Farr, Studies in the Early History of Europe (London: Continuum, 2001), 69–86.
35 All citations of *Guthlac A* will be by line number from Jane Roberts, ed., *The Guthlac Poems of the Exeter Book* (Oxford: Oxford University Press, 1979). See Roberts, *Guthlac Poems*, 12–14 for the manuscript context. The poem's most recent edition is Bernard J. Muir, *The Exeter Anthology of Old English Poetry*, 2 vols. (Exeter: University of Exeter Press, 2000), vol. 1, 111–39 and vol. 2, 429–40, with an accompanying DVD containing a facsimile. The Exeter Book is listed among the items donated by Leofric to Exeter and generally regarded as a tenth-century compilation of earlier Old English poems; see Richard Gameson, 'The origin of the Exeter Book of Old English poetry', *Anglo-Saxon England* 25 (1996): 135–85.
36 See Roberts, *Guthlac Poems*, 15–19, 29–36 and 48–63; 'A metrical examination of the poems "Guthlac A" and "Guthlac B"', *Proceedings of the Royal Irish Academy, Section C: Archaeology, Celtic Studies, History, Linguistics, Literature* 71 (1971): 91–137; and 'Guðlac A, B, and C?', *Medium Ævum* 42 (1973): 43–6.
37 *Guthlac A* is generally considered an early poem; see Roberts, 'Metrical examination', 116–20 and *Guthlac Poems*, 48–71; and R. D. Fulk, *A History of Old English Meter* (Philadelphia: University of Pennsylvania Press, 1992), 400. Critics have noted in defence of its early date the poem's statement that

Guthlac is remembered by men still living; see e.g. Alaric Hall, 'Constructing Anglo-Saxon sanctity: tradition, innovation, and Saint Guthlac', *Images of Sanctity: Essays in Honour of Gary Dickson*, ed. Debra Higgs Strickland, Visualising the Middle Ages 1 (Leiden: Brill, 2007), 207–35 at 209.

38 Daniel G. Calder, '*Guthlac A* and *Guthlac B*: some discriminations', *Anglo-Saxon Poetry: Essays in Appreciation for John C. McGalliard*, ed. Lewis E. Nicholson and Dolores W. Freese (Notre Dame: Notre Dame University Press, 1975), 65–80 at 66. Credit for *Guthlac A*'s redeemed reputation is usually given to Laurence K. Shook, 'The burial mound in *Guthlac A*', *Modern Philology* 58 (1960): 1–10 and 'The prologue of the Old-English "Guthlac A"', *Mediaeval Studies* 23 (1961): 294–304; Shook provides an overview of earlier critical attitudes in 'The burial mound', 2.

39 See Roberts, *Guthlac Poems*, 19–29 for a useful overview of scholarship on this topic; see also her '*Guthlac A*: sources and source hunting', *Medieval English Studies presented to George Kane*, ed. Edward Donald Kennedy et al. (Wolfeboro NH: Brewer, 1988), 1–18.

40 The poet could, of course, have been drawing not on Felix but rather on the broader corpus of legendary material that would have evolved around this saint. For an account of the different kinds of hagiographical materials, see Thomas D. Hill, '*Imago Dei*: genre, symbolism, and Anglo-Saxon hagiography', *Holy Men and Holy Women: Old English Prose Saints' Lives and Their Contexts*, ed. Paul E. Szarmach (Albany NY: SUNY Press, 1996), 35–50. For interpretations of this poem exploring its distinctiveness among Guthlac materials, see in particular Frances Randall Lipp, '*Guthlac A*: an interpretation', *Mediaeval Studies* 33 (1971): 46–62; Thomas D. Hill, 'The middle way: *Idel-Wuldor* and *Egesa* in the Old English *Guthlac A*', *Review of English Studies* NS 30 (1979): 182–7; Christopher A. Jones, 'Envisioning the *cenobium* in the Old English *Guthlac A*', *Mediaeval Studies* 57 (1995): 259–91; Robin Norris, 'The Augustinian theory of use and enjoyment in *Guthlac A* and *B*', *Neuphilologische Mitteilungen* 104 (2003): 159–78; and Hall, 'Constructing Anglo-Saxon sanctity'.

41 Cohen, *Medieval Identity Machines*, 144.

42 Alfred K. Siewers, 'Landscapes of conversion: Guthlac's mound and Grendel's mere as expressions of Anglo-Saxon nation building', *Viator* 34 (2003): 1–39 at 2.

43 Fabienne L. Michelet, *Creation, Migration, and Conquest: Imaginary Geography and Sense of Space in Old English Literature* (Oxford: Oxford University Press, 2006), 164.

44 On the archaeological reality of the Fens, see John Hines, *Voices in the Past: English Literature and Archaeology* (Cambridge: Boydell & Brewer, 2004), 67; Catherine A. M. Clarke, *Literary Landscapes and the Idea of England, 700–1400* (Cambridge: Boydell & Brewer, 2006), 46–7 and Della Hooke, *The Landscape of Anglo-Saxon England* (Leicester: Leicester University Press, 1998), 170–3.

45 Shook, 'The burial mound', 8. Calder, 'Discriminations', 73, describes the *beorg* as the 'spatial symbol of the "center"'; Hall, 'Constructing Anglo-Saxon sanc-

tity', 216, notes that the poem 'specifies the location of Guthlac's struggles as a *beorg* no fewer than fourteen times'.
46 See the entries for *beorg* in Joseph Bosworth and T. Northcote Toller, *An Anglo-Saxon Dictionary* (Oxford: Clarendon Press, 1898); T. Northcote Toller, *An Anglo-Saxon Dictionary Supplement* (Oxford: Clarendon Press, 1921); and Angus Cameron, Ashley Crandell Amos, and Antonette diPaolo Healey et al., *Dictionary of Old English: A to G Online* (Toronto, 1986—), www.doe.utoronto.ca/.
47 See notably Paul F. Reichardt, 'Guthlac A and the landscape of spiritual perfection', *Neophilologus* 56 (1974): 331–8 and David F. Johnson, 'Spiritual combat and the land of Canaan in *Guthlac A*', *Intertexts: Studies in Anglo-Saxon Culture Presented to Paul E. Szarmach*, ed. Virginia Blanton and Helene Scheck (Tempe AZ: ACMRS, 2008), 307–17.
48 See notably Shook, 'The burial mound'; Karl P. Wentersdorf, '*Guthlac A*: the battle for the *beorg*', *Neophilologus* 62 (1978): 135–42; Sarah Semple, 'A fear of the past: the place of the prehistoric burial mound in the ideology of middle and later Anglo-Saxon England', *World Archaeology* 30 (1998): 109–26; and Hall, 'Constructing Anglo-Saxon sanctity'.
49 Colgrave, *Felix's Life of Saint Guthlac*, 92–5.
50 Manish Sharma, 'A reconsideration of the structure of *Guthlac A*: the extremes of saintliness', *Journal of English and Germanic Philology* 101 (2002): 185–200 at 195.
51 Alexandra Hennessey Olsen, *Guthlac of Croyland: A Study of Heroic Hagiography* (Washington DC: University Press of America, 1981), 34–5. A similar argument was made in an unpublished doctoral dissertation by Cynthia Edelstein Cornell, 'Sources of the Old English Guthlac poems' (University of Missouri-Columbia, 1976), 147: the poet 'deliberately chose an ambiguous term which at times suggests Guthlac's literal-historical tumulus dwelling ... and at others carries overtones of the scenes of Christ's temptation and martyrdom or of the earthly and heavenly paradises'.
52 Arthur Groos, 'The "elder" angel in *Guthlac A*', *Anglia* 101 (1983): 141–6 at 141–2 has argued that ambiguity is crucial elsewhere in the poem, in the description of an angel who 'hafað yldran had' (4b): 'it potentially conveys meanings of both greater age and greater rank ... both meanings can be adduced from patristic and medieval conceptions of the relative status of angels and men, and it is precisely this ambiguity which makes the phrase ... an effective introduction to the life of St. Guthlac'.
53 Katherine O'Brien O'Keeffe, 'Guthlac's crossings', *Quaestio: Selected Proceedings of the Cambridge Colloquium in Anglo-Saxon, Norse, and Celtic* 2 (2001): 1–26 at 3.
54 This inconsistency is often criticised, as for instance 'the poet's penchant for giving several versions of the same story', Angela Abdou, 'Speech and power in Old English conversion narratives', *Florilegium* 17 (2000): 195–212 at 206.
55 Roberts, *Guthlac Poems*, 50–2 notes the poem's legal terminology as one of 'two

groups of specialized vocabulary not general in Old English verse' (the other being religious), though she ultimately finds 'little significance' in its presence. Stephanie Clark, 'A more permanent homeland: land tenure in *Guthlac A*', *Anglo-Saxon England*, 40 (2011): 75–102, and Scott Thompson Smith, *Land and Book: Literature and Land Tenure in Anglo-Saxon England* (Toronto: University of Toronto Press, 2012), 190–213, have independently argued for the importance of this legal vocabulary in foregrounding the property dispute within the poem, though both argue that this language is used to bolster Guthlac's claims, ultimately equating the right to land with a reward for the faithful.

56 For the appearance of this tradition in Anglo-Saxon texts see Antonette diPaolo Healey, *The Old English Vision of St. Paul*, Speculum Anniversary Monographs 2 (Cambridge MA: The Medieval Academy of America, 1978), 48–50; see also P. Baum, 'Judas' Sunday rest', *Modern Language Review* 18 (1923): 168–82; L. Gougaud, 'La croyance au répit périodique des damnés dans les légendes irlandaises', *Mélanges bretons et celtiques offerts á M. J. Loth*, ed. H. Champion (Paris–Rennes: H. Champion, 1927), 63–72; and Charles D. Wright, *The Irish Tradition in Old English Literature*, Cambridge Studies in Anglo-Saxon England 6 (Cambridge: Cambridge University Press, 1993; repr. 2006), 109 n.16, 141–5 and 222.

57 Olsen, *Heroic Hagiography*, 33.

58 Jennifer Neville, *Representations of the Natural World in Old English Poetry*, Cambridge Studies in Anglo-Saxon England 27 (Cambridge: Cambridge University Press, 1999), 127.

59 Alvin A. Lee, *The Guest-Hall of Eden: Four Essays on the Design of Old English Poetry* (New Haven: Yale University Press, 1972), 105 (emphasis mine).

60 Roberts, *Guthlac Poems*, 137 n.216, notes the rarity of *eþelriehte* (found only here, in *Beowulf* and in *Exodus*) and suggests 'a translation such as "far from ancestral domain"', which reflects the geography of the Fens.

61 Michelet, *Creation, Migration, and Conquest*, 171.

62 O'Brien O'Keeffe, 'Guthlac's crossings', 21: 'in the ethnic politics of this contest with demons, we see the folding over of political and religious discourses in Felix's discourse of place. This assault of the demons against Guthlac, guardian of the island, is not merely parallel with the depredations of the Welsh against the western border of Mercia – in an analogous folding of the narrative, the demons *are* Britons (or is it that the Britons are demons?) ... we must ask what is achieved by this identification. In the merging of Britons and demons, Felix produces a node in which religious and political discourses, the material and the spiritual, are folded into one'.

63 Michelet, *Creation, Migration, and Conquest*, 171.

64 As Manish Sharma, 'A reconsideration of the structure of *Guthlac A*', 199, notes, 'the use of *mearclond* to describe the site of Guthlac's anchoritic dwelling suggests it is as much a threshold locale as the gates of heaven and hell'.

65 Charles D. Wright, 'The three temptations and the seven gifts of the Holy

Spirit in "Guthlac A", 160b–169', *Traditio* 38 (1982): 341–3, notes that Guthlac's trials reflect the three temptations and are overcome by the seven gifts of the holy spirit.
66 Clarke, *Literary Landscapes and the Idea of England*, 45.
67 See Benjamin P. Kurtz, 'From St. Antony to St. Guthlac: a study in biography', *University of California Publications in Modern Philology* 12 (1925–6): 103–46 and Rosemary Woolf, 'Saints' lives', *Continuations and Beginnings: Studies in Old English Literature*, ed. Eric Gerald Stanley (London: Nelson, 1966), 37–66.
68 Catherine A. M. Clarke, 'The allegory of landscape: land reclamation and defence at Glastonbury Abbey', *On Allegory: Some Medieval Aspects and Approaches from Chaucer to Shakespeare*, ed. M. Carr, K. P. Clarke and M. Nievergelt (Newcastle: Cambridge Scholars, 2008), 87–103 at 98 and 99.
69 Lee, *Guest-Hall of Eden*, 108.
70 Roberts, 'Hagiography and literature', 83.
71 Michelet, *Creation, Migration, and Conquest*, 173.
72 Ibid., 173 and 174.
73 Wentersdorf, 'Battle for the *beorg*' and Hall, 'Constructing Anglo-Saxon sanctity' argue that the *beorg on bearwe* illustrates the conversion of a pagan ritual site to Christianity.
74 The positive qualities of the *beorg* are noted in an unpublished dissertation by Chester Kobos, 'The structure and background of *Guthlac A*' (Fordham University, 1972) at 36, 69, 71 and 130–1. He argues that 'the hermit's joys in his hermitage' is one of three significant motifs and of Irish influence. While I agree that Guthlac takes pleasure from the landscape, its positive nature is not consistent.
75 Ananya Jahanara Kabir, *Paradise, Death and Doomsday in Anglo-Saxon Literature*, Cambridge Studies in Anglo-Saxon England 32 (Cambridge: Cambridge University Press, 2001), 144–5.
76 Ibid., 145.
77 Ibid., 143–4.
78 Clarke, *Literary Landscapes and the Idea of England*, 50–1.
79 Cohen, *Medieval Identity Machines*, 141, 138, 117, 121 and 116.
80 Ibid., 144 and 146.
81 Siewers, 'Landscapes of conversion', 2–3.
82 Ibid., 21 and 25.
83 As Nicholas Howe, *Writing the Map of Anglo-Saxon England: Essays in Cultural Geography* (New Haven: Yale University Press, 2008), 154, notes of the four Old English poetic codices, 'only the Exeter Book registers the presence of England in poems like *Guthlac A* and *B* and more distantly *The Ruin*'.
84 Colgrave, *Felix's Life of Saint Guthlac*, XXXIV, 108–11.
85 About seventy lines of text are missing – see Roberts, *Guthlac Poems*, 12–14. A reconstruction of the missing section has been proposed by Robert D. Stevick, 'The length of "Guthlac A"', *Viator* 13 (1982): 15–48.

86 Shook, 'Burial mound', 2.
87 Colgrave, *Felix's Life of Saint Guthlac*, 2.
88 See *Ibid.*, 1–2 and 185–6.
89 See James Bentham, *The History and Antiquities of the Conventual and Cathedral Church of Ely* (Cambridge: Cambridge University Press, 1771), app. 1, 51; John William Edward Conybeare, *A History of Cambridgeshire* (London: Elliot Stock, 1897), 41–3; Edward Augustus Freeman, *The History of the Norman Conquest of England*, 6 vols. (London: Macmillan, 1873–9), vol. i, 477 and vol. iv, 468–9; Arthur Gray, 'On the late survival of a Celtic population in East Anglia', *Proceedings of the Cambridge Antiquarian Society* 15 (1911): 42–52; and H. C. Darby, 'The fenland frontier in Anglo-Saxon England', *Antiquity* 8 (1934): 185–201.
90 Frank M. Stenton, *Anglo-Saxon England*, 3rd edn (Oxford: Clarendon Press, 1971; repr. 1975), 178.
91 Barbara Yorke, 'The origins of Mercia', *Mercia*, ed. Brown and Farr, 19. The complexity of Mercia's borders is discussed by David Hill, 'Mercians: the dwellers on the boundary', *Mercia*, ed. Brown and Farr.
92 T. M. Charles-Edwards, 'Wales and Mercia, 613–918', *Mercia*, ed. Brown and Farr, 90.
93 Charles-Edwards, 'Wales and Mercia', 94–5.
94 Cohen, *Medieval Identity Machines*, 146.
95 See Roberts, *Guthlac Poems*, 48–71.
96 Stenton, *Anglo-Saxon England*, 206.
97 Yorke, 'The origins of Mercia', 20.
98 *Ibid.*, 19.
99 Charles-Edwards, 'Wales and Mercia', 94.
100 T. A. Shippey, *Old English Verse* (London: Hutchinson, 1972), 129.
101 Michael D. Cherniss, *Ingeld and Christ: Heroic Concepts and Values in Old English Christian Poetry* (The Hague: Mouton, 1972), 229. On the motif of the two contending spirits, see Charles D. Wright, *The Irish Tradition in Anglo-Saxon England*, 260–1; and two entries on the 'Shepherd of Hermas' in *Sources of Anglo-Saxon Literary Culture: The Apocrypha*, ed. Frederick M. Biggs, Instrumenta Anglistica Mediaevalia 1 (Kalamazoo MI: Medieval Institute Publications, 2007), 63–6.
102 Semple, 'A fear of the past', 114.
103 Roberts, 'Hagiography and literature', 86.
104 Roberts, 'Hagiography and literature', 76.
105 Colgrave, *Felix's Life of Saint Guthlac*, ch. XXXIV, 108–9.
106 The *South English Legendary* is a Middle English verse compilation of many varied saints' lives dating to the thirteenth or fourteenth century. The *SEL* itself has been edited, but these editions have used base manuscripts that do not contain the Guthlac poems, which thus are not included in extant editions of the *SEL*. For more on the *SEL*, see Carl Horstmann, *The Early South-*

English Legendary, or Lives of Saints, EETS OS 87 (London: N. Trübner, 1887); Charlotte D'Evelyn and Anna J. Mill, *The South English Legendary*, 3 vols., EETS 235, 236 and 244 (London: Oxford University Press, 1956–9); and Manfred Görlach, *The Textual Tradition of the South English Legendary*, Leeds Texts and Monographs NS 6 (Leeds: University of Leeds, 1974).

107 MS Cotton Julius D ix, line 5; MS Bodleian 779, line 5, and MS Corpus Christi College, Cambridge, 145, line 5, also describe Guthlac's family as being 'from the March of Wales'. Cited from Whitney French Bolton, 'The Middle English and Latin poems of Saint Guthlac' (PhD thesis, Princeton University, 1954), 184. See 139–82 for an overview of manuscripts, previous editions, language, dating, style, etc. The only other complete edition of these poems that I am aware of is that of Hans Forstmann, 'Untersuchungen zur Guthlac-Legende', *Bonner Beiträge zur Anglistik* 12 (Bonn: Hanstein, 1902).

4

The 'dark Welsh' as slaves and slave raiders in Exeter Book riddles 52 and 72[1]

The previous chapter argued that the Latin and vernacular *Lives* of Saint Guthlac show a mixed Anglo-Welsh culture among warrior elites in the borderlands. This conceptualisation of the borderlands was not limited to the learned clerics responsible for Anglo-Saxon hagiography. More popular vernacular literary tradition reflected some of the same ideas. A group of Old English riddles whose setting is the Welsh *mearc* (march or boundary) depict a common culture of the borderlands in the shared values of a warrior elite across an ostensible Anglo/Welsh divide. These riddles, which link the 'dark Welsh' to agricultural labour through the cattle they herd, have long been understood to show the Welsh as slaves, reflecting negative Anglo/Welsh relations and Anglo-Saxon awareness of ethnic and social division. However, it makes greater sense to read the 'captives' in these riddles polysemically, as both cattle and humans, alluding to the fact that the Welsh were as often slave raiders as they were slaves in the Anglo-Saxon period. In this chapter I argue that these riddles hinge on questions not just of ethnicity but also of class. Like the Anglo-Saxons, some Welsh were enslaved and others were warrior elite. The setting of these riddles on the Welsh *mearc* underscores the reputation of the Welsh borderlands as rife with cattle raiding. Contrary to the common perception that the Welsh borderlands in Anglo-Saxon England were defined by Offa's Dyke, these riddles – coupled with historical evidence of drove roads – suggest that this region is better understood as a permeable zone within which both Anglo-Saxons and Welsh travelled, often on cattle and slave raids.

The Welsh borderlands and Offa's Dyke

It is often assumed that, from the mid-eighth century onwards, the Welsh borderlands were defined, and thus sharply divided by, Offa's Dyke. Asser's famous statement in his *Life of King Alfred* that 'fuit in Mercia moderno tempore quidam strenuus atque universis circa se regibus et regionibus finitimis formidolosus rex, nomine Offa, qui vallum magnum inter Britanniam atque Merciam de mari usque ad mare fieri imperavit'[2] (there was in Mercia in fairly recent times a certain vigorous king called Offa, who terrified all the neighbouring kings and provinces around him, and who had a great dyke built between Wales and Mercia from sea to sea)[3] was, until very recently, taken literally. Sir Cyril Fox and Frank Noble – the two scholars whose work was most central in defining twentieth-century understanding of Offa's Dyke – both used Asser's statement as the starting point of their archaeological investigations.[4] In turn, their conclusions that Offa's Dyke was a more-or-less continuous planned earthwork which extended from sea to sea, roughly following the lines of the modern border between Wales and England, were largely accepted by historians of the period. Consequently, Offa's Dyke has long been understood as a defining feature of the Anglo-Saxon landscape and a permanent and inviolable boundary between Anglo-Saxons and Welsh.

However, recent work on Offa's Dyke has begun to revise our understanding of its extent and purpose, though much about this monument remains contested among those who study it. David Hill and Margaret Worthington, after a 31-year archaeological study of Offa's Dyke and its neighbouring earthworks, came to the conclusion that Asser's stock phrase 'from sea to sea' has been a red herring. They suggested that other earthworks in the region, which earlier scholars had sought to connect to Offa's Dyke despite the lengthy gaps between them on the ground, were actually built at various periods. Hill and Worthington concluded that Offa's Dyke (see Map 1) can be narrowly localised in both space and time: it runs only 'between the kingdom of Powys and that part of the western boundary of Mercia that corresponds to it' and was built as a result of military clashes between the Mercian king, Offa, and his Welsh counterpart Eliseg, the king of Powys.[5] These conclusions are attested both from the evidence of the Dyke itself and also from the corresponding Welsh monument known as the Pillar of Eliseg.[6] In their view, Offa's Dyke was constructed at a particular place and time for a particular reason – it was the result of conflict between two strong rulers during Offa's reign. It was not the defining border of Anglo-Saxon England.[7]

Another recent study of Offa's Dyke by Keith Ray and Ian Bapty has argued that it was a more deliberate expression of Mercian political hegemony in the late eighth and early ninth centuries.[8] Their arguments about how Offa's Dyke functioned in the landscape are well aligned with the conclusions of this book. Ray and Bapty suggest that 'despite a greater awareness of the location and form of the earthwork, the focus needs to shift from a border defined simply by the Dyke to a wider frontier territory that was itself transitional: topographically, politically, culturally, and historically'.[9] They conclude further:

> If Offa's Dyke was never conceived as a frontier 'line' or as a stand-alone work, and was instead designed to be the key element in the creation of a frontier zone that with the benefit of hindsight set the framework for the Anglo-Welsh borderland for the next 700 years, the 'March' was as important as the Dyke itself. The Dyke is the main point of historical attention because Asser mentioned it, because it is such an impressive construction, and because it made the longest and deepest impression on medieval and later writers, especially in the role it came to have historically, of defining 'Wales'. However, it was the frontier itself that was arguably the focus of Mercian activity, and for which the Dyke was the principal, but not necessarily the only, manifestation.[10]

The role of Offa's Dyke is being reconsidered from the defining border between Anglo-Saxon England and Wales to one manifestation of a broader frontier zone during the expansionist reign of Offa.

Moreover, while Offa's Dyke has loomed large in modern scholarship on the Anglo/Welsh border, the fact that Asser's *Life of King Alfred* is the only contemporary source to mention the Dyke has gone largely unremarked. Indeed, Paul Russell has recently made the unpublished suggestion that Asser's famous description of Offa's Dyke extending 'de mari usque ad mare' (from sea to sea) is rhetorical convention, following a long tradition describing Hadrian's Wall in this way: the *Scriptores Historiae Augustae* (4th? c.); Eutropius, *Historiae Romanae Breviarium*, 'a mari ad mare' (4th c.); Orosius, *Historiae contra Paganos*, 'a mari ad mare' (5th c.); Gildas, *De Excidio Britanniae*, 'inter duo maria' (6th c.); Bede's *Historia Ecclesiastica*, 'a mari ad mare' (8th c.); and the *Historia Brittonum*, 'a mari usque ad mare' (9th c.), all describe Hadrian's Wall thus, before Asser's *De Gestis Alfredi* (10th c.) borrows the phrase 'de mari usque ad mare' to describe Offa's Dyke instead. It is likely that even the original description of Hadrian's Wall had as much to do with rhetorical effect as with geographical precision, because the phrase seems to be taken ultimately from Psalms 72:8: 'et dominabitur a mari usque ad mare et a flumine usque ad terminos terrae' (and he shall rule from sea to sea and from the river to the ends of the earth).[11] Offa's Dyke did not feature prominently in the Anglo-Saxon textual record and was likely far less central to the Anglo-Saxon spatial imagination than much twentieth-century criticism has believed it to have been. The Exeter Book Riddles serve as an important counterpoint to the image of the Welsh borderlands seemingly provided by Offa's Dyke.

Exeter Book Riddles 12, 52, and 72 are often grouped together because they all link Welsh servitude and oxen.[12] There is a *swearte Wealas* (l. 4) and *wonfeax Wale* (l. 8) in Riddle 12, a *wonfah Wale* (l. 6) in Riddle 52, and the link of *sweartum hyrde* (l. 11) to *mearcpaþas Walas* (l. 12) in Riddle 72. Riddles 52 and 72 are understood to depict cattle herded by the 'dark Welsh', while Riddle 12 has drawn critical attention because its *wonfeax wale* (l. 8a, dark-haired, female Welsh slave) also raises questions of gender.[13] (Although Riddle 12 does connect the Welsh to cattle, it is less relevant to this chapter because it focuses on uses for leather after the ox is dead.)

While studies of these riddles have usefully explored the ethnic and class hierarchies that inevitably accompanied slavery in Anglo-Saxon England,[14] what has gone unnoticed is the important point that the 'dark Welsh' are not the voices of captivity in these riddles, but rather the ones in control of fettered captives. In Riddle 52, 'þara oþrum wæs an getenge / wonfah Wale, seo weold hyra / bega siþe bendum fæstra' (ll. 5–7, near to one was a dark-coloured Welsh woman, she controlled them both on their journey, fixed by bonds), while Riddle 72 links a 'sweartum hyrde' (l. 11a, dark keeper) to 'mearcpaþas Walas' (l. 12a, Welsh border paths).[15] By depicting the Welsh in this position, Riddles 52 and 72 evoke the historical reality that Welsh kingdoms often preyed on one another in slave raids after the Viking attacks had illuminated the profitability of the slave market from the ninth century onwards. These riddles' multilayered solutions and their location on the Welsh *mearc* make clear that the borderlands were depicted in vernacular literary tradition as a site of cattle and slave raiding among a mixed Anglo-Welsh warrior elite.

Slaves and cattle: chattel in early medieval Britain

The argument that the imagery of these riddles alludes to both slaves bound by Welsh raiders and cattle herded by Welsh labourers draws support from the frequent equivalence of slaves and animals in both the Anglo-Saxon textual corpus and Welsh law codes, which makes their parallel captivity in these riddles a natural one. It has long been noted that slaves were 'bought and sold as cattle'[16] in Anglo-Saxon England based on sources such as the

Anglo-Saxon Chronicle, which equates the two as spoils of war. For instance, MS A in 909 describes how King Edward's army 'gehergade swiðe micel on þæm norðhere, ægðer ge on mannum ge on gehwelces cynnes yrfe'[17] (plundered the northern army exceedingly greatly, in respect to both men and also all kinds of cattle), likening men and cattle as equal loot to be taken upon victory. Likewise, an entry for 1052 in MS E shows that slaves, cattle, and property were all understood to belong to the same broad category of possessions, when Harold Godwinson 'nam him on orfe 7 on mannum 7 on æhtum swa him gewearð'[18] (he seized of cattle and of men and of property such as came to be possessed by him).

David Pelteret has demonstrated the legal (and cultural) equivalence of animals and slaves in Anglo-Saxon England, as substantiated by the use of the term *æht* throughout the corpus to refer to property – in the form of slaves, objects and cattle – indiscriminately.[19] The equation of slaves and cattle in particular is striking, as 'a man was thus equivalent to a team of oxen but was assessed at only two-thirds the value of a horse'.[20] The reality that 'slaves were regarded by some members of society as property just like cattle'[21] is affirmed by the language of the 1102 Council of Westminster, which outlawed the trade of slaves in England by stating, 'nequis illud nefarium negotium quo hactenus homines in Anglia solebant uelut bruta animalia uenundari deinceps ullatenus facere praesumat'[22] (that no one is henceforth to presume to carry on that shameful trading whereby heretofore men used in England to be sold like brute beasts).[23] The economic equation of slaves and cattle in Anglo-Saxon England gives their parallel captivities in these riddles significant weight.

This cultural equivalence of slaves and cattle in early medieval Britain is also evident in Welsh law codes, which make it clear that the legal status of slaves and animals was often similar. Although the manuscripts containing these codes were written after the Anglo-Saxon period, it is generally believed that the traditions they preserve are older.[24] The laws provide valuable insight into cultural attitudes towards slavery in medieval Wales. For instance, in one section of the laws detailing the amount that must be paid in compensation for a killing, the subhuman status of both slaves and animals is evident in their lack of *galanas*, the Welsh equivalent of Anglo-Saxon *weregild*: 'trydyd yw, caeth; nyt oes alanas idaw, namyn talu y werth o'e arglwyd ual gwerth llwdyn'[25] (the third is a bondman, there is no *galanas* for him; only payment of his worth to his master, like the worth of a beast).[26] A similar comparison between slaves and beasts is made in regard to the procedure for recovery of a slave, where 'y neb picifo y6reic caeth adiga6n y hatt6yn dracheuen pan ymynno, val y gallei d6yn y anniveil' (the owner of the bondwoman can recover her when he will, as he may his animal).[27] Slaves and animals also have the same worth, 'dyn caeth ... ac anifeil am holi y werth os lleddir' (a bondman [is the same as] an animal to claim his worth if killed),[28] and the same status as other property, 'kanys medyant auẏd ẏdẏn ar ẏ gaeth mal ar ẏaneueil'[29] (for a person has the property of his bondman as of his animal).[30] Their legal equivalence in medieval Britain makes their parallel captivities in the Exeter Book Riddles a natural cultural allusion.

Welsh slaves and raiders in Anglo-Saxon England

Crucial to studies exploring the subjugated status of the 'dark Welsh' in these riddles is an understanding of the *Wealas* as an ethnic and social 'other' in Anglo-Saxon England. Dieter Bitterli encapsulates the current critical position on the role of the Welsh in these texts when he writes:

> as elsewhere in the Exeter Book *Riddles*, the 'dark Welshman' (*swearte Wealas*, 4) represent the enslaved labourers and underdogs of Anglo-Saxon society. They are stereotypically called 'dark' because of their dark hair – as opposed to the 'fair-haired' members of the aristocracy.[31]

Defining the term *wealh* has been a slightly fraught endeavour, for the word, originally meaning simply 'foreigner', came to signify both racial and social difference, referring at first to those of Celtic ethnicity, and then also to slaves more broadly, in Anglo-Saxon England.[32] Margaret Lindsay Faull has argued for a reading simply of 'slave' in the Exeter Book Riddles,[33] but since her interpretation ignores the ethnic difference signified by the characteristic darkness of the Welsh, it has been overturned by more recent criticism: as John W. Tanke argues, 'Faull's argument that *wealas* and *wale* refer not to race but class is open to serious objection'.[34] Etymological differences aside, criticism examining the 'dark Welsh' of the Exeter Book Riddles has generally agreed that 'a servant or a slave, as well as a Welsh person, bound or free, would clearly not have been held in high regard by the "literate elite" who composed and read the poetry in the Exeter Book'.[35] These figures embody the perceived cultural distance between labourers and the aristocratic (either religious or warrior) elite in Anglo-Saxon England.

These riddles are a reminder of the historical reality that Welsh and slave were often synonymous in Anglo-Saxon England, where 'slavery was an integral part' of society.[36] Regardless of its historical accuracy, the narrative that the early Britons had been enslaved by the invading Anglo-Saxons held rhetorical sway from the time when Gildas wrote that 'nonnulli miserarum reliquiarum in montibus deprehensi acervatim iugulabantur: alii fame confecti accedentes manus hostibus dabant in aevum servituri' (a number of the wretched survivors were caught in the mountains and butchered wholesale. Others, their spirit broken by hunger, went to surrender to the enemy; they were fated to be slaves for ever).[37] Indeed, as Pelteret has noted, 'that "Celt" became synonymous with "slave" points to an ominous fate for many of those Celts from the south-west of England'.[38] As Faull has suggested, Riddle 12's *feorran broht* (l. 7b, brought from afar) 'might suggest that this *wealh* had come from Wales, which before the Norse invasions supplied the Anglo-Saxons with slaves taken in border raids'.[39] Scholarship on these riddles has thus found that their depictions of Welsh slaves did mirror historical reality.

Yet the Welsh themselves are not the captives of Riddles 52 and 72. Rather, they are described as controlling fettered figures who are positioned as portraits of human slavery by the repeated imagery of bondage drawn from the 'extensive terminology of servitude and freedom'[40] found throughout the Old English corpus. Six of the fourteen half-lines in the brief Riddle 52 describe scenes of captivity, and the words used are ones whose primary references outside this poem are to human bondage. The noun *ræpingas* (l. 1a) usually refers to people who are bound or taken captive,[41] *gefeterade* (4a) largely describes fettered humans,[42] and *bendum* (3b and 7b) is more often found not with agricultural but with religious terminology,[43] echoing the well-known equation of earthly and spiritual slavery.[44]

Riddles 52 and 72 contain pervasive imagery of bondage which echoes that used to reference human captivity elsewhere in the Old English corpus. While there are a few rare instances where *feter* stands in for a specialised piece of equipment used to train an animal,[45] recent studies have determined that extant fetters from the period were designed for use on humans.[46] This archaeological evidence is borne out by the many literary depictions of fettered slaves that were frequently associated with the cult of St Swithun in Anglo-Saxon England,[47] or the *Vita Wulfstani*'s description of the notorious slave market at Bristol: 'videres et gemeres concathenatos funibus miserorum ordines, et utriusque sexus adolescentes; qui liberali forma, etate integra, barbaris miserationi essent, cotidie prostitui, cotidie venditari'[48] (you might well groan to see the long rows of young men and maidens whose beauty and youth might move the pity of the savage, bound together with cords, and brought to market to be sold).[49] While these riddles' solutions turn fetters into a metaphor for the yokes on cattle, the language of bondage nonetheless suggests their allusion to human captivity. The 'beag ... on healse' (l. 13b, collar on the neck) in Riddle 72 evokes another human adornment or its metaphorical equivalent throughout the corpus, here given the ironic sense of bondage rather than treasure as when glossing *boia*, 'collar or yoke worn by criminals'.[50] The language of bondage in Riddles 52 and 72 echoes that in the Anglo-Saxon corpus used to indicate the captivity of humans.

This imagery resonates within the riddles to emphasise that their bound captives are held in slavery. Yet these captives are under the control of the Welsh, who as Erik I. Bromberg's earlier work has demonstrated, were active slave raiders who frequently supplied captives from neighbouring kingdoms to surrounding markets.[51] When the Viking attacks on Wales began in the ninth century,[52] the Welsh were 'only victims of Viking slave raids', yet they quickly saw the potential profit to be gained and 'became active dealers in slaves'[53] after raiding other kingdoms, often with external assistance. K. L. Maund argues that 'the Hiberno-Scandinavians may have begun as an external threat: by the end of the eleventh century they were a resource to be exploited, to be turned to the ends of individual Welsh kings'.[54] Others turned to 'Ireland [as] a place of refuge for Welshmen' and 'committed the kings of Ireland to military intervention in Wales'[55] that often resulted in the capture of prisoners who would be sold as slaves. Bromberg argues that the slave trade flourished in Wales, in part because

> both Church and state seem not to have interfered with the Welsh slave trade. While the English church from perhaps as early as the ninth century made frequent attempts to halt all sale of Christians to pagans or sales overseas, there is no evidence that the Welsh clergy ever took similar steps.[56]

Of course, this is not to suggest that the Welsh consciously set out to exploit their own people.[57] Rather – as was also the case in Anglo-Saxon England[58] – conflict between kingdoms, combined with the visible profitability of the slave market modelled by the Viking raids, meant that Welsh slaves were often captured by raiders from other kingdoms in Wales. Nor were slave raids geographically restricted – as Pelteret notes, 'from the middle of the eleventh century the "Celtic fringe" began making predatory raids on England'.[59] Slavery in the British Isles during the Middle Ages was a complex issue, but it is clear that to paint the Welsh simply as victims of Anglo-Saxon aggression is too simple a picture, for their involvement in the slave trade was frequently an active one.

Evidence of internal slave raiding can also be found in the Welsh law codes. For instance, the custom of taking prisoners after victory in battle is evidenced by a law governing who gets to keep them:

> O deruyd daly dyn y mywn brwydyr, a bot gwyr deu arglwyd yn y daly, y kyntaf a dotto y law ar y karcharawr, arglwyd hwnnw a'e dyly. Os gwyr un arglwyd vydant y kyntaf a dotto y law arnaw hwnnw bieiuyd y arueu a'e yspeil, kany rann kyfreith yna.[60]
>
> (If a man be taken in battle, and the men of two lords be present at the taking of him, the lord of the first who shall lay his hand upon him is to own the prisoner; if they be the men of one lord, the first who shall lay his hand upon him owns his spoil; since the law does not share in that instance.)[61]

Here, men are casually equated to spoils in battle, and the necessity of rules for the process of their seizure suggests that prisoners of war, whether held for ransom or sold into slavery, were a valuable commodity whose resale was a frequent occurrence. While such evidence demonstrates that 'Welsh law expressly recognised the slave trade',[62] it also seems to have encouraged it by drawing no distinctions between its own people and those of foreign birth:

> G6yr kaith amoda6l ac alldydyon, y rei hynny a dycha6n y hargl6yd y g6erthu a'e rodi o gyfreith, ac ny dylyant gaffel ia6n amdanynt or lledir aghyfreitha6l, kans nid oes genedl ydynt a'e gofyno.[63]
>
> (Conventional bondmen and *alltud*s [foreigners] can be sold by their lord, and given, by law; and amends are not to be made for them, if they be unlawfully killed; because they have no kindred who can demand it).[64]

The fact that Welshmen could be sold as easily as foreign prisoners supports the existence of 'a trade in the Welsh interior as well as along the coast in order to meet the demand',[65] as well as general indifference – unlike the frequently voiced outrage in Anglo-Saxon England[66] – on the part of both religious and secular leaders at the thought of Welshmen sold into slavery on foreign shores. While many slaves in early medieval England were certainly Welsh, it is worth remembering that this was far more likely to have come about as a consequence of warring with a neighbouring kingdom in Wales than it was to have been the result of aggressive raiding on the part of the Anglo-Saxons.

Riddle 52

The cultural equivalence of slaves and cattle in early medieval Britain is most overt in Riddle 52, because it contains details that can refer only to human captivity, signalling the text's analogous enslavement of cattle and humans. Despite its brevity, this riddle neatly encompasses three distinct allusions. It was solved as 'flail' by Moritz Trautmann, an answer accepted with some hesitation by subsequent editors, all of whom express lingering doubts while admitting that no solution more compelling has emerged.[67] The riddle's clear description of a pair of yoked oxen guided into a barn by a female Welsh slave was once proposed as its solution by John A. Walz,[68] but dismissed by Frederick Tupper as one that 'smacks of fatal obviousness'.[69] However, Tupper's objections to the simplicity of this reading may be countered by the dual nature of the pervasive imagery of bondage and captivity within the text, which also alludes to fettered human slaves led into a hall by a dark Welsh trader. Its text reads as follows:

> Ic seah ræpingas   in ræced fergan
> under hrof sales   hearde twegen,
> þa wæron genumne,[70]   nearwum bendum
> gefeterade   fæste togædre;
> þara oþrum wæs   an getenge
> wonfah Wale,   seo weold hyra
> bega siþe   bendum fæstra.

(I saw captives brought into the house
under the roof of the hall, a hard two,
who were seized, by narrow bonds
fettered fast together;
near to one was
a dark-coloured Welsh woman, she controlled them
both on their journey, fixed by bonds.)

The fact that the *wonfah Wale* in this text is clearly female might appear to argue against a reading of the Welsh as slave traders, since it seems unlikely that women acted as slave raiders. Yet the distinction between slaves and property owners in early medieval Britain was one of class, not gender, and so it is unsurprising to find a Welsh woman in control of her own property. Pelteret's study of Anglo-Saxon wills and manumission documents demonstrates that a substantial proportion involve the legal actions of Anglo-Saxon women who owned slaves and other property.[71] Likewise, 'Welsh women were relatively well endowed with marriage property',[72] so much so that divorce laws ensured both men and women would 'start their new lives on a viable and reasonably equal footing'.[73] In Wales, 'women, like men, had honour-price, brought property into marriage, and retrieved their personal shares upon death or divorce'.[74] Thus it is not out of place to find a woman selling her own slaves; rather, her actions reinforce the role of the ethnically distinct 'dark Welsh' as brokers of human merchandise.

Key details in Riddle 52 signify that its captives are human. The *ræpingas* appear indoors, as is emphasised by the use of two distinct words for 'hall', 'in ræced fergan / under hrof sales' (ll. 1b–2a, brought into the house under the roof of the hall). Yet archaeological evidence demonstrates that, in contrast to their Germanic counterparts, the halls built in Anglo-Saxon England were not designed to contain animals. As Martin Welch notes, in continental Germanic halls 'at least half the building was subdivided into stalls, designed to keep cattle and other livestock in good condition through the relatively severe winters of these regions', while 'cattle stalling seems to have been unnecessary in England with its mild, wet climate'.[75] There is no evidence that animals were kept indoors in Anglo-Saxon England, as the weather was not harsh enough to demand it and so halls were not designed to accommodate them. While Riddle 52's solution of course understands these terms metaphorically – as cattle in the 'hall' of the barn, then as components of the flail in the threshing room – this description of 'ræpingas in ræced fergan / under hrof sales' also evokes their more straightforward allusion to human captives brought into a hall by a slave trader.

Riddle 72

Riddle 72 constructs an even more elaborate literary illustration of the historical duality of the Welsh as slaves and slave traders in Anglo-Saxon England by painting a sad portrait of the harsh life of a slave in the Welsh marches under the control of a 'dark keeper'. Its ultimate solution of 'ox' has remained uncontested for quite some time,[76] and the narrative moves from scenes of youth to an expanded depiction of captivity in its undamaged portion:

>Ic wæs lytel ...
>fo ...
>... te geaf ...
>... þe   þe unc gemæne ...
>   ... sweostor min,
>fedde mec ...   oft ic feower teah
>swæse broþor,   þara onsundran gehwylc
>dægtidum me   drincan sealde
>þurh þyrel þearle.   Ic þæh on lust,
>oþþæt ic wæs yldra   ond þæt an forlet
>sweartum hyrde,   siþade widdor,
>mearcpaþas Walas træd,   moras pæðde,
>bunden under beame,   beag hæfde on healse,

wean on laste	weorc þrowade,
earfoða dæl.	Oft mec isern scod
sare on sidan;	ic swigade,
næfre meldade	monna ængum
gif me ordstæpe	egle wæron.

(I was small ...
...
... gave ...
... that mutual to us ...
... my sister,
fed me .... often I pulled four
dear brothers, when separately each one
in day-time gave me drink
in abundance through a hole. I thrived in pleasure
until I was older and let that go
to a swarthy keeper, journeyed widely,
trod the paths of the Welsh marches, traversed the moors,
bound under a beam, I had a collar on the neck,
I suffered pain on the track of woe,
a portion of hardships. Often the iron instrument hurt me
sorely on the side; I was silent,
never accused any men
if the thrusts of that sharp point were painful to me.)

Obvious interpretive difficulties are posed by the gaps in the manuscript, but some critics have also been greatly troubled by line 12a, *mearcpaþas Walas træd*, which taken at face value describes how 'the young ox is kept and reared by the "dark herdsman", until it is made to till the fields and to walk across the moors "in the Welsh borderland", or literally: to tread the "Welsh borderpaths".[77] While George Philip Krapp and Elliot Van Kirk Dobbie give the manuscript this reading, they acknowledge its metrical difficulties if *walas* is retained, observing that Ferdinand Holthausen[78] 'would omit the word entirely, for metrical reasons' and suggesting 'that *paþas* and *walas* represented two attempts by the scribe to reproduce a partly illegible word'.[79] The two most recent editions extend Krapp and Dobbie's unease to omit the word *walas* on metrical grounds. Craig Williamson gives *mearpaþas træd* for *mearc paþas walas træd*,[80] characterising the manuscript reading as 'clearly overburdened':

> The presence of *pæðde* in the next half-line may mean that the scribe wrote *paþas* because he was anticipating *træd* and put in a natural object for it, but even if the original reading had been something like *mearc Wala træd*, it is not

clear why the ox should have been characteristically defined as walking the boundary or country of the Welsh. My own guess, following up on the suggestion of Krapp and Dobbie, is that the original *mearcpaþas* was corrupted into something like *mearcwawas*, and that two scribal conjectures written in above the *-wawas* in the form of *paþas* and *walas* were then both incorporated into the text by a later scribe.[81]

Bernard J. Muir follows this precedent, giving *mearcpaþas træd* and noting, 'the MS has *walas* before *træd*, which is clearly extraneous'.[82]

The omission of *walas*, however, goes against current Anglo-Saxon editorial practice, which as Paul E. Szarmach has noted 'is a tendency towards non-intervention in the textual evidence and an attempt to preserve the text as received'.[83] While a metrically superior emendation is undoubtedly valuable, the text as preserved within its sole extant manuscript deserves equal consideration, for it reveals that at some point in time an Anglo-Saxon scribe thought that *mearcpaþas* and *walas* belonged together. Given the nearly unfailing association between Welsh ethnicity and darkness in the rest of the riddles – the *swearte Wealas* (l. 4) and the *wonfeax Wale* (l. 8) in Riddle 12, and a *wonfah Wale* (l. 6) in Riddle 52[84] – the connection of *sweartum hyrde* (l. 11) to *mearcpaþas Walas* (l. 12) seems simply another natural link between the Welsh and the visible markers of their ethnicity, a link that reveals the cultural values of Anglo-Saxon England.[85] Yet even accepting the metrical emendation leaves a 'dark keeper' who travels the marches or border paths with captives under his control.[86] The strong connections between these elements and the Welsh, here and elsewhere in the Exeter Book Riddles, place even its emended version in the same group of riddles featuring bound captives under the control of the 'dark Welsh'.

The specific geographical terminology used by Riddle 72 to locate the suffering of its captive has never been satisfactorily explained. However, this riddle's geographical precision and its imagery of a journey made in captivity evoke two historical realities for travel along the Welsh borderlands in such conditions: cattle droving and slave raids. Williamson's concern that 'it is not clear why the ox should have been characteristically defined as walking the boundary or country of the Welsh'[87] has been dismissed by Rulon-Miller: 'there may be no cause for puzzlement here, considering the frequent conflation of Welsh and oxen in the riddles'.[88] Yet her solution does not account for the fact that the riddle's speaker suffers on the *mearcpaþas* and *moras*, terms that denote non-arable wastelands too mountainous or swampy to be ploughed,[89] the traditional interpretation of this riddle's solution. What this language does describe perfectly, however, is the journey of cattle herded along drove roads from Wales to England.

Drove roads were wide and well-travelled routes used annually to herd livestock, particularly cattle, from rural Wales to the more fertile pastures to the east where they would be fattened and sold at markets in England.[90] Wales was a large-scale supplier of cattle, herded by 'the drovers who brought northern and Welsh cattle into the beast markets of the Midlands',[91] from the medieval period onwards.[92] Richard J. Moore-Colyer, in his comprehensive study of Welsh cattle droving, has argued that 'undoubtedly there were sporadic movements of cattle from Wales into England since the very earliest times, and the possible existence of a regular traffic in cattle between the two countries during the pre-Norman period is particularly intriguing'.[93] Pointing to gaps in Offa's Dyke, he has proposed that 'it is tempting, although perhaps a little contentious, to suggest that where these openings coincide with established drove track, the track may be of considerable antiquity'.[94]

There is both archaeological and textual evidence to suggest that cattle droving was practised during the Anglo-Saxon period. Della Hooke has argued that 'a pattern of drove ways can be suggested' in Anglo-Saxon England, which archaeologists believe 'probably originated in the late Iron Age or Roman periods, arising out of a system of transhumance when stock was moved seasonally away from cultivated zones to summer and autumn pastures'.[95] The Welsh borderlands, where lowland winter pastures and summer highland pastures meet, would be a natural location of such early drove roads. Moreover, textual evidence for this practice along the Welsh borderlands during the Anglo-Saxon period may exist in the form of the *Dunsæte Agreement* discussed in the Introduction.[96] While earlier I considered what this text might tell us about the laws of the Welsh borderlands, the content of the *Dunsæte Agreement* – namely, its focus on cattle theft— and its location on the lower River Wye along the Welsh borderlands also shed light on the cattle trade in the Anglo-Saxon period. As Margaret Gelling has argued, 'the Ordinance deals with conditions on the English/Welsh border which are likely to have been much the same for several centuries'.[97] Moore-Colyer has suggested that this text 'strongly indicates the existence of a legitimate cattle trade between the Dunsæte and the English ... from the late eighth century'.[98] In light of this evidence, it seems reasonable to suggest that cattle droving along the Welsh borderlands was an established practice during the Anglo-Saxon period, even before frequent post-Conquest references demonstrate its magnitude throughout the later Middle Ages.[99]

The practice of cattle droving across the Welsh borderlands, I argue, explains the imagery of travel present in Riddles 72 and 52. The captives are on a 'siþe' (l. 7a, journey) in Riddle 52, and Riddle 72's speaker 'siþade widdor' (l. 11b, journeyed widely) and 'mearcpaþas Walas træd, moras pædde' (l. 12, trod the paths of the Welsh marches, traversed the moors) 'on laste' (l. 14a, on the track). Such descriptions are more fittingly applied to cattle herded along a drove road in the Welsh borderlands than cattle used in agricultural work. Understanding these riddles' descriptions of 'journeys' as evoking cattle driven along drove roads, rather than ploughing as has been understood, clarifies the puzzle of why they are situated in the Welsh borderlands.

Cattle and slave raids in the borderlands

Understanding the specific geography of these riddles alongside their dual allusions to cattle and human captivity creates a portrait of the Welsh borderlands that mirrors its historical reputation (both before and after the Conquest)[100] as the site of frequent cattle and slave raids. Raiding was central to Welsh warfare and indeed culture from its earliest known history through to the close of the medieval period. In early Britain, 'especially among British and Irish kingdoms, cattle seem to have been a particularly important form of booty, and one whose acquisition was the object of successful lords', so much so that 'cattle raids may in fact have been initiated for the purpose of establishing tribute from other kingdoms'.[101] At the same time, as David Wyatt has thoroughly demonstrated, slave raiding in the early British Isles was not simply a profit of battle but its goal, one which was embedded into the fabric of early Celtic society.[102] Indeed, as the discussion in the beginning of this chapter has indicated, cattle and slaves were equated as property (and plunder) in the early British Isles.

After the Norman Conquest, as John Gillingham in particular has shown, the fact that England moved away from slavery as such (exchanging it, of course, for serfdom) more quickly than did Wales meant that, from the perspective of Anglo-Norman England, Wales became identified as the locus of slavery in Britain.[103] The March of Wales in particular had a reputation for lawlessness tantamount to its identity as a locus of both cattle and slave raiding: 'the men of the March, so it was alleged, raided these border countries, burning and looting, killing or ransoming their victims and then retiring to the sanctuary of their lordships, where English sheriffs were powerless to act against them'.[104] The March was firmly embedded in the Anglo-Norman imagination as the site of violence and cattle theft. Exeter Book Riddles 52 and 72, with their dual layers of allusion to the parallel captivities of cattle droving and slave raiding along the Welsh borderlands, present a portrait of this region as a similar site of lawlessness and danger during the Anglo-Saxon period.

Conclusions

Exeter Book Riddles 52 and 72 have a clever polysemic solution that depicts 'the dark Welsh' as both slaves and slave raiders in Anglo-Saxon England. Understanding this solution shifts the representation of the Welsh in these riddles from a group inferior in both class and ethnicity to the Anglo-Saxons – the way in which these riddles have traditionally been interpreted – to a people, like the Anglo-Saxons, spread across all strata of society in the early British Isles. Significantly, the solution of these riddles as depicting both cattle droving and slave raiding, two activities historically identified with the Welsh borderlands, explains the presence of the Welsh in these riddles and the location of Riddle 72 along the Welsh borderlands. In their linkage of cattle, captivity and the Welsh to the borderlands, these riddles depict this region as a site of cattle and slave raiding before the Conquest, foreshadowing its later notoriety.

In the modern critical imagination, the Anglo/Welsh border in the Anglo-Saxon period has come to be defined by Offa's Dyke. But what Exeter Book Riddles 52 and 72 suggest is that, within popular Anglo-Saxon literary tradition, the Welsh borderlands were perceived not as an impenetrable boundary, but rather as a region associated with cattle and slave raiding, where an elite warrior class could make its own fortune. As Chapter Five will argue, this literary reputation of the Welsh borderlands was well matched by historical reality in the later Anglo-Saxon period, when Welsh rulers and Mercian earls in the borderlands came together to carry out numerous raids on surrounding kingdoms over the course of the tenth and eleventh centuries. In the late Anglo-Saxon period, the *Anglo-Saxon Chronicle* depicts the Welsh borderlands as a distinct region within Anglo-Saxon England, one which acted as a significant, independent political force over the course of the eleventh century.

Notes

1 Part of this chapter appeared in an earlier form as 'The "Dark Welsh" as slaves and slave traders in Exeter Book riddles 52 and 72', *English Studies* 95 (2014): 235–55. It appears here with the permission of Routledge.
2 William Henry Stevenson, *Asser's Life of King Alfred, Together with the Annals of Saint Neots* (Oxford: Clarendon Press, 1959), 12.

3 Simon Keynes and Michael Lapidge, *Alfred the Great: Asser's Life of King Alfred and Other Contemporary Sources* (London: Penguin, 1983), 71.
4 See Sir Cyril Fox, *Offa's Dyke* (London: British Academy, 1955) and Frank Noble and Margaret Gelling, *Offa's Dyke Reviewed* (Oxford: BAR, 1983).
5 David Hill and Margaret Worthington, *Offa's Dyke: History and Guide* (Stroud: Tempus, 2003), 110.
6 See further *ibid.*, 103–28 for conclusions and explanation of evidence, and Appendix 2, 178–80, for transcription and translation of the Pillar of Eliseg.
7 See also the map in David Hill, 'Mercians: the dwellers on the boundary', in *Mercia: An Anglo-Saxon Kingdom in Europe*, ed. Michelle P. Brown and Carol A. Farr (London: Continuum, 2001), 179.
8 Keith Ray and Ian Bapty, *Offa's Dyke: Landscape and Hegemony in Eighth-Century Britain* (Oxford: Oxbow Books, 2016).
9 *Ibid.*, 336.
10 *Ibid.*, 344.
11 Paul Russell, 'The rhetoric and reality of early medieval frontiers in Britain', talk given at the University of Notre Dame, 30 January 2016. I am grateful to him for allowing me to include the argument here.
12 See Nina Rulon-Miller, 'Sexual humor and fettered desire in Exeter Book Riddle 12', in *Humor in Anglo-Saxon literature*, ed. Jonathan Wilcox (Woodbridge, Suffolk: Boydell, 2000), 99–126 at 117. This literary connection between slavery and agrarian work reflects the historical reality of Anglo-Saxon England: see David A. E. Pelteret, 'Slavery in Anglo-Saxon England', in *The Anglo-Saxons: Synthesis and Achievement*, ed. J. Douglas Woods and David A. E. Pelteret (Waterloo, Ontario: Wilfrid Laurier University Press, 1985), 117–33 at 123; and David A. E. Pelteret, *Slavery in Early Mediaeval England: From the Reign of Alfred Until the Twelfth Century*, Studies in Anglo-Saxon History 7 (Woodbridge, Suffolk: Boydell, 1995), 64–5, 116–17 and 268–9 (*dæge*).
13 John W. Tanke, 'Wonfeax wale: ideology and figuration in the sexual riddles of the Exeter Book', in *Class and Gender in Early English Literature: Intersections*, ed. Britton J. Harwood and Gillian R. Overing (Bloomington IN: Indiana University Press, 1994), 21–42 and Rulon-Miller, 'Sexual humor', 99–126.
14 On slavery, see Pelteret, *Slavery in Early Mediaeval England*; 'Slave raiding and slave trading in early England', *Anglo-Saxon England* 9 (1981): 99–114; 'Slavery in Anglo-Saxon England', 117–33; and Oliver Padel, 'Slavery in Saxon Cornwall: the Bodmin manumissions', Kathleen Hughes Memorial Lectures 7 (Cambridge: Department of Anglo-Saxon, Norse and Celtic, 2009).
15 The texts and numbering of the riddles are from Elliot Van Kirk Dobbie and George Phillip Krapp, eds, *The Exeter Book*, Anglo-Saxon Poetic Records 3 (New York: Columbia University Press, 1936). More recent editions are Craig Williamson, ed., *The Old English Riddles of the Exeter Book* (Chapel Hill: University of North Carolina Press, 1977) and Bernard J. Muir, *The Exeter Anthology of Old English Poetry: An Edition of Exeter Dean and Chapter MS 3501*, 2

vols., Exeter Medieval English Texts and Studies (Exeter: University of Exeter Press, 1994). A recent re-evaluation of the riddles' Old English solutions is John D. Niles, *Old English Enigmatic Poems and the Play of the Texts*, Studies in the Early Middle Ages 13 (Turnhout: Brepols, 2006).

16 F. York Powell, 'Britain under English and Danes', in *Social England*, vol. I, *From the Earliest Times to the Accession of Edward the First*, ed. H. D. Traill (New York: G.P. Putnam's Sons, 1894), 125.

17 Janet M. Bately, *The Anglo-Saxon Chronicle: A Collaborative Edition, Volume 3: MS A* (Cambridge, D.S. Brewer, 1986), 63 [909].

18 Susan Irvine, *The Anglo-Saxon Chronicle: A Collaborative Edition*, Volume 7: *MS E* (Cambridge: D.S. Brewer, 2004) 83 [1052].

19 Pelteret, *Slavery in Early Mediaeval England*, 164–84 and 261–2.

20 Ibid., 86, citing *Dunsæte* 7.

21 Ibid., 84–5, citing Alfred and Guthrum 4.

22 Martin Rule, ed., *Eadmeri Historia Novorum in Anglia*, Rolls Series 81 (London: Longman, 1884), 143, canon 28.

23 Geoffrey Bosanquet, trans., *Eadmer's History of Recent Events in England* (London: Cresset Press, 1964), 152.

24 T. M. Charles-Edwards, *The Welsh Laws*, Writers of Wales Series (Cardiff: University of Wales Press, 1989), 6. As he and Robin Chapman Stacey, 'Law and lawbooks in mediaeval Wales', *History Compass* 8 (2010): 1180–90, make clear, the textual history of the medieval Welsh laws is extremely complicated: there are some 40 different manuscripts representing five Latin and three Welsh redactions, all of which date from centuries after these traditions were ostensibly codified in the tenth century during the reign of Hywel Dda. See further Charles-Edwards, *The Welsh Laws*, 16–19, 20–2, 25–48 and 95–102; and the Cyfraith Hywel project funded by the University of Wales at www.cyfraith-hywel.org.uk/en/index.php (accessed 22 March 2016). In what follows I have aimed to quote from the most recent published edition of a given law text whenever possible. I am grateful to Paul Russell for advice and references in the following discussions of Welsh law; all mistakes of course remain my own.

25 Melville Richards, ed., *Cyfrethiau Hywel Dda yn ôl Llawysgrif Coleg yr Iesu LVII Rhydychen*, 2nd edn (Cardiff: University of Wales Press, 1990), 89.

26 Aneurin Owen, ed. and trans., *Ancient Laws and Institutes of Wales* (London: Public Records Commissioners, 1841). Owen's *Ancient Laws* was published in two forms, a single-volume folio and a two-volume quarto, the pagination of which is quite different. For that reason, references will be given by law code (as titled by Owen), book, chapter and paragraph. Owen's 'Venedotian Code' = Iowerth; his 'Gwentian Code' = Cyfnerth; and his 'Demetian Code' = Blegwryd; his 'anomalous laws' are those which did not fit into any of these redactions. Here, Owen, 'Dimetian Code', 3.3.8.

27 Owen, 'Dimetian Code', 2.18.53. This section of text is only in MS Q (NLW, Wynnstay 36), a late medieval manuscript lacking a modern edition. For a

discussion of the letter 'G' in medieval Welsh orthography, see T. M. Charles-Edwards and Paul Russell, 'The Hendregadredd manuscript and the orthography and phonology of Welsh in the early fourteenth century,' *National Library of Wales Journal* 28 (1993/4): 419–62 at 421–3.

28 Owen, 'Welsh laws', 14.6.3. This section of text is only in MS H (NLW, Peniarth 164), a late and difficult manuscript lacking a modern edition.
29 Arthur W. Wade-Evans, ed., *Welsh Medieval Law* (Oxford: Clarendon Press, 1909; repr. Aalen: Scientia Verlag, 1979), 116.
30 Owen, 'Gwentian Code', 2.40.23.
31 Dieter Bitterli, *Say What I Am Called: The Old English Riddles of the Exeter Book and the Anglo-Latin Riddle Tradition*, Toronto Anglo-Saxon Series 2 (Toronto: University of Toronto Press, 2009), 31.
32 See the entry for *wealh*, in Joseph Bosworth and T. Northcote Toller, *An Anglo-Saxon Dictionary* (Oxford: Clarendon Press, 1898) and T. Northcote Toller, *An Anglo-Saxon Dictionary Supplement* (Oxford: Clarendon Press, 1921), Ia, II. For discussion of this terminology in relation to slavery and ethnic difference in Anglo-Saxon England, see Pelteret, *Slavery in Early Mediaeval England*, 43, 51–4, 319–22 (entries on *weale, wealh, weal-sada*) and 325–6 (*wilisc*); Debby Banham, 'Anglo-Saxon attitudes: in search of the origins of English racism', *European Review of History* 1 (1994): 143–56 at 150–3; and Kevin Crossley-Holland, trans., *The Exeter Book Riddles*, revised edn (Harmondsworth, Middlesex: Penguin Classics, 1993), 114–17.
33 Margaret Lindsay Faull, 'The semantic development of Old English *Wealh*', *Leeds Studies in English* NS 8 (1975): 20–44 at 30.
34 Tanke, 'Wonfeax wale', 25; see 25–6 for a full discussion of his objections.
35 Rulon-Miller, 'Sexual humor', 117. She notes an ambiguous potential reference to the Welsh 'in Riddle 49 (Bookcase), where a *þegn* (male servant) in line 5 is *sweart ond saloneb* (dark and dark-faced, possibly also Welsh', 116–17; while this 'is the only riddle featuring a "dark", possibly Welsh, person ... that does not contain references to oxen or binding ... the riddle subject is *eardfæst* (fixed, earth-bound), perhaps an echo of more literal bindings in other riddles dealing with the Welsh', 117 n.68.
36 Pelteret, *Slavery in Early Mediaeval England*, 41.
37 Michael Winterbottom, ed. and trans., *Gildas: The Ruin of Britain and Other Works*, Arthurian Period Sources 7 (Chichester: Phillimore, 1978), 98 and 27.
38 Pelteret, 'Slavery in Anglo-Saxon England', 121.
39 Faull, 'Old English *Wealh*', 30.
40 Pelteret, *Slavery in Early Mediaeval England*, 41; these terms are catalogued in 'Appendix I: The Old English terminology of servitude and freedom', 261–330.
41 See the entries for *ræpan* (to bind [with a rope], make captive), *ge-ræpan* (Bosworth and Toller, *Dictionary*: to bind, Toller, *Supplement*: to fasten with a rope, bind, chain), *ræpling* (one bound, a captive, prisoner, criminal), *ræpling-weard* (a keeper of prisoners), *ræpsan* (to seize [?], to reprove [?]), *ræpsung*

(seizing [?], reproving [?]) in Bosworth and Toller, *Dictionary* and Toller, *Supplement*.

42 See the entries for *ge-fetrian* (to fetter, bind) in Bosworth and Toller, *Dictionary* and Toller, *Supplement*; and Cameron et al., *Dictionary of Old English*, which gives further 'to fetter, shackle, bind (someone/something); also figurative' and makes clear that other instances of *ge-fetrian* (in *The Panther*, *Genesis A*, *Solomon and Saturn*, *The Paris Psalter*, *Exodus* and *The Menologium*) occur in a religious context.

43 See the entry for *bend* (what ties, binds, or bends) in Bosworth and Toller, *An Anglo-Saxon Dictionary and Supplement*; and Cameron, definition 1, 'bond, cord, especially referring to restraining fetters; also figurative'. For Riddle 72, see also entry for *bindan* (to bind, tie) in Bosworth and Toller, *An Anglo-Saxon Dictionary and Supplement*; and Cameron (to bind together).

44 See Pelteret, *Slavery in Early Mediaeval England*, 61–4 and 67–70. Rulon-Miller, 'Sexual humor', 124, has also noted a high concentration of binding imagery in Riddle 12, although she interprets it through the lens of sadomasochism: 'I would suggest, rather, that sexual innuendo permeates Riddle 12 from start to finish. The theme of the use of leather in master–slave relationships resonates throughout the riddle, in what seems an anticipation of modern-day leather fetishism. In this text, masters are served by fettered beings, from the speaking subject, a yoked, and then slaughtered, ox, to the male Welsh slaves bound by leather thongs, to the "better" Anglo-Saxon men, who are similarly bound, to the leather receptacles that serve their masters, the "implicitly well-to-do" *bryd* and *deorum*, to the masturbating female slave who, as we have seen, "serves men" in more ways than one. In addition, in this erotically charged riddle, both the *felawlonc bryd* who treads on leather and the ambiguous leather *bosm* that furnishes drink seem to allude to sexual acts'. I find no evidence of such sexually charged language in Riddles 52 and 72. Seth Lerer, *Literacy and Power in Anglo-Saxon Literature*, Regents Studies in Medieval Culture (Lincoln NE: University of Nebraska Press, 1991), 117–25, interprets binding imagery elsewhere in the Exeter Book Riddles as allusions to intellectual knowledge and bookbinding; I also do not see this as applicable to the bound Welsh/oxen group.

45 Cameron et al., *Dictionary of Old English*, entry for *feter*: 1.c., 'specifically: shackle or restraint, usually for the feet of animals or birds; gin, snare' and 1.c.i., 'glossing *paturum* (*pastorium*) "clog or hobble by which animals were held (? while grazing)"; also in variation with *pedum* "shepherd's crook, sheep-hook", perhaps by confusion with *pedica* "fetter, snare".' The first meaning, 1.c., cites three occurrences in the corpus. Of these, the first refers to a horse: 'gif hit hors sy sing on his feteran oþþe on his bridele', 'if it is a horse sing this over his fetters or over his bridle'; 'Charm 5' in T. O. Cockayne, *Leechdoms, Wortcunning and Starcraft of Early England*, Rolls Series 35, 3 vols. (1864–6; repr. Wiesbaden: Kraus, 1965), III, 286. The second meaning refers to the taming of wild hawks:

'sum sceal wildne fugel wloncne atemian, heafoc on honda, oþþæt seo heoroswealwe wynsum weorþeð; deþ he wyrplas on, fedeþ swa on feterum fiþrum dealne', 'one shall tame the proud wild bird, the hawk on the hand, until that sword-swallow becomes pleasant; he puts *vervelles* [rings attaching the hawk to its jess; see entry for *wyrpel* in Bosworth and Toller, *Dictionary*] on it, so feeds in fetters the wing-proud one'; 'The Fortunes of Men' in Dobbie and Krapp, *Exeter Book*, 156. The third is a gloss on *pedica* which Cameron et al., *Dictionary of Old English*, notes is 'prob. from Iob 18:10 *abscondita est in terra pedica eius*'; in H. D. Meritt, *Old English Glosses: A Collection*, MLA General Series 16 (New York: MLA, 1945), no. 52, 32.2. Similarly, sense 1.c.i. gives two occurrences, both glossing *paturum*, in the glosses: J. H. Hessels, ed., *A Late Eighth-Century Latin-Anglo-Saxon Glossary (Leiden MS. Voss. Qo Lat. No. 69)* (Cambridge: Cambridge University Press, 1906), 46.42 and J. D. Pheifer, ed., *Old English Glosses in the Epinal–Erfurt Glossary* (Oxford: Clarendon Press, 1974), 641.

46 See Pelteret, *Slavery in Early Mediaeval England*, 58–9; I. H. Goodall, 'Locks and keys', in *Object and Economy in Medieval Winchester*, ed. Martin Biddle, Winchester Studies 7.ii (Oxford: Clarendon Press, 1990), 1011–12, par. 3671–5, plate LXIII and figure 314; J. Henning, 'Gefangenenfesseln im slawischen Siedlungsraum und der europäische Sklavenhandel im 6. bis 12. Jahrhundert. Archäologisches zum Bedeutungswandel von "skālbos-saklibasclavus"', *Germania* 70.2 (1990): 403–26; B. G. Scott, 'Iron "slave-collars" from Lagore crannog, Co. Meath', *Proceedings of the Royal Irish Academy* 78C (1978): 213–30; and Harold Mytum, *The Origins of Early Christian Ireland* (London: Routledge, 1992), 144. Pelteret, *Slavery in Early Mediaeval England*, 322 (*wealsada*), notes the existence of a specific term 'a slave shackle' for the Latin *absconderunt superbi laqueum mihi*, Psalm 139:5 in the Paris Psalter, in George Phillip Krapp, ed., *The Paris Psalter and the Metres of Boethius*, Anglo-Saxon Poetic Records 5 (New York: Columbia University Press, 1932), 136. Pelteret glosses *weal* simply as 'slave'; I would note the suggestive connections to the Welsh as well.

47 See Michael Lapidge, *The Cult of St Swithun*, Winchester Studies 4.11 (Oxford: Clarendon Press, 2003): Lantfred of Winchester, *Translatio et Miracvla S. Swithvni*, vi (288–91), xx (302–5), xxxviii (330–3) and xxxix (332–3); see also xxiv (306–7), xxvii (314–17), and xxxiv (322–5) for accounts of fettered prisoners; Wulfstan of Winchester, *Narratio Metrica de S. Swithvno*, I.ix (468–9), II.ii (496–503), II.xxi (548–9), and II.xxii (548–9); see also II.vii (506–7), II.x (518–27), and II.xvii (536–9) for accounts of fettered prisoners; Ælfric of Winchester, *Life of St Swithun*, xii (596–7) and xxv (604–7); see also xxvi (606–7) for account of fettered prisoners; many similar accounts also occur in later post-Conquest texts, for which see 611–796. See Pelteret, *Slavery in Early Mediaeval England*, 57–60, for discussion of these examples.

48 R. R. Darlington, ed., *The Vita Wulfstani of William of Malmesbury* (London: Royal Historical Society, 1928), 43–4.

49 J. H. F. Peile, trans., *William of Malmesbury's Life of St Wulfstan, Bishop of Worcester* (Oxford: Blackwell, 1934), 64–5.
50 See the entry for *beag* in Bosworth and Toller, *An Anglo-Saxon Dictionary and Supplement*; and Cameron et al., which gives most occurrences of *beag* as a literal adornment: a circular metal ornament of some kind (ring, bracelet, torque – see 1., 1.b., 1.c., 1.d., 1.e., 1.f.) with the broader sense of treasure generally (1.a.i., 1.a.ii., 1.a.iii., 1.h.). The word occasionally denotes metaphorical adornments – see 1.c.i. (referring to the circle of feathers around the neck of the Phoenix), 1.d.i. (Christ's crown of thorns), 1.d.ii. (monastic tonsure), 1.d.iii. (iris of the eye), and 1.g. (circular engraving on a chalice). It is also, in one instance, 2., an 'erroneous gloss for *coccineus* "scarlet-coloured"' and 3. appears as an element in personal names corresponding to Latin equivalents *armilla, boia, corona, dextrale, monile, torques*. Significantly, sense 1.c.ii. gives *beag* in one instance as a gloss for *boia*, 'collar or yoke worn by criminals'; W. G. Stryker, 'The Latin–Old English glossary in MS. Cotton Cleopatra A.III', unpublished doctoral dissertation (Stanford University, 1951), 28–367, 737; with corrections by Manfred Voss, 'Strykers Edition des alphabetischen Cleopatraglossars: Corrigenda und Addenda', *Arbeiten aus Anglistik und Amerikanistik* 13 (1988): 123–38.
51 Eric I. Bromberg, 'Wales and the mediaeval slave trade', *Speculum* 17 (1942): 263–9.
52 See B. G. Charles, *Old Norse Relations With Wales* (Cardiff: University of Wales Press, 1934); Poul Holm, 'The slave trade of Dublin, ninth to twelfth centuries', *Peritia* 5 (1986): 317–45; Pelteret, *Slavery in Early Mediaeval England*, 70–4, 74–9 and 139–40; Wendy Davies, *Patterns of Power in Early Wales* (Oxford: Clarendon Press, 1990), 48–60; K. L. Maund, *Ireland, Wales, and England in the Eleventh Century* (Woodbridge, Suffolk: Boydell, 1991), 156–82; Seán Duffy, 'Ostmen, Irish and Welsh in the eleventh century', *Peritia* 9 (1995): 379–96; and Colman Etchingham, 'North Wales, Ireland and the Isles: the insular Viking zone', *Peritia* 15 (2001): 145–87.
53 Bromberg, 'Wales and the mediaeval slave trade', 264.
54 Maund, *Ireland, Wales, and England*, 182.
55 Duffy, 'Ostmen, Irish and Welsh', 396.
56 Bromberg, 'Wales and the mediaeval slave trade', 266.
57 On what precisely it meant to be 'Welsh' in the Middle Ages, see Wendy Davies, *Wales in the Early Middle Ages*, Studies in the Early History of Britain (Leicester: Leicester University Press, 1982), 196–7 and *Patterns of Power*, 88–9; T. M. Charles-Edwards, 'Language and society among the insular Celts, AD 400–1000', in *The Celtic World*, ed. M. J. Green (London: Routledge, 1995), 711–13; and Huw Pryce, 'British or Welsh? National identity in twelfth-century Wales', *English Historical Review* 116 (2001): 775–801. On the difficulties of racial classification in general during the Middle Ages, see Robert Bartlett, 'Medieval and modern concepts of race and ethnicity', *Journal of Medieval and*

Early Modern Studies 31 (2001): 39–56; and Bryan Ward-Perkins, 'Why did the Anglo-Saxons not become more British?', *English Historical Review* 115 (2000): 513–33.

58 Pelteret, 'Slave raiding and slave trading in early England', demonstrates the pervasive capture and sale of slaves amongst warring Anglo-Saxon kingdoms.
59 *Ibid.*, 111.
60 Richards, *Cyfrethiau Hywel Dda*, 145.
61 Owen, 'Welsh laws', 5.2.142.
62 Bromberg, 'Wales and the mediaeval slave trade', 266.
63 Christine James, *Machlud Cyfraith Hywel: golygiad o BL Add 22356* (Cambridge: Seminar Cyfraith Hywel, 2013), 60. Hosted online at www.cyfraith-hywel.org.uk/en/machlud-cyf-hyw.php (accessed 22 March 2016) by the University of Wales.
64 Owen, 'Welsh laws', 11.2.2. While there were no distinctions drawn between the enslavement of native versus non-native peoples, there was, however, a difference in their worth: 'punt a hanner yw gwerth caeth tramor; os o'r ynys honn yd henuyd, punt vyd y werth', Richards, *Cyfreithiau Hywel Dda*, 59 (one pound and a half is the worth of a bondman from beyond sea; if he be a native of this island, a pound is his worth), Owen, 'Dimetian Code', 2.17.38.
65 Bromberg, 'Wales and the mediaeval slave trade', 264.
66 See *ibid.*, 266–9; and Pelteret, 'Slave raiding and slave trading in early England', 107–13.
67 Moritz Trautmann, 'Zu den altenglischen Rätseln', *Anglia* 17 (1895): 396–400 at 396; cited in Dobbie and Krapp, *Exeter Book*, 348. Rejected solutions include 'two pails' by F. Dietrich, 'Die Räthsel des Exeterbuchs. Würdigung, Lösung und Herstellung', *Zeitschrift für deutsches Altertum* 11 (1859): 448–90 at 476; 'well-buckets' by C. W. M. Grein, 'Kleine Mittheilungen', *Germania* 10 (1865): 305–10 at 308; 'yoke of oxen' by John A. Walz, 'Notes on the Anglo-Saxon riddles', *Harvard Studies and Notes* 5 (1896): 261–8 at 265; and 'broom', by Moritz Trautmann, 'Die Auflösungen der altenglischen Rätsel', *Anglia* 5 (1894): 46–51 at 50, before he proposed flail. Dobbie and Krapp, *Exeter Book*, 348, describe this solution as 'evidently correct'; following their lukewarm endorsement, Williamson, *The Old English Riddles of the Exeter Book*, 295–6 (his riddle 50), writes that 'Trautmann's "flail" seems the best solution yet offered ... It must be admitted that there is little in the riddle to define the actual process of the threshing, but the same lack of detail provides problems for almost any solution'. See also Niles, *Enigmatic Poems*, 143.
68 Walz, 'Notes on the Anglo-Saxon riddles', 265: 'a yoke of oxen led into the barn or house by a female slave'; cited in Dobbie and Krapp, *Exeter Book*, 348.
69 Frederick Tupper, Jr, *The Riddles of the Exeter Book* (Boston: Ginn, 1910), 185; cited in Dobbie and Krapp, *Exeter Book*, 348.
70 Here the MS reads *genamne*. Two solutions have been proposed. F. Holthausen, 'Zur Textkritik altenglischer Dichtungen', *Englische Studien* 37 (1907):

198–211 at 209, 'proposed *genamnan*, plur. of a noun *genamna*, "namensvetter, gleighnamiger, genosse", citing O[ld] H[igh] G[erman] *ginamno*'; cited in Dobbie and Krapp, *Exeter Book*, 348. Dobbie and Krapp accept Holthausen's emendation, noting 'If we solve the riddle as "flail", we can hardly accept *genamnan* in the narrow meaning "gleichnamiger", but as "genosse" it makes excellent sense'. I follow the emendation first proposed by Benjamin Thorpe, *Codex Exoniensis: A Collection of Anglo-Saxon Poetry* (London: Society of Antiquaries of London, 1842), 435 (his riddle 53), to *genumne*, the past participle of *geniman*. See Williamson, *The Old English Riddles of the Exeter Book*, 296 for discussion; he accepts it and notes that 'the evidence for the existence of a noun, *genamn* from the verb, *genemnan*, in Old English is slight', giving the translation of this line as 'which were seized (held) by tight bonds'.

71 Pelteret, *Slavery in Early Mediaeval England*, 112–63.

72 Dorothy Dilts Swartz, 'The legal status of women in early medieval Ireland and Wales in comparison with western Europe and Mediterranean societies: environmental and social correlations', *Proceedings of the Harvard Celtic Colloquium* 13 (1993): 107–18 at 111.

73 Robin Chapman Stacey, 'Divorce, medieval Welsh style', *Speculum* 77 (2002): 1107–27 at 1112.

74 Nerys Patterson, 'Women as vassal: gender symmetry in medieval Wales', *Proceedings of the Harvard Celtic Colloquium* 8 (1988): 31–45 at 31. See also the essays collected in Dafydd Jenkins and Morfydd E. Owen, eds, *The Welsh Law of Women: Studies Presented to Professor Daniel A. Binchy on his Eightieth Birthday* (Cardiff: University of Wales Press, 1980), particularly Christopher McAll, 'The normal paradigms of a woman's life in the Irish and Welsh law texts', 7–22; Rees Davies, 'The status of women and the practice of marriage in late-medieval Wales', 93–114; and D. B. Walters, 'The European legal context of the Welsh law of matrimonial property', 115–31.

75 Martin Welch, *Discovering Anglo-Saxon England* (University Park PA: Pennsylvania State University Press, 1992), 36; see also 39–42. His points are re-emphasised by Nicholas Howe, *Writing the Map of Anglo-Saxon England: Essays in Cultural Geography* (New Haven: Yale University Press, 2008), 52–3. See also Stephen Pollington, *The Mead Hall: The Feasting Tradition in Anglo-Saxon England* (Norfolk: Anglo-Saxon Books, 2003), 65–98; Frands Herschend, *The Idea of the Good in Late Iron Age Society*, Occasional Papers in Archaeology 15 (Uppsala: Department of Archaeology and Ancient History, 1998); and Raymond Ian Page, *Life in Anglo-Saxon England* (London: Batsford, 1970), 136–54.

76 Dietrich, 'Die Räthsel des Exeterbuchs', 480, originally solved this as 'axle and wheels'; C. W. M. Grein, *Sprachschatz der angelsächsischen Dichter*, in collaboration with F. Holthausen, revised by J. J. Köhler (Heidelberg: Carl Winter, 1912), 527, interpreted *feower broþor* as 'mamillas vaccae'; and Stopford A. Brooke, *The History of Early English Literature* (New York: Macmillan, 1892), 189, solved as

'ox'; see Dobbie and Krapp, *Exeter Book*, 370; Williamson, *The Old English Riddles of the Exeter Book*, 342–4 (his 70); and Niles, *Enigmatic Poems*, 143. This is one of three Exeter Book Riddles with accepted solutions of 'ox' (12, 38 and 72); for discussion of their Latin analogues, see Bitterli, *Say What I Am Called*, 26–34.
77 Bitterli, *Say What I Am Called*, 32–4.
78 F. Holthausen, 'Zu altenglischen Denkmälern', *Englische Studien* 51 (1917): 180–8 at 188.
79 Dobbie and Krapp, *Exeter Book*, 370.
80 Williamson, *The Old English Riddles of the Exeter Book*, 108 (his 70).
81 Ibid., 344.
82 Muir, *The Exeter Anthology of Old English Poetry*, vol. 1, 368.
83 Paul Szarmach, 'Introduction', in *The Editing of Old English: Papers from the 1990 Manchester Conference*, ed. Donald G. Scragg and Paul E. Szarmach (Cambridge: D. S. Brewer, 1994), 3; see also Helmut Gneuss, 'Guide to the editing and preparation of texts for the Dictionary of Old English', 15; Antonette diPaolo Healey, 'The search for meaning', 87; and Michael Lapidge, 'On the emendation of Old English texts', 53–67 in the same volume. Lapidge thoughtfully argues for the opposite point to the one I am trying to make here: 'we have a responsibility as editors to conserve the transmitted text when it is sound, but – and here I dissent from prevailing opinion – to emend it when it is not', 67. While I fully agree with his argument that correct and incorrect texts can and should be discerned, my point is that while there may indeed be a lost, better version of the text that deserves our attention, so too do the surviving words on the page.
84 Williamson, *The Old English Riddles of the Exeter Book*, 296–7, groups these in his notes to Riddle 52 (his 50), calling attention to 'the clearly defined *wonfah Wale* (6), who is mentioned several times in the Riddles'; this group encompasses riddles 12 (lines 4 and 8), 52 (line 6) and 72 (line 12) – his riddles 10, 50 and 70 – even though he omits *walas* from the text of Riddle 72. The only possible exception to this constant link of Welsh to darkness is Riddle 49, with its *þegn* (4) who is *sweart ond saloneb* (5) with no mention of his being Welsh; see Rulon-Miller, 'Sexual humor', 116–17 and Bitterli, *Say What I Am Called*, 31–2.
85 See Rulon-Miller, 'Sexual humor', 116–17. Pelteret, *Slavery in Early Mediaeval England*, 51 n.6, takes this riddle to refer solely to ethnic distinction: 'Riddle, §52, 71, and possibly 88 contain the words *wealh* (m) and *wale* (f). In the first two the words seem to mean "Celt"; the riddles would have an ironic impact if they meant "slave" as well, but there is no evidence within the poems for assigning this sense to them'. While the agricultural labour performed by these figures seems to stand against the latter half of this statement, he does interpret Riddle 72 (his 71) as referring to Celtic ethnicity, even emphasising this quality at the expense of social status.
86 *Mearc* appears to have had a fluid range of meanings (see entries in Bosworth and Toller, *Dictionary*, and Toller, *Supplement*), but always carried some conno-

tation of border, boundary, limit or frontier. Primary meanings of *mearc* given by Bosworth and Toller are limit, boundary, confine of a district, border, 'the territory within the boundaries' (with many Germanic cognates). Bosworth and Toller define *mearcpæð* as 'path leading through a country' or 'paths across the marches?'

87   Williamson, *The Old English Riddles of the Exeter Book*, 34.
88   Rulon-Miller, 'Sexual humor', 117.
89   See the entries for *mearcpæþ*, *mearcland* I, *mearcstapa*, *mearc* II, and *mor* I and particularly II, in Bosworth and Toller, *Dictionary* and Toller, *Supplement*.
90   See Frank M. Stenton, 'The road system of medieval England', *Economic History Review* 7 (1936): 1–21 at 17–19 for an account given by a medieval drover.
91   Christopher Dyer, *Everyday Life in Medieval England* (London: Continuum International, 1994; repr. 2000), 278.
92   Caroline Skeel, 'The cattle trade between Wales and England from the fifteenth to the nineteenth centuries', *Transactions of the Royal Historical Society*, Fourth Series 9 (1926): 135–58 at 136, notes: 'Wales has been always noted for cattle ... it was natural that the surplus cattle of Wales should find their way to the rich feeding-grounds of England'. See also David Walker, *Medieval Wales*, Cambridge Medieval Textbooks (Cambridge: Cambridge University Press, 1990; repr. 1999), 61–2. Two classic studies of Welsh cattle droving attest to its rich history from the Middle Ages onwards: Richard J. Moore-Colyer, *The Welsh Cattle Drovers: Agriculture and the Welsh Cattle Trade Before and During the Nineteenth Century* (Cardiff: University of Wales Press, 1976; 2nd edn. Ashbourne: Landmark, 2002) and P. G. Hughes, *Wales and the Drovers* (1943; 2nd edn, Carmarthen, Dyfed, Wales: Golden Grove Editions, 1988), 1–3 and 27–50.
93   Moore-Colyer, *Welsh Cattle Drovers*, 59.
94   Ibid., 59; see also Frederick C. Suppe, *Military Institutions on the Welsh Marches: Shropshire, A.D. 1066–1300*, Studies in Celtic History XIV (Woodbridge, Suffolk: Boydell, 1994), 35.
95   Della Hooke, 'Mercia: landscape and environment', in *Mercia: An Anglo-Saxon Kingdom in Europe*, ed. Michelle P. Brown and Carol A. Farr, Studies in the Early History of Europe (Leicester: Leicester University Press, 2001), 163–5. In support of the theory that Anglo-Saxon drove roads evolved from an early system of transhumance, Hooke cites W. J. Ford, 'Settlement patterns in the central region of the Warwickshire Avon', in *Medieval Settlement, Continuity and Change*, ed. P. H. Sawyer (London: Edward Arnold, 1976), 274–94; Steven Bassett, *The Wootton Wawen Project: Interim Report No. 4* (Birmingham: University of Birmingham School of History, 1986), 15, fig. 7; and Della Hooke, 'Reconstructing Anglo-Saxon landscapes in Warwickshire', *Transactions of the Birmingham and Warwickshire Archaeological Society* 100 (1996): 99–116.
96   See Chapter One: Introduction, 1–6, for bibliography and discussion; also Carole Hough, 'Cattle-tracking in the Fonthill letter', *English Historical Review* 115 (2000): 864–92.

97 Margaret Gelling, *The West Midlands in the Early Middle Ages*, Studies in the Early History of Britain (Leicester: Leicester University Press, 1992), 113.
98 Moore-Colyer, *Welsh Cattle Drovers*, 59.
99 See *ibid.*, 58–74, for evidence of cattle droving in the medieval and early modern periods.
100 For conditions after the Conquest, see Rees Davies, *Lordship and Society in the March of Wales, 1282–1400* (Oxford: Clarendon Press, 1978), 3, and Geraint H. Jenkins, *A Concise History of Wales* (Cambridge: Cambridge University Press, 2007), 119.
101 Stephen S. Evans, *The Lords of Battle: Image and Reality of the Comitatus in Dark-Age Britain* (Woodbridge, Suffolk: Boydell, 1997), 126. Medieval Irish literature in particular provides many vivid illustrations of such raiding via the genre of *táin bó* (cattle raid) tales, the most famous of which is the *Táin Bó Cúailnge*.
102 David Wyatt, *Slaves and Warriors in Medieval Britain and Ireland, 800–1200* (Leiden: Brill, 2009).
103 John Gillingham, *The English in the Twelfth Century: Imperialism, National Identity and Political Values* (Woodbridge, Suffolk: Boydell, 2000), particularly Chapter 3 (41–58). As he concludes, 58, 'as a result of twelfth-century developments in the conduct and perception of war, the Irish, the Irish-speaking Scots and the Welsh all came to be seen as barbarous savages who fought war in an uncivilised fashion'. See also Brock Holden, *Lords of the Central Marches: English Aristocracy and Frontier Society, 1087–1265* (Oxford: Oxford University Press, 2008), 48ff.
104 Davies, *Lordship and Society*, 3.

5

The Welsh borderlands in the *Anglo-Saxon Chronicle*

The previous chapters of this book have proposed that the Welsh borderlands had a culture of their own and were understood as a distinct region by the authors of those early Anglo-Saxon texts that mention this territory. This chapter moves forward chronologically to the tenth and eleventh centuries and suggests that political alliance in the Welsh borderlands during the later Anglo-Saxon period was a significant pattern across time. The *Anglo-Saxon Chronicle*, a major historical source for the later Anglo-Saxon period, depicts the Welsh borderlands acting as an independent political force throughout the eleventh century. Moreover, a pattern of sustained political alliance between Mercia and northern Wales is evident in the tenth century within a corpus of mostly Welsh historical sources. This pattern of alliance continues in the *Anglo-Saxon Chronicle* throughout the eleventh century, across the Norman Conquest. At the moment of the Norman arrival in England, the Welsh borderlands were a significant political force in Anglo-Saxon England.

The *Anglo-Saxon Chronicle* is frequently cited as a paradigm of Anglo/Welsh antagonism. Yet, while its early annals certainly record a great deal of this type of conflict, as noted in Chapter One, it is important to remember that such annals were written centuries after the events they purport to describe. 'The *Anglo-Saxon Chronicle*' is a shorthand way of referring to seven surviving manuscripts of the same text, which originated in a Common Stock but diverged in tone, style and content when they were disseminated and continued at separate locations across Anglo-Saxon England. The origins of the *Anglo-Saxon Chronicle* as a cohesive record are disputed, but the most widely accepted suggestion for its genesis is that it was begun in the late-ninth-century court of King Alfred as part of his vernacular translation and education programme.[1] Regardless of whether or not Alfred deserves credit for its creation, it is important to remember that those entries in the *Anglo-Saxon Chronicle* which predate the moment of its creation, while not historically 'inaccurate' *per se*, were written later, in many cases centuries later, at a moment in time which many have argued saw an increased sense of 'Englishness' in the face of the Viking attacks.

Thus while the traditional interpretation of Anglo/Welsh relations in the *Anglo-Saxon Chronicle* has found 'British subordination' against which 'English identity was ethnically defined',[2] this book has argued that all Anglo/Welsh encounters cannot be subsumed under that paradigm. Even in the eleventh century – despite the arguments of such scholars as James Campbell, Patrick Wormald, Sarah Foot, Kathleen Davis and Nicholas Brooks for a 'maximalist view' of Anglo-Saxon England, a greater sense of Anglo-Saxon 'national' identity before the Norman Conquest than had been traditionally understood[3] – it is impossible to collapse the many kingdoms, powerful families and political actors in Britain into a uniform 'Anglo-Saxon' identity, as those arguing for the 'minimalist view' of Anglo-Saxon government, such as Paul R. Hyams and Andrew Rabin, have noted.[4] In spite of the rise of Wessex and King Alfred's promotion of some sense of Anglo-Saxon unity in the face of the Viking attacks, the Welsh borderlands retained their identity as a distinct region in the texts of the later Anglo-Saxon period. The *Anglo-Saxon Chronicle* continues to depict the borderlands as an independent political force throughout the eleventh century.

Alliances between Mercian earls and Welsh leaders have not gone unnoticed. However, these partnerships have been treated as exceptional. It has been understood that, occasionally, 'renegade English nobles were useful to political interests in eleventh-century Wales'[5] or, when an Anglo-Saxon earl 'felt himself increasingly isolated, surrounded and threatened', he 'fought his way back again in arms and in alliance with the kingdom's enemies'.[6] Because each alliance has been assigned an individual motivation, the pattern as a whole – that the borderlands acted as a political force across the eleventh century – has been explained away. Likewise, the political alliances within this region have been interpreted in a different light after the Norman Conquest. Despite the prevalence of such pacts after 1066, they have been treated as exceptional circumstances brought about by the Norman presence in England and romanticised as outlaw narratives. Without denying the importance of individual actors and circumstances in forging political relationships, considering these moments of unity together – reading both Welsh and Anglo-Saxon sources and moving across the eleventh century – reveals a broader pattern in which the *Anglo-*

Saxon Chronicle depicts the Welsh borderlands as a distinct political actor throughout the century, before and after the arrival of the Normans.[7]

The tenth-century background

A longer period of political alliance in the Welsh borderlands is suggested by half a dozen tenth-century battles in which troops from Mercia and northern Wales fought together against other Welsh and Anglo-Saxon kingdoms. While these battles have gone largely unrecognised as part of a broader pattern because they are described mostly by Welsh sources,[8] work by Charles Insley has convincingly placed these events in the context of calculated political cooperation between northern Wales and Mercia at the expense of southwestern Wales in the tenth century.[9] I argue that these events together show sustained political alliance within the Welsh borderlands throughout the tenth century, a unity which runs deeper than the desperate collective resistance to the Viking attacks that underlies so much of the narratives of this period.[10] Evidence for this pattern begins with two battles in the late ninth century: combined Mercian and Welsh forces fought against the Vikings in 893, and forces led by Æthelred of Mercia and Anarawd of Gwynedd attacked South Wales in 894. The long entry for 893 in the *Anglo-Saxon Chronicle* records that the Danes at Buttington were besieged by an army led by ealdormen Æthelred of Mercia, Æthelhelm and Æthelnoth which also included 'sum dæl þæs Norðwealcynnes'[11] (some portion of the north Welsh). Æthelred appears to have been in charge of this army,[12] indicating that in the late ninth century a Mercian leader's forces included a northern Welsh division.

In 894, further evidence for political alliance in the Welsh borderlands is provided by the *Annales Cambriae*, which record that 'Anaraut cum Anglis uenit uastare Cereticiam et Strat Tiui' (Anarawd came with the English to ravage Ceredigion and Ystrad Tywi).[13] As T. M. Charles-Edwards has argued, the chronicler's choice of the word *Angli* – instead of *Saxones*, which he uses to indicate the English as a whole – suggests that Anarawd's allies in this raid were the (Anglian) Mercians in particular.[14] The likelihood that this attack reflects an alliance between Anarawd of Gwynedd and Æthelred of Mercia is further substantiated by the complicated series of events related in Chapter 80 of Asser's *Life of King Alfred*, which appears to depict the same outcome.[15] Asser notes that South Wales was squeezed by both Anarawd ap Rhodri from the north and Æthelred of Mercia from the east, a parallel to the *Annales Cambriae* annal which suggests cooperation between these two leaders at the expense of southern Welsh territory.[16]

Further evidence for this alliance between Mercia and northern Wales at the expense of southern Wales appears a few decades later when Alfred's successor, Edward the Elder, seized Mercia from Ælfwynn in 918 after the death of his sister Æthelflæd. The *Anglo-Saxon Chronicle* records that, as he did so, he also gained the submission of those Welsh kings who had been formerly subject to Mercia: Hywel and Clydog ap Cadell of South Wales, and Idwal ap Anarawd of Gwynedd.[17] These details are indicative that an agreement existed between the rulers of Gwynedd and Mercia by which their aggression would be directed jointly at South Wales in exchange for Gwynedd's recognition of Mercian overlordship, which was then inherited by Edward.[18] At the end of the ninth and beginning of the tenth centuries, then, there is evidence that alliances in the Welsh borderlands were beginning to have an impact on the broader political landscape of other Anglo-Saxon and Welsh kingdoms.

Surviving evidence from a variety of sources indicates that the Welsh borderlands continued to act with the same political goals throughout the tenth century. William of Malmesbury is the sole source to record a 924 revolt at Chester, which saw Mercians and Welsh allied against Edward when 'Rex Eduardus, post multa et in bello et in toga nobiliter consummate, paucis ante obitum Vrbem Legionum fidutia Britonum rebellantem a contumatia compescuit' (King Edward, after many famous achievements in both war and peace, a few days before his death suppressed the rebellious spirit of the City of Legions, which was in revolt, relying on the support of the Britons).[19] William claims as his source a (now lost) panegyric for the reign of Athelstan. If this story is true, the revolt at Chester fits into a broader pattern of political alliance in the Welsh borderlands directed outwards against the rest of Anglo-Saxon England. Yet even if William invented this revolt, his having done so would nonetheless reflect the reputation of the Welsh borderlands as a politically aligned region.

Close connections between Mercia and northern Wales continued under the reign of Edward's son Æthelstan, who became king of Mercia in 924 and England in 925. Æthelstan was linked to Mercia all his life, beginning with the story – also recorded only by William of Malmesbury – that as a child, he was fostered in Mercia in the household of Æthelred and Æthelflæd.[20] There also exists a strong possibility that Edward had intended his two sons to rule simultaneously: Ælfweard over Wessex and Æthelstan over Mercia.[21] Ælfweard died shortly after Edward, so it is impossible to know what would have happened if both brothers had remained alive, but it is clear that Æthelstan had strong Mercian support both before and during his kingship. Æthelstan's background appears to have promoted the role of Welsh leaders

The borderlands in the Anglo-Saxon Chronicle

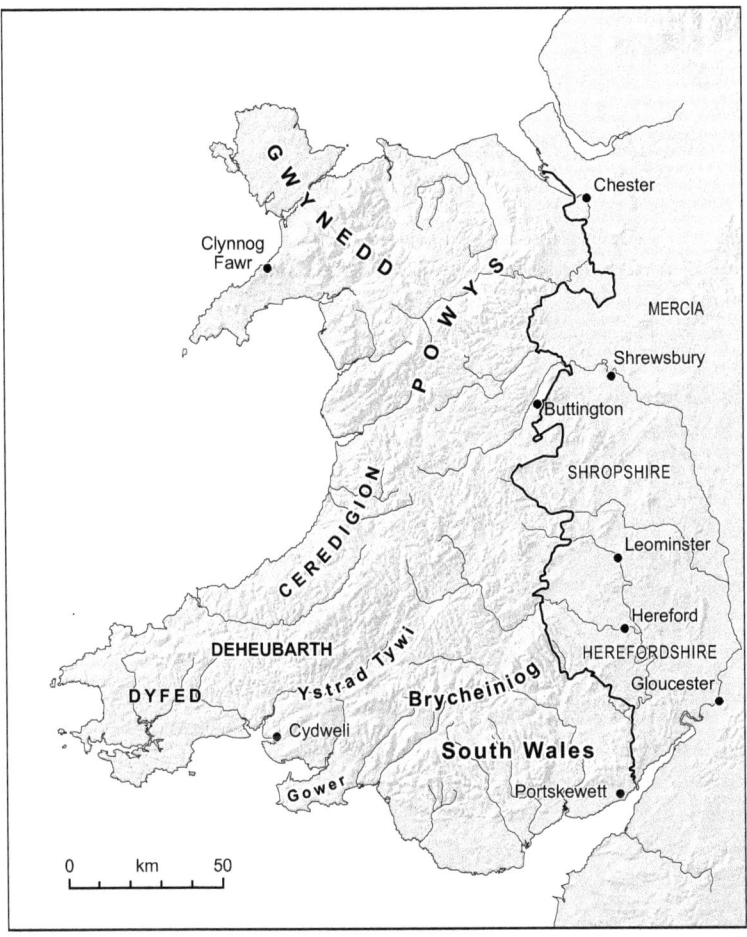

Map 3 Southern Wales in the tenth century, with locations of raids[22]

in Anglo-Saxon politics to match their relationship with Mercia, as Welsh rulers gained increasing prominence at politically significant moments during Æthelstan's reign. A meeting to pledge peace was convened in 926 between Æthelstan and all the kings he is said to have ruled over: Hywel of the West Welsh, Constantine king of Scots, Owain of Gwent and Ealdred of Bamburgh.[23] While the *Anglo-Saxon Chronicle* emphasises Æthelstan's overlordship, it is clear that the Welsh had a significant presence in the politics of his reign. Further evidence suggests that three Welsh kings –

Hywel, Idwal of Gwynedd and Morgan of Gwent – supported Æthelstan on his Scottish campaign in 934.[24] These rulers may have been subordinate to Æthelstan – although D. P. Kirby has argued otherwise[25] – but the continuity of alliance between the Welsh and Æthelstan is notable and presumably a consequence of his strong Mercian connections.

Close political connections between Mercia and Wales continued in the second half of the tenth century. After Eadred's death in 955, Eadwig ruled Wessex while Edgar ruled Mercia, continuing the pattern in which Mercian political interests remained distinct from those of Wessex.[26] At the same time, several raids in the last quarter of the tenth century offer glimpses of continued political alliance in the Welsh borderlands. In 978, the Welsh chronicle *Brut y Tywysogyon*[27] records a raid in which 'ac y diffeithyawd hywel van yeuaf ar saesson gyueilyawc vawr'[28] (and Hywel ap Ieuaf and the Saxons ravaged Clynnog Fawr).[29] These 'Saxons' were likely Mercians under the command of Ælfhere of Mercia, an ealdorman first appointed by Eadwig in 956,[30] because a few years later in 983[31] the *Brut y Tywysogyon* records a similar attack: 'Blwydyn wedy hyny y diffeithwyd brycheinyawc a holl wladoed eynyawn ap ywein ygan y saesson ac alfred yn dywyssawc vdunt a hywel ap yeuaf. ac eyn. aladawd llawer oylluoed'[32] (a year after that, Brycheiniog and all the lands of Einion ab Owain were ravaged by the Saxons, with Aelfhere as their leader, and Hywel ap Ieuaf and Einion slew many of their hosts).[33] These raids suggest a pattern of political alliance within the Welsh borderlands in which attacks were directed outward against other Anglo-Saxon and Welsh kingdoms.

Political alliance within the Welsh borderlands transcended individual rulers, suggesting its stability across time. While both Ælfhere and Hywel died shortly after their raid on Brycheiniog,[34] another joint offensive by a Welsh leader and a Mercian earl took place in 992[35] when Æthelsige of Mercia and Edwin ab Einion ab Owain raided Deheubarth: 'Dec mlyned aphedwarugeint a nawkant oed oed krist pan diffeithyawd maredud ap ywein vaeshyueid. Blywydyn wedy hyny y diffeithyawd edwin fab eynyon ac edylfi seis a llu mawr ygyd ac ef holl gyfoeth maredud yn neheubarth nyd amgen keredigyawn adyued a gwyr a chedweli. A gwystlon agymyrth or holl gyfoeth ar dryded weith ydiffeithyawd vynyw'[36] (Nine hundred and ninety was the year of Christ when Maredudd ab Owain ravaged Maeshyfaidd. A year after that, Edwin ab Einion and Edylfi the Saxon, and with him a great host, ravaged all the territory of Maredudd in Deheubarth, that is, Ceredigion and Dyfed and Gower and Cydweli. And he took hostages from the whole territory. And for the third time he ravaged Menevia).[37] As David E. Thornton has argued, this was likely a direct response to an attack in which Maredudd raided Mercian territory the year before.[38] The fact that retaliation for a raid on Mercia was undertaken jointly by local Mercian and Welsh leaders (indeed, Edwin ab Einion ab Owain was Maredudd's nephew)[39] speaks to the strength of this political alliance in the Welsh borderlands at the end of the tenth century. This background provides an important context for political alliances in the Welsh borderlands in the eleventh century, suggesting continuity and stability within the region.

The Welsh borderlands in the *Anglo-Saxon Chronicle* before 1066

The alliances between Mercian earls and Welsh rulers depicted in the eleventh century by the *Anglo-Saxon Chronicle* continue this pattern. In six significant incidents before the Norman Conquest, the Welsh borderlands are depicted as a region with distinct political interests apart from other Anglo-Saxon kingdoms. MS C is the only recension of the *Anglo-Saxon Chronicle*[40] to record a 1046 raid on South Wales by Sweyn Godwinson and the northern Welsh king Gruffudd ap Llewelyn.[41] In 1043, Sweyn had been granted an earldom bordering South Wales. A few years later, he attacked the southern Welsh together with Gruffudd ap Llewelyn, at that point king of Gwynedd and Powys: 'Her on þysum geare for Swegn eorl into Wealan 7 Griffin se norþerna cyng forð mid him, 7 him man gislode'[42] (in this year Earl Sweyn went into Wales and Gruffudd the northern king went with him, and he [or they] was [or were] given hostages). This raid has not been granted much political significance because Sweyn abducted the abbess of Leominster on his way back, for which he was later exiled.[43] Yet if emphasis is placed on the hostage-taking raid of South Wales rather than the scandal of the abbess's abduction, this attack continues the pattern of political alliance between Mercian earls and northern Welsh rulers from the tenth to the eleventh centuries.

Political alliance in the Welsh borderlands is further evident in the coordinated attacks by Earl Ælfgar of Mercia and King Gruffudd ap Llywelyn (first of Gwynedd, later of all Wales) described in the *Anglo-Saxon Chronicle*'s annals for 1055 and 1058. These detailed narratives show sustained political alliance in the Welsh borderlands alongside a military culture distinct from that of other Anglo-Saxon kingdoms, so much so that these narratives prefigure the borderlands' later literary reputation as the home of outlaws. In 1055 and again in 1058, Earl Ælfgar was outlawed, then raised an army and successfully regained his lands in alliance with Gruffudd ap Llywelyn. While these events have traditionally been understood as an isolated pact between two mercenary individuals,[44] placed in context, they continue the pattern of political alliance in the Welsh borderlands in the eleventh century.

The events of 1055 are described from three distinct perspectives: MS C has a Mercian bias, MS E supports the Godwinsons and so is anti-Mercian, and MS D tries to remain neutral.[45] Yet the events surrounding Ælfgar's exile are clear, regardless of each chronicle's political leanings, and show the impact of alliance in the Welsh borderlands on the broader Anglo-Saxon political landscape. MS C relates that shortly after the death of Earl Siward in 1055, 'Ða ðæræfter binnan lyttlan fyrste wæs witena gemot on Lundene, 7 man geutlagode þa Ælfgar eorl Leofrices sunu eorles butan ælcan gylte, 7 he gewende ða to Irlande 7 begeat him ðær lið, þæt wæs .xviii. scipa butan his agenan, 7 wendan ða to Brytlande to Griffine cinge mid þam werede, 7 he hine underfeng on his griðe'[46] (then a little while after there was a council meeting in London, and men outlawed Earl Ælfgar, Earl Leofric's son, without any guilt. Then he went to Ireland and got himself a fleet – that was eighteen ships besides his own – and he went then to Wales to King Gruffudd with that army, and he took him in under his protection). MS E places the blame on Ælfgar, recording that 'utlagode mann Ælfgar eorl, forðon him man wearp on þet he wæs þes cynges swica 7 ealra landleoda'[47] (men outlawed Earl Ælfgar, because he was accused as a traitor to the king and everyone in the land), and 'he þæs geanwyrde wes ætforan eallum þam mannum þe þær gegaderode wæron, þeah him þet word ofscute his unnþances'[48] (he admitted this to all the men who were meeting there, though the words shot out against his wishes), but ultimately it describes the same series of events. So too does MS D in its attempt at neutrality: '7 þæræfter sona man utlagode Ælfgar eorl, Leofrices sunu eorles, forneh butan gylte'[49] (and soon thereafter men outlawed Earl Ælfgar, Earl Leofric's son, almost without guilt).

The aftermath of Ælfgar's exile demonstrates both the continuity of political alliance in the Welsh borderlands over the eleventh century and also the ways in which the borderlands were positioned against the rest of Anglo-Saxon England. MS C says of Gruffudd and Ælfgar that 'hig gegaderadan ða mycle fyrde mid ðam yriscan mannan 7 mid Walkynne, 7 Rawulf eorl gaderade mycel fyrde agean to Herefordport, 7 hi sohtan hi ðær'[50] (they brought together a great army with the Irish men and with the Welsh people, and Earl Ralph brought together a great army against them at Hereford, and they sought them there). MS E relates that 'Ælfgar eorl gesohte Griffines geheald on Norðwealan, 7 on þisum geare Griffin 7 Ælfgar forbærndon Sancte Æðelbryhtes mynster 7 ealle þa burh Hereford'[51] (Earl Ælfgar sought Gruffud's protection in North Wales, and in this year Gruffudd and Ælfgar burned Saint Æthelberht's minster and all the town of Hereford), and MS D that Ælfgar 'he gewende to Hirlande 7 Brytlande, 7 begeat him þær micel genge, 7 ferde swa to Hereforda'[52] (he went to Ireland and Wales, and there got himself a great band, and went thus to Hereford).

The borderlands are characterised as having a distinctive style of fighting in the narratives of this battle at Hereford. MS C reports that 'Ac ær þær wære ænig spere gescoten ær fleah ðæt englisce folc forðan þe hig wæran on horsan, 7 man sloh ðær mycel wæl – abutan feower hund manna oððe fife – 7 hig nænne agean'[53] (but before there was any spear cast the English people had fled because they were on horse, and many men were slain there – about four or five hundred men – and they killed none in return). As is also the case after the Battle of Hastings, a distinction is drawn between the troops of the Welsh borderlands, who fight on foot, and an English army that remains on horseback to its detriment.[54] The English army's use of cavalry here underscores its cowardice, as what should be a military advantage only enables a quicker retreat and, even on horseback, hundreds of English troops are killed without inflicting any damage in return. MS D also distinguishes between the two military forces in its characterisation of Ælfgar's troops as a *genge* (band) in contrast to Earl Ralph's *here* (army).[55] The word *genge* is used – almost solely within the *Anglo-Saxon Chronicle* – to describe smaller raiding parties rather than large armies,[56] as when, for instance, 'Hereward 7 his genge'[57] (Hereward and his band) attack Peterborough. While the difference may seem a subtle one, it reinforces the distinctive fighting style of the Welsh borderlands: small bands on foot, not large armies on horseback.

The forces of the Welsh borderlands are depicted like outlaws – heroic in certain ways, yet still on the margins of society. After defeating the English army, Ælfgar and Gruffudd 'hig gewendan ða to ðam porte 7 ðæt forbærndan 7 þæt mære mynster, ðe Æþelstan se arwurða biscop ær let getimbrian, þæt hig beryptan 7 bereafodan æt haligdome 7 æt hreaue 7 æt eallon ðingan, 7 þæt folc slogan 7 sume on weg læddan'[58] (they turned then to the town and burned it and the great minster which the honourable Bishop Æthelstan had built earlier – they plundered it and looted it of holy things and spoil and all things, and slew the people and led some away). The annalist naturally disapproves of the minster being looted and burned. However, the details of this annal place Ælfgar and Gruffudd within a broader literary tradition of outlaw narratives. In its tension between approving the righting of wrongs and condemning sacrilege and violence, this annal parallels an episode from the life of the post-Conquest outlaw Hereward (discussed further in Chapter Six).[59] Hereward's looting and burning of Peterborough – ostensibly so the Normans could not do it first – demonstrates the tension between heroic resistance and violence above the law so common in post-Conquest outlaw narratives.[60] The burning of Æthelstan's minster encapsulates the same tensions.

The extent of the violence caused by the aftermath of this battle – hundreds of soldiers dead, the town burned, the minster looted and Hereford's civilians killed or enslaved – reflects the strength of the military forces that the Welsh borderlands could muster at this time. It also reflects the perception, as this book has argued, that the Welsh borderlands were viewed by outsiders as a site of exceptional violence where a culture of raiding and aggression towards noncombatants persisted.[61] Indeed, the consequences of the raid demonstrate that the Welsh borderlands were treated as a distinct military threat by the rest of Anglo-Saxon England: 'Ða gaderade man fyrde geond eall Engla land swyðe neah, 7 hig coman to Gleaweceastre 7 wendan swa uneorr ut on Wealas 7 þær lagon sume hwile, 7 Harald eorl let dician ða dic abutan þæt port þa hwile'[62] (an army was brought together throughout all the land of England nearby, and they came to Gloucester and went a little way into Wales and stayed there for a while, and Earl Harold had a dyke built around the town during that time). Harold led an attack into Wales even though it was Ælfgar who had been outlawed, indicating that Ælfgar and Gruffudd were viewed as a united front. Because of their success in battle, 'man geinlagode þa Ælfgar eorl, 7 man ageaf him eall þæt him wæs ær ofgenumen'[63] (men then restored Earl Ælfgar, and they gave him back all that had been taken from him before). The alliance between Ælfgar and Gruffudd had a significant impact on the political landscape of Anglo-Saxon England, and its narratives underscore the perception of the Welsh borderlands as a distinct region.

The partnership between Ælfgar and Gruffudd is only explicitly mentioned in 1055 and 1058. However, it seems likely that a more stable political alliance in the Welsh borderlands also stands behind the death of Bishop Leofgar in 1056. MSS C and D both record that Leofgar, a priest of Earl Harold's who improperly wore moustaches, became bishop after Athelstan's death.[64] Leofgar's embrace of secular values only worsened upon his new appointment:

> Se forlet his crisman 7 his hrode his gastlican wæpna 7 feng to his spere 7 to his sweorde æfter his biscuphade 7 swa for to fyrde ongean Griffin þone wyliscan cing, 7 hine man ðar ofsloh 7 his preostas mid him 7 Ælfnoð scirgerefan 7 manega gode menn mid heom, 7 ða oðre ætflugon.[65]
>
> (He abandoned his chrism and his cross – his spiritual weapons – and took up his spear and his sword after he was appointed bishop, and he went like

this to the battle against Gruffudd the Welsh king, and they slew him there and his priests with him and the sheriff Ælfnoth and many good men with them, and the others fled.)

This annal underscores both Gruffudd's skill as a secular leader and Leofgar's failure as a spiritual one. The bishop prioritises earthly over eternal glory, and he is also depicted as rash (attacking Gruffudd without provocation), ill-prepared (losing quickly) and irresponsible, having brought about the deaths of 'many good men' whom he led to battle.

This annal indicates that the alliance between Gruffudd and Ælfgar was more stable than two isolated moments in 1055 and 1058. Indeed, it is difficult to imagine how Leofgar's death could have taken place if Gruffudd and Ælfgar were not in alliance, given both its timing of 1056 and location in the Welsh borderlands (in Mercia, at Hereford). Ælfgar's absence from this battle is surprising, given that he fought alongside Gruffudd at Hereford in the previous year, and one wonders if the annalist of MS C may have been willing to record that Gruffudd killed a bishop but hesitated when it came to the direct involvement of a Mercian earl. Yet regardless of whether or not Ælfgar participated in this battle, the circumstances of Leofgar's death indicate the continuity of political alliance in the Welsh borderlands in 1056. This annal also distinguishes between the military tactics of the two armies, noting that 'Earfoðlic is to atellanne seo gedrecednes 7 seo fare eall 7 seo fyrdung 7 þæt geswinc 7 manna fyll 7 eac horsa þe eall Engla here dreah'[66] (it is difficult to tell of the troubles, and the journeys, and the fighting, and all the labour and the loss of men and also horses, that all the English army suffered). As in the earlier defeat of Earl Ralph's forces at Hereford, the English troops are unsuccessful in a way that highlights their dependence on cavalry. Leofgar's death shows that the troops of the Welsh borderlands continued to be distinguished from an English army.

MS D is the sole source to record a second rebellion of Ælfgar and Gruffudd in 1058. The narrative is sparse, but indicates that the events of 1055 were repeated a few years later. In 1058, 'Her man ytte ut Ælfgar eorl, ac he com sona inn ongean mid strece þurh Gryffines fultum. 7 her com scyphere of Norwegan. Hit is langsum to atellanne eall hu hit gefaren wæs'[67] (here men exiled Earl Ælfgar, but he quickly came back again with violence through Gruffudd's aid. And here came a ship army from Norway. It is tiresome to tell how it all happened). Even the sparse details of this attack – Ælfgar's return 'with violence' – echo previous characterisations of warfare along the Welsh borderlands as that of outlaws, furthering the perception that this region stands apart from the rest of Anglo-Saxon

England. The annal itself makes clear that a great deal of information has been deliberately left out, and Welsh and Irish sources indicate the extent of this omission. The *Annales Cambriae* record an attack by Magnus, the son of Harald Hardrada, carried out with Gruffudd's aid,[68] and the Irish *Annals of Tigernach* preserve the gathering of 'Longes la mac rig Lochland, co nGallaib Indsi Orcc 7 Indsi Gall 7 Atha cliath, do gabail rigi Saxan, acht nocor' deonaig Dia sin' (a fleet [led] by the son of the king of Norway, with the foreigners of the Orkneys and the Hebrides and Dublin, to seize the kingdom of England; but to this God consented not).[69] This revolt, then, was much more serious than the annalist of MS D lets on.

Yet while MS D downplays the scale of these events, textual omissions can be as interesting as inclusions. In minimising the role of the Norwegian fleet and omitting the Irish altogether, this annal elevates the centrality of Ælfgar and Gruffudd to this attempted invasion. The Mercian earl and Welsh king are again depicted as a significant political bloc in Anglo-Saxon England. Because there is no clear reason (as in MS C's Mercian perspective) for MS D to sympathise with Ælfgar and Gruffudd, it seems likeliest that the chronicler depicts the two as a significant military force simply because that is how they were perceived. MS D represents the Welsh borderlands as a significant political and military presence in the eleventh century.

The perception that the Welsh borderlands formed a politically allied region is further suggested by the circumstances of Gruffudd ap Llewelyn's death in 1063. He was killed by the Godwinsons after Ælfgar disappears from historical records in 1062 (when he likely died, although no chronicle notes the date of his death), indicating both that the loss of Gruffudd's ally made him vulnerable and that the Welsh borderlands was perceived as a significant political threat by the powerful Godwinson family. Harold and Tostig attacked Wales in 1063, forcing its people into submission. After this, the Welsh (probably in South Wales) killed Gruffudd and brought his head to Harold. MS E records that,

> Her for Harold eorl 7 his broðor Tostig eorl, ægðer ge mid landfyrde ge mid sciphere, into Brytlande 7 þet land geeodon, 7 þet folc heom gislodon 7 to bugon 7 foron syððan to 7 ofslogon heora cyng Griffin 7 brohton Harolde his heafod, 7 he sette oþerne cyng þærto.[70]

> (Here Earl Harold and his brother Earl Tostig went together – with a land-army and a ship-army – into Wales and defeated that land. And all the people gave them hostages and submitted to them, and afterwards they went out and slew their King Gruffudd, and brought Harold his head, and he appointed another king there.)

King Edward appointed Gruffudd's half-brothers Bleddyn and Rhiwallon as rulers in Wales after they swore loyalty to him. The longer narrative in MS D makes the role of other Welsh kingdoms in these events even clearer:

> On þissum geare for Harold eorl æfter middanwintre of Gleaweceastre to Rudelan, þe Griffines wæs, 7 þonne ham forbærnde, 7 his scipa 7 alle þa gewæda þe þærto gebyrede, 7 hine on fleame gebrohte, 7 þa to þam gongdagan for Harold mid scipum of Brycgstowe abutan Brytland, 7 þæt folc griþede 7 gisledon, 7 Tostig for mid landferde ongean, 7 þæt land geeodon. Ac her on ðissan illcan geare on herfeste wearþ Griffin kync ofslangen on nonas Agusti fram his agenum mannum, þurh þæt gewinn þe he won wiþ Harold eorl, se wæs keening ofer eall Wealcyn, 7 man brohte his eafod to Harolde eorle, 7 Harold hit þam kynge brohte, 7 his scipes heafod, 7 þa bone þermid, 7 se kyng Eadward betæhte þæt land his twam gebroþran Bleþgente 7 Rigwatlan, 7 hig aþas sworon 7 gislas saldan þæm cynge 7 þæm eorle þæt heo him on allum þingum unswicende beon woldon, 7 eighwar him gearwe on wætere 7 on lande, 7 swylc of þam lande gelæstan swylc man dyde toforan ær oþrum kynge.[71]

> (In this year Earl Harold went after midwinter from Gloucester to Rhuddlan, which was Gruffudd's, and burned his home, and his ships and all the things which belonged to them, and brought him to flight. And then, near Rogation Days, Harold went with ships from Bristol around Wales, and that people made peace and gave hostages, and Tostig went against them with a landarmy, and he conquered that land. But here in the same year at harvest King Gruffudd was slain on August 5th by his own men, because of the battle he was waging with Earl Harold. He was king over all the Welsh people. And men brought his head to Earl Harold, and Harold brought it to the king, and his ship's head, and its ornament also. And King Edward gave that land to his [Gruffudd's] two brothers, Bleddyn and Rhiwallon. And they swore oaths, and gave hostages to the king and to the earl, that they would be true to him in all things, and everywhere ready on water and on land, and also to give him from that land such as men did before to that other king.)

As Frederick C. Suppe has argued, decapitation was often used as a political tool against Welsh rulers in the high Middle Ages.[72] It formed a very public statement of humiliation and suppression, both for a ruler and for his people. Gruffudd ap Llewelyn's death clearly held such political symbolism – not only is he himself decapitated, but so too is his ship of its figurehead, and both are brought by the Welsh people first to Harold and then to Edward.[73] Gruffudd's death appears to have been intended as a powerful statement of subjugation after the death of his strongest ally. The circumstances of Gruffudd's death underscore how Anglo-Saxon England perceived the Welsh borderlands as a politically aligned region in the eleventh century.

The Welsh borderlands in the *Anglo-Saxon Chronicle* after 1066

Political cooperation in the Welsh borderlands did not end with the Norman Conquest. Although a distinction has been drawn in scholarship between alliances formed before and after the Battle of Hastings, that distinction is not present in the *Anglo-Saxon Chronicle* itself. Rather, several incidents indicate continuity in this region. Bleddyn and Rhiwallon, Gruffudd's successors, have been characterised as 'puppet rulers' of Edward,[74] yet they continued the pattern of alliance in the borderlands evident when Gruffudd was king, uniting with Ælfgar's sons Eadwine and Morcar in 1065, 1068 and 1071, and with the Mercian landowner Eadric 'the Wild' in 1067. Throughout the eleventh century, the Welsh borderlands was a politically allied region.

In 1065, a series of events centred around the ongoing rivalry between the Godwinsons and Leofricsons occurred when Northumbria deposed and banished Earl Tostig and set Morcar, son of Earl Ælfgar, in his place. Morcar had the support of both the Northumbrians and his brother Eadwine, whose troops included the men of his (Mercian) earldom and a large number of Welsh. The combined forces successfully installed Morcar in Northumbria, while Tostig fled to the continent. MSS C and D introduce these events by noting a successful raid by Caradog ap Gruffudd ap Rhydderch against a hunting lodge that Earl Harold had built in Wales, at Portskewett,

> 7 þa hyt eall mæst gegaderod wæs, þa for Cradoc Griffines sunu to mid eallum þam þe he begytan mihte 7 þæt folc mæst eall ofsloh þe þar timbrode 7 þæt god genam þe þar gegaderod wæs.[75]

> (And when it was almost ready, then Caradog, Gruffudd's son, came with all those who he could gather, and slew almost all the people who were building there, and took the goods which were collected there.)

Caradog's raid appears to have been a response to Harold's incursion onto Welsh lands. Yet the location of this attack – Portskewett is just inside Wales, 10 miles from Bristol, at the point where the Severn estuary narrows – coupled with the lack of any Mercian retaliation, suggests political alliance in this region even though no Mercian participation in the raid is recorded. The attack on Harold's hunting lodge continues the pattern of opposition between the borderlands and the Godwinsons that had coloured so much of the political landscape of the eleventh century.

This opposition is equally evident in the narrative of Tostig's deposition, which is described in largely similar language in MSS C, D and E. In 1065, the people of Yorkshire and Northumberland banded together, exiled Tostig and killed his men:

> 7 sona æfter þisan gegaderedon þa þegenas hi ealle on Eoforwicscire 7 on Norðhymbralande togædere, 7 geutlagedan heora eorl Tosti, 7 ofslogon his hiredmen, ealle þe hig mihten to cumen, ægþær ge Englisce ge Denisce, 7 naman ealle his wæpna on Eaforwic, 7 gold 7 seolfer 7 ealle his sceattas þe hig mihton ahwær þær geacsian.[76]
>
> (And soon after this all the thanes of Yorkshire and Northumberland banded together, and they outlawed their earl, Tostig, and slew his men – all that they were able to get to – English and Danish alike, and took all his weapons in York, and gold and silver and all his money which they could find anywhere there.)

After banishing Tostig, the people of Northumbria 'sendon æfter Morkere, Ælfgares sunu eorles, 7 gecuron hine heom to eorle'[77] (they sent for Morcar, Earl Ælfgar's son, and they chose him as their earl). The military support that Morcar received reveals political continuity in the borderlands, as '7 his broþor Eadwine him com togeanes mid þam mannum þe on his eorldome weron, 7 eac fela Brettas comon mid him'[78] (his brother Edwin came to him with the men who were in his earldom [Mercia], and likewise many Welsh came with him). The threat was significant enough that Edward installed Morcar as earl of Northumbria, while Tostig fled with his family and supporters to the continent. In two key incidents in 1065, then, the Welsh borderlands were united against the Godwinsons and defeated them. Stephen Baxter has noted that the Welsh component of Eadwine's army suggests that he 'had managed to revive the Cambro-Mercian alliance which had been such a prominent feature of his father's survival strategies',[79] but it is unnecessary to interpret these events as a revival. Ælfgar and Gruffudd died only a few years earlier, and Ælfgar had married his daughter to Gruffudd sometime before his death, creating kinship ties between the two families that outlasted both men.[80] The rapid response of Eadwine's forces suggests continuity in politics.

The *Anglo-Saxon Chronicle* depicts a continuous pattern of political alliance in the Welsh borderlands in the eleventh century before the Battle of Hastings. Examining the rebellions that took place after 1066 in light of this pattern reveals continuity in the politics of the region. The numerous revolts which were led jointly by Mercian earls and Welsh rulers after 1066 were not just a product of desperation in the wake of the Norman presence, but rather arose from an older and more stable political alliance. Such an alliance in the Welsh borderlands was not limited to the families of Gruffudd and Ælfgar. The first recorded rebellion to arise in the borderlands after 1066 involved an alliance between Welsh rulers and Eadric 'the Wild' or 'Cild', a Mercian landowner with no ties to the house of Leofric. While not denying the significant impact of the Norman Conquest on Anglo-Saxon England,[81] the narrative of this 1067 revolt testifies to the perception that rebellion was an inherent part of the cultural fabric of the Welsh borderlands. Eadric's legend grew increasingly romantic in post-Conquest sources,[82] but the succinct account of his revolt in the *Anglo-Saxon Chronicle* mirrors narratives of political alliance in the borderlands throughout the eleventh century, demonstrating the continued perception that the Welsh borderlands were a politically aligned region both before and after 1066.

In 1067, MS D is the sole recension to record a rebellion in which '7 Eadric cild 7 þa Bryttas wurdon unsehte 7 wunnon heom wið þa castelmenn on Hereforda, 7 fela hearmas heom dydon'[83] (Eadric 'cild' and the Welsh grew hostile and they attacked the castle-men in Hereford, and did them great harm). Subsequently, 'her se kyng sette micel gyld on earm folc, 7 þeahhwæðre let æfre herigan eall þæt hi oferforon'[84] (the king set a great tax on the poor people, and regardless he always let it be harried, all that they travelled over). Eadric was a landowner with significant holdings in Herefordshire and Shropshire, both Mercian territories in the Welsh borderlands. This annal treats Eadric and the Welsh ('Eadric cild 7 þa Bryttas')[85] as a unit, and the ease and speed with which this rebellion formed after the Battle of Hastings reflects the underlying pattern of alliance in the Welsh borderlands. Moreover, while the rebels are initially characterised as 'hostile', their revolt gains sympathy in light of the king's ineffectual response. Eadric and the Welsh do great damage to Hereford, and even a tax on the 'poor people' cannot prevent further raids. This rebellion continues the representation of the Welsh borderlands as a locus of outlaws throughout the eleventh century in the *Anglo-Saxon Chronicle*.

The *Chronicle* of John of Worcester also preserves a record of the 1067 rebellion, in slightly more detail than MS D. Eadric is described as 'eo tempore extitit quidam prepotens minister, Edricus, cognomento Siluaticus, filius Alfrici, fratris Edrici Streone' (at that time there lived a powerful thegn Eadric, called *Silvaticus*, son of Ælfric, brother of Eadric

Streona),[86] suggesting an elevated social status that explains why he would have the political capital to muster the forces of the Welsh borderlands. After the Battle of Hastings, 'cuius terram, quia se dedere regi dedignabatur, Herefordenses castellani, et Ricardus filius Scrob, frequenter uastauerunt, sed quotienscunque super eum irruerant, multos e suis militibus et scutariis perdiderunt' (the Hereford castle garrison as well as Richard, son of Scrob, frequently laid waste his land, which he had refused to hand over to the king, but whenever they attacked him they lost many of their knights and soldiers).[87] John of Worcester provides even greater justification and sympathy for the rebellion than MS D: because of this land seizure, 'iccirco asscitis sibi in auxilium regibus Walanorum Blethgento, uidelicet, et Riuuatlo, idem uir Edricus, Herefordensem prouinciam usque ad pontem amnis Lucge deuastauit, ingentemque predam reduxit' (Eadric, calling on the help of the kings of the Welsh, Bleddyn and Rhiwallon, laid waste Herefordshire up to the bridge over the River Lugg, and brought back great spoil).[88] As in the *Anglo-Saxon Chronicle*, political alliance in the Welsh borderlands is depicted as having persisted past 1066. Whereas MS D notes that simply 'the Welsh' were partners in this rebellion, John of Worcester's version names Bleddyn and Rhiwallon. As we will see in a moment, these two Welsh rulers also rebelled with the Mercian earls Eadwine and Morcar in 1068, testifying further to the continued political alliance in the borderlands after 1066.

There is separate evidence of the rebellious combination of Eadric and the Welsh in the *Ecclesiastical History* of Orderic Vitalis, which links that alliance with a revolt by the men of Chester (see below).[89] Orderic's narrative also depicts the Welsh borderlands as a politically allied region, demonstrating the strength of a cultural memory that saw this area united in opposition to the Normans. Another passage from the same book of the *Ecclesiastical History* reinforces this impression, when Orderic relates: 'Circa terminos regni occidentem aut plagam septentrionalem uersus effrenis adhuc ferocia superbiebat; et Angliæ regi nisi ad libitum suum famulari sub rege Eduardo aliisque prioribus olim despexerat' (but in the marches of his kingdom, to the west and north, the inhabitants were still barbarous, and had only obeyed the English king in the time of King Edward and his predecessors when it suited their ends).[90]

Orderic's *Ecclesiastical History* is the sole surviving record of three rebellions led jointly by the Mercian earls and Welsh rulers of the borderlands in the years immediately after the Norman invasion: the revolt of Mercian earls Edwin and Morcar alongside Bleddyn of Gwynedd in 1068, a rebellion at Shrewsbury by the forces of the Mercian city of Chester and its Welsh neighbours in 1069, and the Mercian Earl Edwin's last stand at Ely in 1071, supported by a significant Welsh coalition. These rebellions continue the pattern of alliance in the Welsh borderlands evident over the course of the tenth and eleventh centuries.[91] Orderic, whose source was the now-lost ending of the *Gesta Guillelmi* written by William of Poitiers,[92] records the only surviving narrative of Eadwine and Morcar's 1068 rebellion. This revolt was provoked by William's withdrawn promise to give his daughter to Eadwine in marriage. Orderic records that the king failed to keep his word, 'sed postmodum fraudulento consultu Normannorum qui nimis inuidi sunt et cupidi' (but later, listening to the dishonest counsels of his envious and greedy Norman followers).[93] Eventually, 'Vnde iratus cum fratre suo ad rebellionem incitatus est; eumque magna pars Anglorum et Gualorum secuta est' (at last his patience wore out and he and his brother were roused to rebellion, supported by a great many of the English and Welsh).[94] Orderic emphasises the nobility of the Mercian earls – to a surprising extent – in order to justify their campaign against William. Eadwine and Morcar are pious, generous, handsome, of noble lineage and beloved by the people; their rebellion is supported by clergy and commoners alike.[95] His narrative grants Eadwine, Morcar and their Welsh allies a just cause to rebel. Indeed, while William is represented fairly neutrally (if too easily swayed by the opinions of others), his Norman followers are cast as envious and greedy, inflicting injustice and tyranny on an innocent populace.

Significantly, Orderic emphasises the kinship ties between the Mercian earls and their Welsh partners in this rebellion, naming Earl Ælfgar and Lady Godiva's children as 'Eduinum, Morcarum; et unam filiam nomine Aldit quæ primo nupsit Gritfrido regi Gualorum, post cuius mortem sociata est Heraldo regi Anglorum' (Edwin, Morcar and one daughter called Edith, who married first Gruffydd king of the Welsh and after his death Harold king of England).[96] These kin relationships are characterised as a significant component in the political alliance in the borderlands. Orderic writes that 'Tempore Normannicæ cladis quæ nimiis oppressionibus Anglos immoderate conquassauit; Blidenus rex Gualorum ad auunculos suos suppetias uenit, secumque multitudinem Britonum adduxit' (when the Norman conquest had brought such grievous burdens upon the English, Bleddyn king of the Welsh came to the help of his uncles, bringing a great army of Welshmen with him).[97] While the relationship is described slightly inaccurately (Bleddyn was Gruffudd's half-brother, not son), these kinship ties are clearly important. The Welsh borderlands were again perceived as a region with a common cause: 'Congregatis autem in unum multis Anglorum et Gualorum optimatibus, fit generalis querimonia de iniuriis et oppressionibus; quibus intolerabiliter Angli affligebantur a Normannis et eorum contubernalibus' (after large numbers of the leading men of England and Wales had met together, a general outcry arose against the injustice and tyranny which the Normans and their comrades-in-arms had inflicted on the English).[98] While this particular rebellion ended when William embarked on a campaign of castle-building and Edwin and Morcar settled for peace, the combined interests of the borderlands remained unsatisfied, and rebellion against the Conqueror continued.

In the autumn of 1069, 'Guali et Cestrenses præsidium regis apud Scrobesburiam obsederunt; quibus incolæ ciuitatis cum Edrico Guilda potenti et bellicoso uiro aliisque ferocibus Anglis auxilio fuerunt' (the Welshmen and men of Chester besieged the royal stronghold at Shrewsbury, and were assisted by the native citizens, the powerful and warlike Edric the Wild, and other untameable Englishmen).[99] Once again, the Welsh borderlands were united in rebellion against the Conqueror. This particular revolt appears to have been at least temporarily successful, because William sent his earls (William fitzOsbern and Count Brian) to suppress it. However, 'Verum priusquam illi Scrobesburiam peruenissent; urbe combusta hostes discesserant' (before they could reach Shrewsbury the enemy had burned the town and scattered).[100] The king retaliated in the winter of 1070 when 'Deinde mouet expeditionem contra Cestrenses et Gualos; qui præter alias offensas nuperrime Scrobesburiam obsederunt' (then he undertook an expedition against the Welsh and the men of Chester, who had recently crowned their many lawless acts by besieging Shrewsbury).[101] William's response demonstrates that he understood the Welsh borderlands as a cohesive unit, which had acted as one and deserved to be punished as one.

William's army was reluctant to embark on this campaign. As Orderic records, 'Verebatur enim locorum asperitatem hiemis intemperiem, alimentorum inopiam et hostium terribilem ferociam' (they feared the wildness of the region, the severity of winter, the scarcity of food and the terrible ferocity of the enemy).[102] These fears suggests that the Norman troops also saw the Welsh borderlands as a distinct region, one known for the harshness of its landscape and the ferocity of its warriors. While this expedition did end successfully for the king, who 'Tandem exercitum incolumem usque Cestram perduxit; et in tota Merciorum regione motus hostiles regia ui compescuit' (at last he brought his army safely to Chester and suppressed all risings throughout Mercia with royal power),[103] William's response to the rebellion at Shrewsbury indicates that he too saw the Welsh borderlands as a distinct political entity and one that required more caution than the rest of England.

The heroic last stand of Eadwine and Morcar at Ely in 1071 is narrated by several manuscripts of the *Anglo-Saxon Chronicle*. I will discuss these entries at greater length in Chapter Six, arguing that they represent a moment when the Welsh borderlands became more explicitly aligned with outlawry. First, Orderic's version of Eadwine's death merits discussion as a coda to political alliances in the Welsh borderlands in the tenth and eleventh centuries. As in his description of Eadwine's and Morcar's first rebellion, Orderic's narrative is sympathetic to the Mercian earls. William is again 'Nam rex Guillelmus consilio prauorum male usus laudi suæ dampnum ingessit; dum fraudulenter inclitum comitem Morcarum in Eliensi insula conclusit, sibique confederatum et nil mali machinatem uel suspicantem obsedit' (for King William, ill-advisedly relying on evil counsellors, brought great harm to his reputation by treacherously surrounding the noble Earl Morcar in the Isle of Ely, and besieging a man who had made peace with him and was neither doing nor expecting any harm).[104] Orderic reiterates the deceit of the king's messengers, Morcar's naïvety in agreeing to the promised peace, and the king's injustice in condemning Morcar to prison without trial until his death.[105]

Moreover, this narrative again casts its hero in the role of sympathetic outlaw, as 'Quod formosissimus iuuenis Eduinus comes ut audiuit, emori quam uiuere peroptauit; nisi Morcarum fratrem suum iniuste captum liberasset, aut uberrimo sanguine Normannorum sese uindicasset' (when the fair youth Earl Edwin learned of this, he determined to prefer death to life unless he could free his brother Morcar from unjust captivity, or avenge him fully in Norman blood).[106] Thus, 'Sex igitur mensibus a Scottis et Gualis uel Anglis auxilia sibi quæsiuit' (for six months he sought support amongst the Scots, Welsh and English).[107] While this rebellion ultimately results in Eadwine's heroic death – even King William mourns him and exiles the traitors who killed him – in his last stand, Eadwine is seen to rely on the same borderlands army as he had all his life. Even Eadwine's death shows continued political alliance in the Welsh borderlands.

Conclusions

Throughout the tenth and eleventh centuries, the Welsh borderlands acted as a politically allied region, with interests that were recognised as distinct from the rest of Anglo-Saxon England. Many of the defining qualities of those living in this region are those ascribed to outlaws in later romance texts. Yet while the Welsh borderlands in the Anglo-Saxon period were conceptualised as a distinctive space, this region was not yet viewed as the wilderness refuge of outlaws seen in post-Conquest romances. The Welsh borderlands in this period stood as a society apart, not a space apart from society as a whole. Chapter Six moves forward in time to explore the transitional moment between these two conceptualisations. Whereas this chapter has approached the different manuscripts of the *Anglo-Saxon Chronicle* as a relatively cohesive narrative tradition (albeit one that occasionally offers diverse perspectives on the same event), Chapter Six narrows its focus to the *Peterborough Chronicle*, the surviving manuscript of the *Anglo-Saxon Chronicle* that was continued for the longest period after Hastings, almost a full century, until it ends in 1154.

Chapter Six argues that the *Peterborough Chronicle* began an important conceptual shift that would be fully realised in later Anglo-Norman texts: namely, that the defining characteristics of the borderlands were shifted solely onto the Welsh. In the *Peterborough Chronicle*, Anglo-Saxon earls from the Welsh borderlands are characterised, at the beginning of the post-Conquest period, in the same ways as the Welsh are by the end of the eleventh century. The *Peterborough Chronicle* illustrates a transitional moment in the relationship between exiles and the Welsh borderlands, as the characteristics of outlaws shift from borderland rebels to the Welsh alone. This shift in the perception of the borderlands at the end of the eleventh century shows how much was lost with the arrival of the Normans in England. The Welsh borderlands' shift in literary representation to become a home of Welsh outlaws alone was part of a larger impact of the Norman Conquest and perhaps indicates a greater divide between English and Welsh, in the years after the Norman arrival, than has been previously realised.

Notes

1 For an overview of trends in scholarship on the *Anglo-Saxon Chronicle*, see Jacqueline Stodnick, 'Second-rate stories? Changing approaches to the *Anglo-Saxon Chronicle*', *Literature Compass* 3 (2006): 1253–65. Two full-length studies of the *Anglo-Saxon Chronicle* as a political text in its contemporary setting are Thomas Bredehoft, *Textual Histories: Readings in the Anglo-Saxon Chronicle* (Toronto: University of Toronto Press, 2001) and Alice Sheppard, *Families of the King: Writing Identity in the Anglo-Saxon Chronicle* (Toronto: University of Toronto Press, 2004); see also Janet Bately, *The Anglo-Saxon Chronicle: Texts and Textual Relationships* (Reading: Reading Medieval Studies Monograph, 1991).

2 Ryan Lavelle, *Alfred's Wars: Sources and Interpretations of Anglo-Saxon Warfare in the Viking Age* (Woodbridge, Suffolk: Boydell, 2010), 19.

3 James Campbell, 'The late Anglo-Saxon state: a maximum view', *Proceedings of the British Academy* 87 (1994): 39–65 and *The Anglo-Saxon State* (London: Hambledon, 2000); Nicholas Brooks, 'English identity from Bede to the millenium', The Henry Loyn Memorial Lecture, *Haskins Society Journal* 14 (2005): 33–51; Kathleen Davis, 'National writing in the ninth century: a reminder for postcolonial thinkers about the nation', *Journal of Medieval and Early Modern Studies* 28 (1998): 611–37; Sarah Foot, 'The making of Angelcynn: English identity before the Norman Conquest', *Transactions of the Royal Historical Society* 6 (1996): 25–49; Patrick Wormald, 'Bede, the Bretwaldas and the origins of the gens Anglorum', in *Ideal and Reality in Frankish and Anglo-Saxon Society: Studies Presented to J.M. Wallace-Hadrill*, ed. Patrick Wormald with Donald Bullough and Roger Collins (Oxford: Blackwell, 1983), 99–129; and Patrick Wormald, '*Engla Lond*: the making of an allegiance', *Journal of Historical Sociology* 7 (1994): 1–24.
4 For the 'minimalist view' of Anglo-Saxon England, see Paul R. Hyams, *Rancor and Reconciliation in Medieval England* (Ithaca NY: Cornell University Press, 2003), and Andrew Rabin, 'Capital punishment and the Anglo-Saxon judicial apparatus: a maximum view?', in *Capital and Corporal Punishment in Anglo-Saxon England*, ed. Jay Paul Gates and Nicole Marafioti (Woodbridge, Suffolk: Boydell, 2014), 181–99.
5 Lavelle, *Alfred's Wars*, 25.
6 R. Allen Brown, *The Normans and the Norman Conquest* (Woodbridge, Suffolk: Boydell, 1968; repr. 2000), 71.
7 For the historically mixed Anglo-Welsh nature of this region during this time period, see C. P. Lewis, 'Welsh territories and Welsh identities in late Anglo-Saxon England', in *Britons in Anglo-Saxon England*, ed. N. J. Higham, (Woodbridge: Boydell, 2007) 130–43; David E. Thornton, 'Some Welshmen in Domesday Book and beyond: aspects of Anglo-Welsh relations in the eleventh century', in *Britons in Anglo-Saxon England*, ed. Higham, 144–64; Frederick C. Suppe, 'Interpreter families and Anglo-Welsh relations in the Shropshire-Powys marches in the twelfth century', *Anglo-Norman Studies: Proceedings of the Battle Conference* 30 (2007): 196–212; and Frederick C. Suppe, 'Who was Rhys Sais? Some comments on Anglo-Welsh relations before 1066', *Haskins Society Journal* 7 (1995): 63–73.
8 The fact that the *Anglo-Saxon Chronicle* does not record these events is likely due to a combination of two factors – the disruption of the Viking attacks on the historical records of the tenth century in general and the known bias of the *Anglo-Saxon Chronicle* generally towards Wessex (with the exception of MS C, as discussed in greater detail below).
9 Charles Insley, 'Collapse, reconfiguration or renegotiation? The strange end of the Mercian kingdom, 850–924', *Reti Medievali Rivista* 17.2 (2016): 1–19; and two unpublished conference papers: 'The Mercians, the North-West, and the Anglo-Welsh frontier, 900–950' at the International Medieval Congress (IMC), University of Leeds, July 2015 and 'The Mercians, the Merfynion and

the Irish Sea world, 880–920' at the 'Interaction and identity in the Irish Sea region c.400–1100' conference, University of Liverpool, July 2016. I am grateful to Charlie for sharing his unpublished and forthcoming work with me, as well as to all the other participants in the session strand on 'The Anglo-Welsh frontier in the middle ages' at the IMC at Leeds in 2015 and the 'Interaction and identity' conference at Liverpool in 2016 for fruitful discussion around these topics, particularly Marios Costambeys and Charles Insley for spearheading and organising.

10 See Lavelle, *Alfred's Wars*; Frank M. Stenton, *Anglo-Saxon England*, 3rd edn (Oxford: Clarendon Press, 1971; repr. 1975), 239–75, 320–63 and 394–431; H. R. Loyn, *The Vikings in Britain* (New York: St Martin's Press, 1977; repr. 1994); M. K. Lawson, *Cnut: the Danes in England in the Early Eleventh Century* (New York: Longman, 1993); and A. R. Rumble, ed., *The Reign of Cnut, King of England, Denmark and Norway* (London: Leicester University Press, 1994).

11 All citations of the *Anglo-Saxon Chronicle* will be by manuscript and year to the following volumes of *The Anglo-Saxon Chronicle: A Collaborative Edition*, gen. ed. David N. Dumville and Simon Keynes (Cambridge: D.S. Brewer, 1983–): Janet M. Bately, *Volume 3: MS A* (1986); Simon Taylor, *Volume 4: MS B* (1983); Katherine O'Brien O'Keeffe, *Volume 5: MS C* (2001); Patrick W. Conner, *Volume 10: The Abingdon Chronicle, AC 956–1066 (MS C, with Reference to BDE)* (1996); G. P. Cubbin, *Volume 6: MS D* (1996); Susan Irvine, *Volume 7: MS E* (2004); and Peter S. Baker, *Volume 8: MS F* (2000); here *MS A*, ed. Bately, 893.

12 T. M. Charles-Edwards, *Wales and the Britons, 350–1064* (Oxford: Oxford University Press, 2013), 507–8. While all errors remain my own, the present chapter is enormously indebted to this book.

13 All citations of the *Annales Cambriae* before 955 will be by annal year to David N. Dumville, ed. and trans., *Annales Cambriae, A.D. 682–954: Texts A–C in Parallel* (Cambridge: Department of Anglo-Saxon, Norse and Celtic, 2002), here, 893 (A). Variant readings: 'Anaraut cum Anglis uenit uastare Ceredig' et Stratewy' (B) and 'Anaraud cum Saxonibus uastauit Keredigaun' (C).

14 Charles-Edwards, *Wales and the Britons*, 507.

15 William Henry Stevenson, *Asser's Life of King Alfred, together with the Annals of Saint Neots Erroneously Ascribed to Asser* (Oxford: Clarendon Press, 1959), 66–7.

16 See further Simon Keynes and Michael Lapidge, trans., *Alfred the Great: Asser's Life of King Alfred and Other Contemporary Sources* (Harmondsworth, Middlesex: Penguin, 1983), 96 and 262–3 n.183.

17 *MS A*, ed. Bately, 918. See further Charles-Edwards, *Wales and the Britons*, 495–500.

18 Charles-Edwards, *Wales and the Britons*, 504–10, noting further that, 'in the early years of Edward the Elder's reign', 'the conquest of Dyfed was accomplished, very probably with the consent if not the active participation of the Mercians, as in 894' (509).

19 William of Malmesbury, *Gesta Regum Anglorum: The History of the English Kings*,

ii.133, ed. and trans. R. A. B. Mynors and completed by R. M. Thompson and M. Winterbottom (Oxford: Clarendon Press, 1998; repr. 2006), 2 vols; text vol. I, 210–11, and notes vol. II, 114–20.
20 *Ibid.*, ii.133. The authenticity of this story is believed by Charles-Edwards, *Wales and the Britons*, 510 n.59 and doubted by David N. Dumville, *Wessex and England from Alfred to Edgar* (Woodbridge, Suffolk: Boydell, 1992), 146.
21 Charles-Edwards, *Wales and the Britons*, 510.
22 See further David Hill, 'Mercians: the dwellers on the boundary', in *Mercia: An Anglo-Saxon Kingdom in Europe*, ed. Michelle P. Brown and Carol A. Farr (London: Continuum, 2001), 173–82 at 174.
23 *MS D*, ed. Cubbin, 926. A slightly more elaborated version of this incident is recorded in 926 in *The Chronicle of John of Worcester, Volume II: The Annals from 450 to 1066*, ed. R. R. Darlington and P. McGurk and trans. Jennifer Bray and P. McGurk (Oxford: Clarendon Press, 1995), 386–7.
24 Charles-Edwards, *Wales and the Britons*, 511.
25 D. P. Kirby, 'Hywel Dda: Anglophil?', *Welsh History Review* 8 (1976): 1–13.
26 *MS D*, ed. Cubbin, 955; *The Abingdon Chronicle*, ed. Conner, 956, 957, 959. For a detailed discussion of these events, see Frederick M. Biggs, 'Edgar's path to the throne', in *Edgar: King of the English, 959–975*, ed. Donald Scragg (Woodbridge, Suffolk: Boydell, 2008), 124–39, who convincingly argues that Eadwig and Edgar ruled Wessex and Mercia as a planned joint kingship.
27 The *Brut y Tywysogyon* exists in three versions: the MS Peniarth 20 version, Thomas Jones, ed., *Brut y Tywysogyon, Peniarth MS 20* (Cardiff: University of Wales Press, 1941) and Thomas Jones, translated with introduction and notes, *Brut y Tywysogyon, or, The Chronicle of the Princes: Peniarth MS 20 Version*, Board of Celtic Studies, University of Wales, History and Law Series 11 (Cardiff: University of Wales Press, 1952); the Red Book of Hergest version, Thomas Jones, ed. and trans., *Brut y Tywysogyon or The Chronicle of the Princes, Red Book of Hergest Version* (Cardiff: University of Wales Press, 1955); and Brenhinedd y Saeson, Thomas Jones, ed. and trans., *Brenhinedd y Saeson or The Kings of the Saxons* (Cardiff: University of Wales Press, 1971). These chronicles are 'three authentic versions of the *Brut* representing three independent Welsh translations of three slightly different texts of a Latin chronicle compiled towards the end of the thirteenth century by an anonymous historiographer who probably worked in the Cistercian abbey of Strata Florida', Jones, *Red Book Version*, p. xii. The *Brut y Tywysogyon* is related to other Welsh chronicle traditions – 'although the original Latin compilation does not appear to have survived, certain sections of it are still to be found embedded in the three texts of the *Annales Cambriae* and in the *Cronica de Wallia*', Jones, *Red Book Version*, p. xii. For a discussion of textual issues, see Jones, *Peniarth 20 Version*, pp. xi–lxxv. Citations to the *Brut y Tywysogyon* will be by annal year and page number to Jones, *Peniarth MS 20* and translations to Jones, *Peniarth 20 Version*, with variant readings from the Red Book provided in the notes, because

Peniarth 20 is believed to be the earlier version – see Jones, *Peniarth 20 Version*, p. lx.
28 Jones, *Peniarth MS 20*, 10.
29 Jones, *Peniarth 20 Version*, 977–8, 9. Alternate reading from Jones, *Red Book Version*, 978, 14–15: 'Ac y diffeithwyt Llyyn a Chelynawc Vawr y gan Hwel ap Jeuaf a'r Saesson' (And Llŷn and Clynnog Fawr were ravaged by Hywel ap Ieuaf and the Saxons).
30 On Ælfhere, see Ann Williams, 'Princeps Merciorum: the family, career and connections of Ælfhere, ealdorman of Mercia, 956–983', *Anglo-Saxon England* 10 (1982): 143–72. D. J. V. Fisher, 'The anti-monastic reaction in the reign of Edward the Martyr', *Cambridge Historical Journal* 10 (1952): 254–70, has demonstrated that Ælfhere's ostensible 'anti-monastic' policies had nothing to do with an anti-monastic stance *per se*, but rather, were simply attacks against his enemies at their most politically vulnerable points.
31 This incident is also recorded in the *Annales Cambriae*; Williams ab Ithel, *Annales Cambriae*, 20. For discussion, see Charles-Edwards, *Wales and the Britons*, 548.
32 Jones, *Peniarth MS 20*, 11.
33 Jones, *Peniarth 20 Version*, 982–3, 9. Alternative reading from Jones, *Red Book Version*, 983, 16–17: 'Ac yna y diffeithwyt Brecheinawc a holl gyuoeth Einawn ap Ywein y gan y Saesson, ac Aluryt yn dywyssawc arnunt, a Hywel ap Jeuaf ac Einawn a ladawd llawer o'e lu' (And then Brycheiniog and the whole territory of Einion ab Owain were ravaged by the Saxons, with Aelfhere as their leader, and Hywel ap Ieuaf and Einion slew many of his host).
34 Ælfhere in 983 and Hywel in 985.
35 This incident is also recorded in the *Annales Cambriae*; Williams ab Ithel, *Annales Cambriae*, 21. For background and discussion on 'Edylfi the Saxon', see David E. Thornton, 'Maredudd ab Owain (d. 999): the most famous king of the Welsh', *Cylchgrawn hanes cymru / Welsh History Review* 18 (1996): 567–91.
36 Jones, *Peniarth MS 20*, 12.
37 Jones, *Peniarth 20 Version*, 990–1 and 991–2, 10. Alternative reading from Jones, *Red Book Version*, 992, 18–19: 'Degmlyned a phetwar ugein a naw cant oed oet Crist pan diffeithawd Etwin vab Dinawn ac Eclis Vawr, tywyssawc Seis y ar uoroed y Deheu, holl vrenhinaetheu Meredud, nyt amgen, Dyfet a Cheredigyawn a Gwhyr a Chetweli. Ac eilweith y kymerth wystlon o'r holl gyfoeth. A'r dryded weith y diffeithawd Vynyw' (Nine hundred and ninety was the year of Christ when Edwin ab Einion and Eclis the Great, a Saxon leader from the seas of the South, ravaged all the kingdoms of Maredudd, that is, Dyfed and Ceredigion and Gower and Cydweli. And a second time he took hostages from the whole territory. And for the third time he ravaged Menevia).
38 Thornton, 'Maredudd ab Owain', 581–2. He notes further that Simon Keynes, 'The historical context of the Battle of Maldon', in Donald Scragg (ed.), *The Battle of Maldon* (Oxford, 1991): 81–113 at 110, n.46, has suggested that Æthelsige

could also be an otherwise-unknown figure who held some position of responsibility in Mercia in the gap between Ealdorman Ælfric (banished in 985) and Eadric Streona (appointed 1007).

39 K. L. Maund, *Ireland, Wales, and England in the Eleventh Century* (Woodbridge, Suffolk: Boydell, 1991), 42–43, has suggested that Edwin received English help because of the strength of his claim to the kingship of Deheubarth. Edwin's English name may be significant in this context, but unfortunately, this incident is his only appearance in the historical records and very little is known about him.

40 Stephen Baxter, 'MS C of the Anglo-Saxon Chronicle and the politics of mid-eleventh-century England', *English Historical Review* 122 (2007): 1189–1227, argues that MS C displays a Mercian bias in the eleventh century and is likely Mercian in origin.

41 A good biography of Gruffudd ap Llywelyn is Michael and Sean Davies, *The Last King of Wales: Gruffudd ap Llywelyn, c. 1013–1063* (Stroud: The History Press, 2012).

42 *MS C*, ed. O'Brien O'Keeffe, 1046.

43 Ibid., 1046.

44 See for example Ann Williams, 'England in the eleventh century', in *A Companion to the Anglo-Norman World*, ed. Christopher Harper-Bill and Elisabeth Van Houts (Woodbridge, Suffolk: Boydell, 2003), 1–18 at 11; K. L. Maund, 'The Welsh Alliances of Earl Ælfgar of Mercia and his Family in the Mid-Eleventh Century', *Anglo-Norman Studies* 11 (1988): 181–90 at 185.

45 Baxter, 'MS C'.

46 *MS C*, ed. O'Brien O'Keeffe, 1055.

47 *MS E*, ed. Irvine, 1055.

48 Ibid., 1055.

49 *MS D*, ed. Cubbin, 1055.

50 *MS C*, ed. O'Brien O'Keeffe, 1055.

51 *MS E*, ed. Irvine, 1055.

52 *MS D*, ed. Cubbin, 1055.

53 *MS C*, ed. O'Brien O'Keeffe, 1055.

54 As described most famously by Gerald of Wales, in Book II, Ch. 8 of his *Description of Wales*, 'How the Welsh can be conquered'; James F. Dimock, ed., *Giraldi Cambrensis opera, Vol. VI, Itinerarium Kambriae et Descriptio Kambriae*, Rolls Series (London: Longmans, 1868) and Lewis Thorpe, trans., *Gerald of Wales: The Journey through Wales and the Description of Wales* (New York: Penguin, 1978). As discussed below in Chapter Six, this distinction between fighting styles gradually shifted from the Welsh borderlands to the Welsh alone.

55 *MS D*, ed. Cubbin, 1055.

56 A. Cameron, A. C. Amos and A. di P. Healey, eds, *Dictionary of Old English* (Toronto: PIMS, 1986–), entry for 'genge'. Of the eight attestations of the

word, seven are in the *Anglo-Saxon Chronicle*; of which five are in MS D and two in MS E – the only other use is in one of Wulfstan's homilies.
57 *MS E*, ed. Irvine, 1070.
58 *MS C*, ed. O'Brien O'Keeffe, 1055.
59 *MS E*, ed. Irvine, 1070 and 1071.
60 Timothy S. Jones, *Outlawry in Medieval Literature* (New York: Palgrave Macmillan, 2010), 76.
61 See David Wyatt, *Slaves and Warriors in Medieval Britain and Ireland, 800–1200* (Leiden: Brill, 2009) and John Gillingham, *The English in the Twelfth Century: Imperialism, National Identity, and Political Values* (Woodbridge, Suffolk: Boydell, 2000), 58.
62 *MS C*, ed. O'Brien O'Keeffe, 1055.
63 Ibid., 1055.
64 Ibid., 1056 and *MS D*, ed. Cubbin, 1056.
65 *MS C*, ed. O'Brien O'Keeffe, 1056.
66 Ibid., 1056.
67 *MS D*, ed. Cubbin, 1058.
68 Williams ab Ithel, *Annales Cambriae*, 25: 'Magnus filius Haraldi, vastavit regionem Anglorum, auxiliante Grifino rege Britonum'.
69 Whitley Stokes, ed. and trans., 'The Annals of Tigernach: the fourth fragment, A.D. 973–1088', *Revue Celtique* 17 (1896): 337–420 at 399.
70 *MS E*, ed. Irvine, 1063.
71 *MS D*, ed. Cubbin, 1063.
72 Frederick C. Suppe, 'The cultural significance of decapitation in high medieval Wales and the Marches', *Bulletin of the Board of Celtic Studies* 36 (1989): 147–60.
73 Elaine M. Treharne has noted the political symbolism of heads in a unique pseudo-Augustinian Old English text that 'exemplifies a variation of the organological concept of the state' which was developed more fully in the twelfth century by John of Salisbury in his *Policraticus*; Elaine M. Treharne, 'The form and function of the twelfth-century Old English "Dicts of Cato"', *Journal of English and Germanic Philology* 102 (2003): 465–85 at 474. See further Nicole Marafioti, *The King's Body: Burial and Succession in Late Anglo-Saxon England* (Toronto: University of Toronto Press, 2014).
74 Rees Davies, *The Age of Conquest: Wales, 1063–1415* (Oxford: Oxford University Press, 1987; repr. paperback 1991, 2000), 24.
75 *MS C*, ed. O'Brien O'Keeffe, 1065.
76 *MS D*, ed. Cubbin, 1065.
77 Ibid., 1065.
78 Ibid., 1065.
79 Stephen Baxter, *The Earls of Mercia: Lordship and Power in Late Anglo-Saxon England* (Oxford: Oxford University Press, 2007), 49.
80 Marjorie Chibnall, ed. and trans., *The Ecclesiastical History of Orderic Vitalis*, 6

vols. (Oxford: Clarendon Press, 1969–80); vol. 2 (Books III–IV, 1969); vol. 2, Book III, 138–9 and vol. 2, Book IV, 216–17.

81 Elaine M. Treharne, *Living Through Conquest: The Politics of Early English, 1020–1220* (Oxford: Oxford University Press, 2012).

82 Eadric appears in Walter Map's *De Nugis Curialium*, ed. and trans. M. R. James, revised by C. N. L. Brooke and R. A. B. Mynors (Oxford: Clarendon Press, 1983, repr. 2002), dist. ii, c. 12; dist. ii, c. 13; and dist. iv, c. 10. See Joshua Byron Smith, *Walter Map and the Matter of Britain* (Philadelphia: University of Pennsylvania Press, 2017), ch 2, 58–9. He appears as a romance character under very different circumstances: as one of several knights or kings who marry, and have children by, a fairy bride who vanishes years later upon the man's thoughtless breaking of a *geis*.

83 *MS D*, ed. Cubbin, 1067.

84 *Ibid.*, 1067.

85 Named as Bleddyn and Rhiwallon in the *Chronicle* of John of Worcester; discussed further below.

86 P. McGurk, ed. and trans., *The Chronicle of John of Worcester, Volume III: The Annals from 1067 to 1140 with the Gloucester Interpolations and the Continuation to 1141* (Oxford: Clarendon Press, 1998), 1067, 4–5.

87 *Ibid.*, 4–5.

88 *Ibid.*, 4–5.

89 Chibnall, *Orderic Vitalis*, vol. 2 (Books III and IV, 1969). All citations and translations are from this edition, by volume and page number. Orderic Vitalis was born in England (in Mercia) in 1075, was put to school in Shrewsbury in 1080 and was sent to the monastery of Saint-Évroul (in Normandy) in 1085, where he wrote his *Ecclesiastical History*. For the background to Orderic's life, see Chibnall, vol. 1, 1–44; for the background to the *Ecclesiastical History*, see vol. 1, 45–125.

90 Chibnall, *Orderic Vitalis*, vol. 2, Book IV, 210–11.

91 Baxter, *Earls of Mercia*, 286, has suggested that William was aware of the potential for Anglo-Welsh alliances and installed earls on the border as a means of trying to prevent them: 'To summarize, King William installed at least one and probably three new earls to commands along the Welsh border while Eadwine remained in power. In this respect, William's policy resembles that of Cnut, for it will be recalled that Cnut installed Eilífr, Hrani, and Hákon in earldoms along the Welsh border shortly after 1016. William, like Cnut, would have been keen to install trusted magnates along the border with Wales, partly to make arrangements for its defence, and partly to prevent the nobility of Mercia forming dangerous cross-border alliances'.

92 *The Gesta Guillelmi of William of Poitiers*, ed. and trans. R. H. C. Davis and Marjorie Chibnall (Oxford: Clarendon Press, 1998).

93 Chibnall, *Orderic Vitalis*, vol. 2, Book IV, 214–16.

94 *Ibid.*, vol. 2, Book IV, 216–17.

95　*Ibid.*, vol. 2, Book IV, 216–17: 'Feruens affectus erat præfatis fratribus erga Dei cultum; et bonorum reuerentiam hominum. Erat eis ingens pulchritudo, nobilis et ampla cognatio; late ualens potentatus et nimia in eos popularium dilectio. A clericis et monachis ad Deum crebra pro illis fiebat oratio; et a turbis pauperum cotidiana supplicatio' (These brothers were zealous in the Service of God, and well-disposed to good men. Both were remarkably handsome, nobly connected with kinsfolk whose power and influence were widespread, and well-loved by the people at large. Clerks and monks ceaselessly offered prayers to God on their behalf; and throngs of the poor daily made supplication).
96　*Ibid.*, vol. 2, Book IV, 216–17.
97　*Ibid.*, vol. 2, Book IV, 216–17.
98　*Ibid.*, vol. 2, Book IV, 216–17.
99　*Ibid.*, vol. 2, 228–9. Orderic does not give a date here, but places this event after the fall of York, which as Chibnall, 228 n.1, notes, took place on 20 September 1069.
100　*Ibid.*, vol. 2, Book IV, 228–9.
101　*Ibid.*, vol. 2, Book IV, 234–5.
102　*Ibid.*, vol. 2, Book IV, 234–5.
103　*Ibid.*, vol. 2, Book IV, 236–7.
104　*Ibid.*, vol. 2, Book IV, 256–7.
105　*Ibid.*, vol. 2, Book IV, 256–9.
106　*Ibid.*, vol. 2, Book IV, 258–9.
107　*Ibid.*, vol. 2, Book IV, 258–9.

6

The transformation of the borderlands outlaw in the eleventh century

Chapter Five argued that the Welsh borderlands are depicted as a politically allied and distinctive territory throughout the eleventh century in the *Anglo-Saxon Chronicle*. The military customs of this region are also singular in being closely aligned with a culture of outlawry, but those living in the borderlands during the Anglo-Saxon period were not divorced from society in the same ways as the outlaws of later romances. As Chapter Five has discussed, the characterisation of the borderlands in the *Anglo-Saxon Chronicle* remained consistent across the Norman Conquest. Yet by the end of the eleventh century this region was seen as not just distinctive, but often beyond the law.

This moment of transition is evident in the *Peterborough Chronicle*, the recension of the *Anglo-Saxon Chronicle* continued for the longest period following the Norman Conquest.[1] The *Peterborough Chronicle* has received a great deal of attention for having been 'continued in the vernacular at a time when most contemporary historiography was in Latin'.[2] Yet at the same time, Malasree Home in her recent study of this work has called attention to the the ways in which 'this vernacular text interacts with Latin texts of Peterborough origin, and even incorporates generic features of alternative forms of historiography (for example, cartularies), something not sufficiently recognised in critical considerations of post-Conquest historiography in general, and the *Chronicle* in particular'.[3] The *Peterborough Chronicle*'s fortuitous survival can be used as a window into shifting representation of the Welsh borderlands in the period after the Normans' arrival. This text marks the beginning of an important conceptual shift that would be fully evident in later Anglo-Norman literature: the transfer of a culture of outlawry from the mixed Anglo-Welsh inhabitants of the borderlands to the Welsh alone by the end of the eleventh century.

The transformation of the borderlands outlaw

In the immediate aftermath of the Conquest, when an alliance of Mercian earls and Welsh nobles rebelled against the Normans, the borderlands were the home of outlaws sympathetically depicted. Yet such was the impact of the Norman presence on the borderlands that within thirty years that role of sympathetic outlaw had been transferred to the Welsh alone. The region was seen as transformed from a mixed culture to the refuge of only the Welsh, driving a wedge between English and Welsh and setting the stage for hostilities against Wales in the ensuing centuries. The *Peterborough Chronicle* illustrates this transition in the perceived relationship between outlaws and the borderlands, from a society whose inhabitants fought like outlaws to a lawless space outside society, a place where outlaws hid in Anglo-Norman romances. The Welsh are the crucial intermediaries between these conceptions of the borderlands.

Rebels in the Welsh borderlands

The *Ecclesiastical History* of Orderic Vitalis, an English-born monastic chronicler in the Norman abbey of Saint-Evroul, illustrates how contemporaries perceived those who rebelled against the Normans: 'Plures in tabernaculis morabantur, in domibus ne mollescerent requiescere dedignabantur; unde quidam eorum a Normannis siluatici cognominabantur' (many men lived in tents, disdaining to sleep in houses lest they should become soft; so that the Normans called them 'wild men').[4] It is this link between rebellion and wilderness that shifts over the course of the late eleventh century from the Welsh borderlands to the Welsh alone.

Orderic's sympathetic characterisation of these rebels as guerrilla fighters in just opposition to a foreign conquest has been often noted. However, resistance to the Normans is largely treated as a particularly English phenomenon in which the last Anglo-Saxons stood firm against alien oppression. Dominique Battles's recent study of cultural difference between Normans and Saxons in Middle English romance, for example, is typical in its remarks that 'chronicle accounts of the years following the Norman Conquest capture the political reality of so many Anglo-Saxon noblemen who, upon losing their lands and positions, retreated into exile', while 'the English who did not die in this process, fled'.[5] These 'disenfranchised Anglo-Saxons' are understood to have 'sought exile on their native soil', where they 'used the forest as a base of operation for the guerrilla war they would wage against the Normans for several years after the Conquest'.[6] Thus while, after the Battle of Hastings, 'the forests ... became associated with political resistance', that resistance is understood to have been of a particularly 'English' nature.[7] But whereas Orderic's sympathetic portrait of native resistance to the Normans has been widely recognised, the rebels he describes here are not Anglo-Saxon earls, broadly speaking, but the same political allies in the Welsh borderlands that were discussed in Chapter Five. His widely excerpted description of these rebels is drawn from a longer narrative of one revolt in particular – that of the northern Welsh ruler Bleddyn and the Mercian earls Eadwine and Morcar, mentioned in the previous chapter. This characterisation of the rebels as 'wild men' in the period immediately after 1066 does not describe a collective English response to the Norman presence in England, but rather one that is particularly associated with the Welsh borderlands.

The full account of this rebellion helps to contextualise Orderic's description of those involved. He begins not with the English but with the Welsh, writing: 'Tempore Normannicæ cladis quæ nimiis oppressionibus Anglos immoderate conquassauit; Blidenus rex Gualorum ad auunculos suos suppetias uenit, secumque multitudinem Britonum adduxit' (when the Norman conquest had brought such grievous burdens upon the English, Bleddyn king of the Welsh came to the help of his uncles, bringing a great army of Welshmen with him).[8] As Chapter Five argued, a longstanding culture of political and military alliance in the borderlands stood behind this rebellion, and Orderic's account underscores the importance of Anglo-Welsh kin ties in this region. Yet in his extended description of these events we can see that, as the rebellion expanded, one of its defining characteristics was the unity of English and Welsh throughout Britain in revolting against the Normans:

> Tempore Normannicæ cladis quæ nimiis oppressionibus Anglos immoderate conquassauit; Blidenus rex Gualorum ad auunculos suos suppetias uenit, secumque multitudinem Britonum adduxit. Congregatis autem in unum multis Anglorum et Gualorum optimatibus, fit generalis querimonia de iniuriis et oppressionibus; quibus intolerabiliter Angli affligebantur a Normannis et eorum contubernalibus. Legationibus quoscunque poterant; per omnes Albionis terminos in hostes clam palamque stimulabant. Fit ex consensu omnium pro uendicanda libertate pristina procax conspiratio; et obnixa contra Normannos coniuratio. Exoritus in finibus Transhumbranis uehemens perturbatio. Seditiosi siluas, paludes; æstuaria et urbes aliquot in munimentis habent. Eborachensis ciuitas ardentissime furit; quam sanctitas pontificis sui sedare nequit. Plures in tabernaculis morabantur, in domibus ne mollescerent requiescere dedignabantur; unde quidam eorum a Normannis siluatici cognominabantur.
>
> (When the Norman conquest had brought such grievous burdens upon the English, Bleddyn king of the Welsh came to the help of his uncles, bringing

a great army of Welshmen with him. After large numbers of the leading men of England and Wales had met together, a general outcry arose against the injustice and tyranny which the Normans and their comrades-in-arms had inflicted on the English. They sent envoys into every corner of Albion to incite men openly and secretly against the enemy. All were ready to conspire together to recover their former liberty, and bind themselves by weighty oaths against the Normans. In the regions north of the Humber violent disturbances broke out. The rebels prepared to defend themselves in woods, marshes and creeks, and in some cities. The city of York was seething with discontent, and showed no respect for the holy office of its archbishop when he tried to appease it. Many men lived in tents, disdaining to sleep in houses lest they should become soft; so that the Normans called them 'wild men'.)[9]

Anglo-Welsh political alliance drove this revolt, and the characterisation of those involved mirrors the ways in which the inhabitants of the Welsh borderlands were described by the *Anglo-Saxon Chronicle* throughout the eleventh century.

However, an important conceptual shift in the identity of these rebels took place in the last years of the eleventh century. As the Mercian earls and landowners involved in the revolts against the Normans were defeated, imprisoned or killed, the same types of rebellious outlaw with ties to the same marginal areas of the landscape of Britain were identified as solely Welsh. The landscape of rebellion underwent a parallel shift. While any wilderness space served as a base for guerilla-style revolts in the immediate aftermath of the Battle of Hastings, a few decades later, the Welsh borderlands became the only marginal geographical area linked to resistance. By the end of the eleventh century, the characterisation and location of rebellion had shifted from the borderlands to the Welsh alone, setting the stage for the reputation of the March of Wales as a place of outlawry in later Anglo-Norman England.

In the immediate aftermath of the Battle of Hastings, the *Peterborough Chronicle* links the rebel Mercian earls Eadwine and Morcar to the landscape of Britain. The annal for 1071 records that 'Her Ædwine eorl 7 Morkere eorl ut hlupon 7 mislice ferdon on wudu 7 on felda'[10] (here Earl Edwin and Earl Morcar leapt out and journeyed varyingly in woods and in fields). An association with the wilderness, also evident in Orderic Vitalis's description of this revolt, defines early rebels against the Normans. Indeed, as Susan Reynolds has noted, Orderic 'is not the only chronicler to make it clear that the English resistance was very widespread or to describe the rebels as taking to the woods and marshes'.[11] Rebellion was firmly linked in the Anglo-Saxon literary record to the *wudu 7 felda* where Eadwine and Morcar fled.

Writing the Welsh borderlands

This connection between rebellion and wilderness is heightened in textual descriptions of Eadwine and Morcar's last stand at Ely, islanded among the treacherous swamps of the Fens. While Ely itself is not in the Welsh borderlands, the participants in this revolt – Mercian earls and Welsh rulers – were from that region and used its political alliances as their basis for rebellion. The revolt at Ely illustrates the rhetorical associations that will be discussed in connection with the landscape of the Welsh borderlands later in this chapter. As the *Peterborough Chronicle* reports, after Eadwine and Morcar took to the *wudu 7 felda*, 'Þa gewende Morkere eorl to Elig on scipe, and Eadwine eorl wearð ofslagen arhlice fram his agenum mannum'[12] (then Earl Morcar went by ship to Ely, and Earl Edwin was traitorously slain by his own men). The noted treachery of Eadwine's men reinforces the sympathetic perspective that the *Peterborough Chronicle* adopts towards these outlaws, as does the groundswell of support for their cause: '7 com se biscop Egelwine 7 Siward Bearn 7 fela hund manna mid heom into Elig'[13] (then came Bishop Æthelwine, and Siward Bearn, and several hundred men with them, into Ely). Indeed, Ely's reputation as being in an inaccessible wilderness is reinforced by William's strategies in attacking it, as '7 þa þe se cyng Willelm þet geaxode, þa bead he ut scipfyrde 7 landfyrde 7 þet land abutan sæt 7 brycge gewrohte 7 inn for, 7 seo scipfyrde on þa sæhealfe'[14] (and when King William learned that, he commanded that a ship-army and a land-army go out, and surround that land, and he built a bridge and went in, and the ship-army was facing the sea-side).

The slightly longer narrative of this event in Orderic Vitalis's *Ecclesiastical History* places even greater emphasis on the remoteness and inaccessibility of the fenlands while describing Morcar's last stand. Orderic relates: 'Nam rex Guillelmus consilio prauorum male usus laudi suæ dampnum ingessit; dum fraudulenter inclitum comitem Morcarum in Eliensi insula conclusit, sibique confederatum et nil mali machinantem uel suspicantem obsedit' (for King William, ill-advisedly relying on evil counsellors, brought great harm to his reputation by treacherously surrounding the noble Earl Morcar in the Isle of Ely, and besieging a man who had made peace with him and was neither doing nor expecting any harm).[15] These treacherous counsellors persuade Morcar to surrender to the king, even though 'Obsessus nempe diu poterat ibidem sese inaccessibilitate loci defendere; aut nimia ui accidente per circumfluens flumen usque in Oceanum nauigio diffugere' (for the besieged could have held out almost indefinitely thanks to the inaccessibility of the place; or if the attacking forces seemed too great might have slipped away by boat along the surrounding rivers to the sea).[16] Eadwine and Morcar's last stand at Ely underscores the link between rebellion and wilderness after the arrival of the Normans.[17]

Yet as we have seen, Eadwine and Morcar were not just any Anglo-Saxon rebels fighting in isolation. Their revolt was a product of political alliance in the borderlands. Orderic's account of their last stand further emphasises this fact when he reiterates that 'Sex igitur mensibus a Scottis et Gaulis uel Anglis auxilia sibi quæsiuit' (So for six months [Edwin] sought support among the Scots, Welsh and English).[18] This link between the borderlands, rebellion and wilderness spaces in the years immediately following the Battle of Hastings is also evident in Orderic's description of William's 1070 expedition against the borderlands forces that had recently raided Shrewsbury (here encapsulated as the Welsh and the men of Chester). As discussed in Chapter Five, William displays a perception of the borderlands as a united military force when in the winter of 1070, 'Deinde mouet expeditionem contra Cestrenses et Gualos; qui præter alias offensas nuperrime Scrobesburiam obsederunt' (then he undertook an expedition against the Welsh and the men of Chester, who had recently crowned their many lawless acts by besieging Shrewsbury).[19]

This expedition is defined by the difficult terrain that William's army must traverse in order to prevent such rebellions. Immediately before this attack, 'Mense ianuario rex Guillelmus Haugustaldam reuertebatur a Tesia, uia quæ hactenus exercitui erat intemptata; qua crebro acutissima iuga et uallium humillimæ sedes, cum uicinia serenitate uerna gaudet, niuibus compluuntur' (in January King William left the Tees and returned to Hexham, following a route no army had hitherto attempted, where towering peaks and the precipitous valleys between them would be deep in snow even when the countryside around blossomed with the spring).[20] William's attempts to suppress these rebellions require fortitude in the face of difficult terrain, as 'At ille in acerrimo hiemis gelu transiuit; animosque militum alacritate sua confirmauit' (undeterred, he crossed them in the depths of a bitter winter, encouraging his soldiers by his own cheerfulness).[21] The landscape in which the rebels are hiding is remote and difficult to access – Orderic relates that 'Illud iter difficulter peractum est; in quo sonipedum ingens ruina facta est' (with great difficulty they struggled on, losing many horses on the way),[22] one of the key characteristics of a dangerous border landscape that will later become associated only with the Welsh by the end of the eleventh century.

Yet here, the borderlands form a daunting landscape in the eyes of William's men. On this expedition, 'Exercitus autem qui dura tolerauerat; in hoc itinere multo duriora restare timebat' (his army, which had already endured great hardship, feared that even greater trials were in store in

Writing the Welsh borderlands

this journey).[23] Their unease is linked directly to the wildness and inaccessibility of the region: 'Verebatur enim locorum asperitatem hiemis intemperiem, alimentorum inopiam et hostium terribilem ferociam' (they feared the wildness of the region, the severity of winter, the scarcity of food and the terrible ferocity of the enemy).[24] William perseveres, as 'Indefessim itaque pergit uia equiti nunquam ante experta, in qua sunt montes ardui et ualles profundissimæ; riui et amnes periculosi, et uoraginosa uallium ima' (and so he pushed on with determination along a road no horseman had attempted before, over steep mountains and precipitous valleys, through rivers and rushing streams and deep abysses).[25] The inhospitable nature of the terrain is frequently referenced – 'In hac uia gradientes sepe nimio uexabantur imbre; mixta interdum grandine' (as they stumbled along the path they were lashed with rain and hail).[26]

Here too a large part of the danger stems from the particularly Norman style of fighting on horseback which is ill-suited to the landscape, its hazards manifest, as 'Aliquando præstabant cunctis usum equi in paludibus enecti' (sometimes all were obliged to feed on horses which had perished in the bogs).[27] Yet the Norman army prevails in the end, due to the fact that 'Ipse rex multoties agiliter pedes cunctos præcedebat, et laborantes manibus impigre adiuuabat' (the king himself, remarkably sure-footed, led the foot-soldiers, readily helping them with his own hands when they were in difficulties),[28] and 'Tandem exercitum incolumem usque Cestram perduxit; et in tota Merciorum regione motus hostiles regia ui compescuit' (so at last he brought his army safely to Chester and suppressed all risings throughout Mercia with royal power).[29] William's response to the uprising at Shrewsbury reflects the link between borderlands rebellions and inaccessible wilderness spaces in the years immediately following the Norman Conquest.

Rebellion and wilderness

Over the course of the late eleventh century, this association between outlaws and wilderness shifted from the rebels of the borderlands, to outlaws more broadly, to the Welsh alone. The first stage in this process is evident in the 1071 annal of the *Peterborough Chronicle*, which relates Hereward's continued resistance when Eadwine and Morcar are defeated. After Ely is surrounded, '7 þa utlagan þa ealle on hand eodan, þet wæs Egelwine biscop 7 Morkere eorl 7 ealle þa þe mid heom wæron butan Herewarde ane 7 ealle þa þe mid him woldon, 7 he hi ahtlice ut lædde'[30] (and the outlaws all went into hand – that was Bishop Æthelwine and Earl

Morcar and all those who were with them – except for Hereward alone, and all those who wished to go with him, and he led them out bravely). After Eadwine's death and Morcar's defeat,[31] Hereward's escape from Ely represented a new generation of rebels. The uprisings shifted from efforts coordinated by the politically allied Welsh borderlands immediately after 1066 to the more isolated revolts that persisted after the first wave of coordinated resistance had been suppressed, and individual rebellion was the only option left – as Reynolds has observed, 'national solidarity had developed at a political level before the Norman invasion, but, given the lack of leadership, guerrilla warfare was the best the English resistance could manage by now'.[32] Hereward embodies this second wave of resistance, and the strength of the narrative connection between his revolt and the landscape of Ely underscores the transition from identifying wilderness spaces with the borderlands to identifying them with rebellion more broadly.

The annal for 1071 in the *Peterborough Chronicle* contrasts Hereward's continued heroic resistance with others' submission. After this escape, Hereward is not mentioned again in most manuscripts of the *Anglo-Saxon Chronicle*. However, a later interpolation into the annal for 1070 in the *Peterborough Chronicle* links heroic rebellion and the marginal spaces on the landscape. As Susan Irvine notes, 'unique to the E-text among the extant versions of the *Anglo-Saxon Chronicle* is a series of twenty passages relating to Peterborough which were apparently incorporated by the first scribe in the course of copying the annals up to 1121 from their exemplar' which can be identified 'not only by their subject-matter but also by the distinctively late characteristics of their language'.[33] This interpolated passage takes up the middle part of the annal for 1070, which was restructured to fit it in, and its account of the raid on Peterborough follows closely the *Chronicle of Hugh Candidus*, which is true of many other interpolations in MS E as well.[34]

The 1070 interpolation narrates a growing rebellion – spurred by the arrival of King Sweyn II of Denmark into northern England – at Ely, where 'þet englisce folc of eall þa feonlandes comen to heom, wendon þet hi sceoldon winnon eall þet land'[35] (the English people from all the fenlands came to them, because they hoped that they would win all that land). As the rebellion gathered strength, 'Þa herdon þa munecas of Burh sægen þet heora agene menn wolden hergon þone mynstre, þet wæs Hereward 7 his genge'[36] (then the monks of Peterborough heard it said that their own men wished to plunder the minster. That was Hereward and his band). The annalist makes clear that while Hereward's raid is ostensibly motivated by the desire to 'protect' Peterborough's treasures from the Norman abbot whom, it is rumoured, William will soon appoint, the outlaw's real purpose in seizing this wealth is to support the growing Danish and Anglo-Saxon rebellion centred at Ely. As Malasree Home has argued, 'the entry in E not only demonstrates the subtle stylistic strategies by which the event is narrated from a purely Peterborough point of view (where Hereward is constructed as villain rather than hero), but also shows the way in which the original entry in the base text was transformed to accommodate the abbey's agenda'.[37] Hereward and his band loot and burn Peterborough, and 'Syððon geden heom to scipe, ferden heom to Elig, betæhtan þær þa ealla þa gærsume'[38] (after that they went to ship, and travelled to Ely, and delivered all the treasures there). When the Norman abbot arrives, 'Þa wæron þa utlagas ealle on flote, wistan þet he scolde þider cumen'[39] (the outlaws were all afloat then, because they knew that he would come there). The rebels' use of Ely as their home base reinforces the link between rebellion and wilderness throughout the *Peterborough Chronicle*.

Reynolds has noted the widespread nature of this connection between rebels and wilderness spaces in post-Conquest chronicles.[40] The *Historia Ecclesie Abbendonensis* relates that 'Interim ceperunt multa in regno Anglico machinari molimina … Horum pars siluarum, quidam in locis insularum sese abdere, piratarum more raptim uiuere, quosque obuios obtruncare' (meanwhile many plots began to be hatched in the English kingdom … some hid themselves away in woods, some in islands, living by plunder like pirates, slaughtering those who came their way).[41] Likewise, the *History of the Abbey of Evesham* preserves a story of how 'Nam in primis temporibus sui regni rex Willelmus fecit deuastari quasdam sciras istis in partibus propter exules et latrones qui in siluis latitabant ubique' (indeed, in the early years of his reign, King William had some shires in these regions of England laid waste because of the exiles and outlaws who were hiding in the woods everywhere).[42] William of Malmesbury, in his *Gesta Regum Anglorum*, relates that, after Harold was killed at Hastings, 'germani, ad terras suae potestatis profugientes, aliquot annis pacem Willelmi turbauerunt, clandestinis latrociniis siluas infestantes nec umquam comminus et aperte martem agentes' (the brothers [Edwin and Morcar] escaped to regions which were under their own control, and there disturbed William's peace for some years by infesting the forests with covert brigandage and never fighting openly and at close quarters).[43] Similarly, the romanticised twelfth-century versions of Hereward's legend portray him living as an outlaw in the woods with a large band.[44] The period immediately following the Norman Conquest, then, saw a link between rebellion and wilderness when 'the silvatici were for some years a widespread and well-known phenomenon'.[45]

Indeed, throughout Orderic's *Ecclesiastical History*, rebellions are staged from the woods, marshes and fenlands. William's response to the joint Danish and Anglo-Saxon rebellion in Northumbria and York underscores this link, as 'Ipse illuc cum equitatu contendit, nefarios quosdam in paludibus pene inaccessibilibus reperit, gladioque punit, et aliquot latibula diruit' (the king hastened to the spot with his knights, hunted out some of the ill-doers who had taken refuge in the almost inaccessible marshes, put them to the sword, and wiped out their hiding places).[46] An inaccessible landscape facilitates rebellion: 'Dani aliquandiu delituere. Verum postquam tuta sunt opinati; conuiuiis prouincialium quæ uulgo firmam appellant illecti ad terram egrediuntur' (for a while the Danes lay in hiding; but when they judged it safe they came out of the marshes to share the feasts of the country people which are colloquially known as 'feorms');[47] the route to the northern rebels 'Itur per siluas, paludes, montana, ualles, artissimo tramite qui binos lateraliter ire non patiebatur' (their route now lay through woods, marshes, mountains, valleys, along paths so narrow that two men could not walk abreast);[48] and the king 'Ipse uero in saltuosa quædam et difficillime accessibilia loca contendit; et abditos illic hostes persequi summopere studuit' (he himself continued to comb forests and remote mountainous places, stopping at nothing to hunt out the enemy hidden there).[49]

Likewise, 'Rursum comperit hostile collegium in angulo quodam regionis latitare, mari uel paludibus undique munito' (he learned that another enemy band was lying hidden in a narrow neck of land sheltered on all sides by sea or marshes),[50] so inaccessible that 'Vnicus aditus per solidum intromittit; latitudine tantum uiginti pedum patens' (it could be reached only by one narrow causeway, no more than twenty feet wide),[51] and the rebels 'Prædam abundantem contraxerant, securi agitabant; nullam sibi uim nocere posse putabant' (had laid in ample supplies and believed themselves safe, regarding their position as impregnable).[52] In response, 'Rex ardens infestos sibi hostes ad flumen Tesiam insequitur, et auia perrumpit; quorum asperitas interdum peditem eum ire compellit' (the king, raging, pursued his bitter enemies to the River Tees, forcing his way through trackless wastes, over ground so rough that he was frequently compelled to go on foot).[53] The hazards of the king's pursuit and the remoteness of the rebels' bases reinforce the connection between rebellion and wilderness in the post-Conquest landscape.

Welsh rebellion

By the end of the eleventh century, however, when all the Mercian earls involved in these early revolts were defeated or had surrendered, textual linkage of rebellion and wilderness shifted to Wales and the Welsh alone. In 1087 the *Peterborough Chronicle* recorded treasonous plotting all over England, but banditry now emanated only from the borderlands and Wales.[54] In the borderlands, '7 ða men þe yldest wæron of Hereforde 7 eall þeo scir forð mid 7 þa men of Scrobscyre mid mycele folce of Brytlande comon 7 hergodon 7 bærndon on Wiðreceastrescire forð þet hi comon to þam porte sylfan 7 woldon þa ðæne port bærnen 7 þet mynster reafian 7 þæs cynges castel gewinnan heom to handa'[55] (then those men who were the leaders of Hereford went forth, and all the shire with them, and the men of Shropshire with many people from Wales came and harried and burned in Worcestershire. They kept coming until they came to the town itself, and wished to burn the town and plunder the minster, and take the king's castle into their hands). This raid continues the pattern of attacks carried out by the borderlands in the tenth and eleventh centuries, as discussed in Chapter Five.

Indeed, as John of Worcester's version of these events makes clearer, the only difference between this raid and those carried out before 1066 was the added participation of Norman Marcher lords. As he relates,

> Dum autem hec interim circumquaque perpetrantur mala, Bernardus de Nouo Mercatu, Rogerius de Laceio, qui iam super regem inuaserat Herefordam, Rauulfus de Mortuo Mari, coniurationis socii, cum hominibus comitis Rogeri de Scrobbesbyria, congregato magno Anglorum, Normannorum, et Walensium exercitu, Wigornensem irruperunt in prouinciam, affirmantes se igne crematuros ipsam ciuitatem Wigreceastram, spoliaturos Dei et sancte Marie ecclesiam, grandem de regis incolis fidelibus sumpturos uindictam.

> (While these evils were being committed everywhere, Bernard of Neufmarché, Roger de Lacy, who had just attacked Hereford against the king, and Ralph Mortimer, their fellow conspirators, with the men of Earl Roger of Shrewsbury, brought together a large army of English, Normans and Welsh, broke into Worcestershire, intending to burn down the city of Worcester, to despoil the church of God and St Mary, and to wreak heavy vengeance on the local supporters of the king.)[56]

John of Worcester's description of this raid underscores the continuity of political alliance within the borderlands and its reputation as a lawless space.

The transformation of the borderlands outlaw

At the end of the eleventh century, however, the identity of those understood to be in rebellion against the Normans shifted from the borderlands as a whole to the Welsh alone. At the end of a long entry for 1094, the *Peterborough Chronicle* records that 'Eac on þisum ylcan geare þa wylisce men hi gegaderodon 7 wið þa Frencisce, þe on Walon oððe on þære neawiste wæron 7 hi ær belandedon, gewinn up ahofon 7 manige festena 7 castelas abræcon 7 men ofslogon'[57] (Also in this same year, the Welsh men gathered themselves together against the French who were in Wales or nearby and had earlier deprived them of lands. They raised up war against them; they destroyed many strongholds and castles and slew the men). The rebellion is a significant one: 'An syððan heora gefylce weox, hi hi on ma todældon'[58] (after their army grew, they divided it into more parts) and 'Wið sum þæra dæle gefeaht Hugo eorl of Scrobscire 7 hi aflymde, ac þeahhweðer þa oðre ealles þæs geares nanes yfeles ne geswicon þe hi don mihton'[59] (Earl Hugh of Shropshire fought against one of these divisions and scattered them, but regardless, throughout all of that year none of the others stopped doing all of the evil that they were able).

The *Chronicle of John of Worcester* likewise notes that 'Interea graui et assiduo tributo, hominumque mortalitate, presenti et anno sequenti, tota uexabatur Anglia' (meanwhile all England was oppressed by heavy and persistent taxation, and a mortality of men, both in this and in the following year),[60] but then 'Ad hec etiam primitus North Walani, deinceps West Walani et Suth Walani, seruitutis iugo, quo diu premebantur, excusso, et ceruice erecta, libertatem sibi uindicare laborabant' (in addition first the North Welsh, then the West and South Welsh, shaking off the yoke of slavery, which they had long endured, and holding their heads up high, sought to recover their liberty).[61] Thus, 'Vnde collecta multitudine, castella, que in West Walania firmata erant, frangebant, et in Castrensi, Scrobbesbyriensi, et Herefordensi prouincia frequenter uillas cremabant, predas agebant, et multos ex Anglis et Normannis interficiebant. Fregerunt et castellum in Meuania insula, eamque sue dicioni subiciebant' (assembling a multitude of men, they razed the castles which had been built in West Wales, and often ravaged townships in Cheshire, Shropshire and Herefordshire, taking booty, and killing many of the English and Normans. They demolished the castle on Anglesey, and reduced the island to their control).[62]

This rebellion was clearly quite significant in scale, and the *Peterborough Chronicle* and John of Worcester agree in highlighting two crucial elements: it is brought about solely by the actions of the Welsh, yet the heroic nature of their revolt is never in doubt. The Welsh rebels are described in the same way as the borderlands had been throughout the eleventh century, namely, successfully fighting for a just cause – here to 'shak[e] off the yoke of slavery' and reclaim their lands and liberty. Yet where earlier annals depicted the borderlands rebelling as a whole, here only the Welsh stand in heroic revolt. This shift is evident at the end of this same annal in the *Chronicle of John of Worcester*, which records that 'Post hec rex Wilelmus .iiii. .kal. Ianuarii Angliam rediit, et ut Walanos debellaret, mox exercitum in Waloniam duxit, ibique homines et equos perdidit multos' (after this King William on 29 December went back to England and led an army into Wales in order to fight the Welsh, and there lost many men and horses).[63] This emphasis on the difficulty of fighting in this landscape, earlier attached to the borderlands as a whole, marks a shift in perception that Wales alone is now the space of inaccessibility, danger, wilderness and outlaws in Britain.

At the end of the eleventh century, the *Peterborough Chronicle* consistently characterised Wales as a dangerously inaccessible space where men and horses perished. As was the case with the borderlands immediately after the Norman Conquest, the link between geography and revolt became a defining factor in the identity of this territory. The Welsh, like the earlier rebels, were described as fleeing to geographically inaccessible spaces – the woods, mountains and moors – and in consequence were perceived as impossible to defeat. The *Peterborough Chronicle* also continued the pattern that Chapter Five found in the *Anglo-Saxon Chronicle* as a whole, namely, that the military culture of the borderlands was distinguished from the rest of England because the more agile foot-soldiers of this region could defeat Norman cavalry, ill-suited to the terrain. Yet by the end of the eleventh century, this distinction in fighting styles had been transferred to the Welsh alone, as every battle fought against them was said to result in loss of men and horses, inextricably linking inaccessible terrain and rebellion with this region.

This narrative link between the Welsh, rebellion and the inaccessibility of a hostile landscape is evident in the *Peterborough Chronicle*'s annal for 1095. Among other troubles, 'Onmang þison wearð þam cynge cuð þet þa wylisce men on Wealon sumne castel heafdon tobroken Muntgumni hatte 7 Hugon eorles men ofslagene þe hine healdon sceoldan'[64] (among all this, it became known to the king that the Welsh men had destroyed a certain castle called Montgomery in Wales, and slain Earl Hugh's men who were supposed to hold it). In response, 'he forþi oðre fyrde het fearlice abannan 7 æfter Sancte Michaeles mæsse into Wealan ferde'[65] (he therefore commanded another army to be mustered quickly, and after Michaelmas journeyed into Wales). Once they were there, 'his fyrde toscyfte 7 þet land eall þurhfor swa þet seo fyrde eall togædere com to ealra halgena to Snawdune; ac þa Wylisce a toforan into muntan and moran ferdan þet hem man to cuman ne mihte'⁶⁶ (his army divided and went all through that land so that the army came all together to Snowdon, but the Welsh always went in front of them into the mountains and the moors so that no one could reach them). Defeated, 'se cyng þa hamweard gewende, forþam he geseah þet he þær þes wintres mare don ne mihte'⁶⁷ (the king went homeward, because he saw that he was not able to do any more that winter). The characterisation of the Welsh in this annal mirrors the ways in which the rebels of the Welsh borderlands were depicted in the immediate aftermath of the Battle of Hastings – as taking to the inaccessible wilderness spaces of Britain to stay one step ahead of a slower Norman army. Yet, at the end of the eleventh century, it is the Welsh alone who are represented as outlaws linked to a dangerous landscape.

The annal for the same year in the *Chronicle of John of Worcester* gives a shorter version of these events but depicts the Welsh in the same way. He writes, 'Interea Walenses castellum Muntgumri fregerunt, et Hugonis Scrobbesbyrie comitis homines in illo nonnullos occiderunt' (meantime the Welsh stormed the castle of Montgomery, and there slew many of Earl Hugh of Shrewsbury's men).⁶⁸ Just as in the *Peterborough Chronicle*, 'Vnde rex iratus, expeditionem cito mandauit, et post festiuitatem sancti Michaelis exercitum in Waloniam duxit, ibique homines et equos quamplures perdidit' (this angered the king, he quickly mounted an expeditionary force, and after the feast of St Michael led an army into Wales, there losing many men and horses).⁶⁹ Wales is an inaccessible space, home to rebels, with danger for men and animals. Yet here too these qualities are attached solely to the Welsh and not the borderlands as a whole.

The same perception of the Welsh is evident in the *Peterborough Chronicle* in its annal for the following year, 1096, when the king's failure to subdue this difficult and rebellious landscape is linked to general misery in England at the time: 'Ðis wæs swiðe hefigtime gear geond eall Angelcyn, ægðer ge þurh mænigfealde gylda 7 eac þurh swiðe hefigtymne hunger þe þisne eard þæs geares swiðe gedrehte'⁷⁰ (this was a very heavy year among all the English, both through manifold taxes and also through a most severe famine which greatly afflicted this land in this year). In addition to taxes and famine, 'Eac on þison geare þa heafodmen þe þis land heoldan oftrædlice fyrde into Wealon sendon 7 mænig man mid þam swiðe gedrehtan, ac man þær ne gespædde butan manmyrringe 7 feohspillinge'⁷¹ (also in this year the leaders who held this land often sent an army into Wales and many men were greatly afflicted by that, but there was no success in that except for loss of life and waste of money). The futility of sending an army into Wales and the constant loss of troops and resources underscores the characterisation of this region as a dangerous landscape.

An entry for 1097 in the *Chronicle of John of Worcester* places similar emphasis on the significance of the Welsh landscape: 'Rex Anglorum Willelmus Quadragesimali tempore Angliam rediit, et post Pasca cum equestri et pedestri exercitu secundo profectus est in Waloniam, ut omnes masculini sexus internitioni daret, at de eis uix aliquem capere aut interimere potuit, sed de suis nonnullos, et equos perdidit multos' (William, king of the English, returned to England during Lent, and after Easter set out a second time for Wales with an army of horse and foot with the intention of killing all the male population; but he was barely able to capture or kill anyone, but lost many men and horses).[72] The familiar patterns of distinction between English and Welsh armies are present in this annal, namely, the prominent role of cavalry in the Norman forces and its apparent role in their lack of success. The Welsh are painted as outlaws, and their territory has become a dangerous place where English armies can only lose.

The long annal for 1097 in the *Peterborough Chronicle* speaks of Wales with an air of defeated finality and underlines its inaccessibility and danger from an English standpoint: 'þæræfter mid mycclum here into Wealon ferde 7 þet land swiðe mid his fyrde þurhfor þurh sume þa Wyliscean þe him to wæron cumen 7 his lædteowas wæron; 7 þærinne wunode fram middesumeran forneah oð August 7 mycel þærinne forleas on mannan 7 on horsan 7 eac on manegan oðran þingan'[73] (thereafter [William] went into Wales with a great army to raid, and he went greatly into that land with his army through some of the Welsh who came to him and were his guides. He stayed there from midsummer well into August and there suffered great loss in men and in horses and also in many other things). Wales is again a complete disaster for the Norman forces. Despite the size of William's army, the duration of his campaign, and the aid of native guides, he is unable to successfully attack Wales because the danger and remoteness of the landscape continually causes the loss of troops and cavalry. Even in the midst of internal Welsh unrest,[74] William abandons his expedition, as 'Ac þa ðe se cyng geseah þet he nan þinge his willes þær geforðian ne mihte, he ongean into þison lande for, 7 hraðe æfter þam he be þam gemæron castelas let gemakian'[75] (but when the king saw that he was able to accomplish none of his desires there, he came back into this land, and shortly after that he had castles built along the boundaries).

At the end of the eleventh century in the *Peterborough Chronicle* and related texts, there is a shift from the borderlands to Wales alone as the landscape that is portrayed as the centre of rebellion: remote, dangerous and with a fighting style culturally distinct from that of the English army. By 1097, Wales is cast as a permanently inaccessible place. Indeed, this failed campaign, which William abandoned in favour of defensive castle-building, marked the end of early Anglo-Norman attempts to conquer Wales and the effective beginning of the March of Wales as its own 'lawless' space.

Conclusions

At the end of the eleventh century, those qualities which had defined the inhabitants of the borderlands – viewed as outlaws, rebels and guerrilla fighters based among inaccessible marshes, woods and mountains – shifted to the Welsh alone in the *Peterborough Chronicle* and related texts. Orderic Vitalis's *Ecclesiastical History* is a fitting conclusion for this chapter because it illustrates the rapid shift in the Norman political imagination of an outlaw identity from the borderlands to Wales alone. Orderic continued his *Ecclesiastical History* after his source text, the now-lost history written by William of Poitiers,[76] had ended, providing us with a valuable description of conditions in the decades after the arrival of the Normans. In the Norman narrative of conquest, after the Mercian rebels are defeated, the Welsh are the next step: 'Rex Guillelmus deiectis ut diximus Merciorum maximis consulibus, Eduino scilicet interfecto, et Morcaro in uinculis constricto; adiutoribus suis inclitas Angliæ regiones distribuit, et ex infimis Normannorum clientibus tribunos et centuriones ditissimos erexit' (after King William had defeated the leading Mercian earls as I have related – Edwin being dead, and Morcar languishing in prison – he divided up the chief provinces of England amongst his followers, and made the humblest of the Normans men of wealth, with civil and military authority).[77]

The defeat of the Mercian earls is immediately linked to the continuing fight against the Welsh: 'Willelmo dapifero Normanniæ Osberni filio insulam Vectam et comitatum Herfordensem dedit; eumque cum Gualterio de Laceio aliisque probatis pugilibus contra Britones bellis inhiantes opposuit' (William gave William fitzOsbern, steward of Normandy, the Isle of Wight and county of Hereford, and set him up in the marches with Walter of Lacy and other proved warriors, to fight the bellicose Welsh).[78] The initial purpose of these Marcher lords is to fight the Welsh, the last remaining rebels after the Mercian earls have been defeated. While some Marcher lords enjoy initial success – 'Horum audacia Brachaniaunos primitus inuasit, et Gualorum reges Risen et Caducan ac Mariadoth aliosque plures prostrauit' (since his followers would dare anything, fitzOsbern made a first attack on Brecknock, and defeated the Welsh kings Rhys, Cadwgan, Maredudd, and many others)[79] – others fail, as 'Cestram et comitatum eius Gherbodo Flandrensi iamdudum rex dederat; qui magna ibi et difficilia tam ab Anglis quam a Gualis aduersantibus pertulerat' (the king had already given the city and county of Chester to the Fleming Gerbod, but he was continually molested by the English and Welsh alike).[80]

Likewise, 'rex Cestrensem consulatum Hugoni de Abrincis filio Ricardi cognomento Goz concessit, qui cum Rodberto de Rodelento et Rodberto de Malopassu aliisque proceribus feris multum Gualorum sanguinem effudit' (the king granted the county of Chester to Hugh of Avranches, son of Richard called Goz, who with Robert of Rhuddlan, Robert of Malpas, and other fierce knights, wrought great slaughter amongst the Welsh),[81] and 'Warino autem Caluo corpore paruo sed animo magno Amieriam neptem suam et præsidatum Scrobesburiæ dedit; per quem Gualos aliosque sibi aduersantes fortiter oppressit, et prouinciam totam sibi commissam pacificauit' (to Warin the Bald, a man small in body but great in spirit, he gave his niece Amieria and the sheriffdom of Shrewsbury, employing him to crush the Welsh and other opponents and pacify the whole province placed under his rule).[82]

Orderic's narrative indicates that, after the initial wave of revolts is crushed and the Mercian earls are captured or killed, the locus of rebellion shifts to Wales and the Welsh. Yet interestingly, so too do Orderic's sympathies. As he condemns the cruelties of the Norman lords and their devastations of the native land and peoples, Orderic's sympathy holds steady even once the consequences of Norman excess are directed solely against Wales. By the end of the eleventh century, it is the Welsh who hold the insular role as outlaws: the source of rebellion, linked to inaccessible wilderness spaces, and depicted sympathetically, suffering at the hands of the Normans.

Throughout the Anglo-Saxon period, the distinctive region of the Welsh borderlands functioned as a cultural nexus between Welsh and Anglo-Saxons. The shift to a perception that it was the Welsh alone who acted like outlaws highlights the loss of the borderlands' distinct culture after the arrival of the Normans. In Chapter Seven, the Conclusion to this book, I explore a text which reflects on this distinctive borderlands culture from a perspective long after the Norman arrival. The Latin *Life of Harold Godwinson*, written 140 years after the Norman Conquest, nonetheless preserves the myth that Harold survived the Battle of Hastings and lived for years in anonymity in the Welsh borderlands. This remarkable story reinforces this region's reputation as a place of lawlessness where identities are blurred, as Harold moves about after his supposed death in the guise of a hermit. In the *Vita Haroldi*, the Welsh borderlands retain their identity as a cultural nexus between Anglo-Saxons and Welsh. Yet at the same time, this region also becomes the place of intersection between Anglo-Saxon and Anglo-Norman England. This nebulous territory is the last place where English identity can survive after the arrival of the Normans. Yet what survives in this region is something more than English identity alone. The *Vita Haroldi* depicts the borderlands as a mixed Anglo-Welsh region whose cultural stability throughout the Anglo-Saxon period was lost in Norman violence towards Wales in the centuries after the Battle of Hastings.

Notes

1. For a recent study of the *Peterborough Chronicle*, see Malasree Home, *The Peterborough Version of the Anglo-Saxon Chronicle: Rewriting Post-Conquest History* (Woodbridge, Suffolk: Boydell, 2015).
2. *Ibid.*, 4.
3. *Ibid.*, 4–5.
4. Marjorie Chibnall, ed. and trans., *The Ecclesiastical History of Orderic Vitalis*, 6 vols. (Oxford: Clarendon Press, 1969–80), vol. 2, Book IV, 216–19.
5. Dominique Battles, *Cultural Difference and Material Culture in Middle English Romance: Normans and Saxons*, Routledge Studies in Medieval Literature and Culture (New York: Routledge, 2013), 140.
6. *Ibid.*, 140.
7. *Ibid.*, 140.
8. Chibnall, *Orderic Vitalis*, vol. 2, Book IV, 216–17.
9. *Ibid.*, vol. 2, Book IV, 216–19.
10. Susan Irvine, *Volume 7: MS E* (Cambridge: D. S. Brewer, 2004), 1071. This annal is repeated nearly verbatim in G. D. Cubbin *Volume 6: MS D* (Cambridge: D. S. Brewer, 1996), 1072: 'Her Eadwine eorl 7 Morkere eorl hlupon ut, 7 mislice ferdon on wuda 7 on feldon'.
11. Susan Reynolds, 'Eadric Silvaticus and the English resistance', *Historical Research* 54 (1981): 102–5 at 104.
12. *MS E*, ed. Irvine, 1071. *MS D*, ed. Cubbin, 1072, reports events in a slightly different order: 'Her Eadwine eorl 7 Morkere eorl hlupon ut, 7 mislice ferdon on wuda 7 on feldon oð þæt Eadwine wearð ofslægen fram his agenum mannum, 7 Morkere mid scype gewende to Helig' (here Earl Edwin and Earl Morcar leapt out and journeyed varyingly in woods and in fields, until Edwin was slain by his own men, and Morcar went by ship to Ely).
13. *MS E*, ed. Irvine, 1071. MS D repeats this nearly verbatim.
14. *MS E*, ed. Irvine, 1071.
15. Chibnall, *Orderic Vitalis*, vol. 2, Book IV, 256–7.
16. *Ibid.*, vol. 2, Book IV, 256–7.

17 A nearly identical account of Edwin's death, Morcar's surrender and Hereward's continued resistance at Ely in 1071 appears in *The Chronicle of John of Worcester, Volume III: The Annals from 1067 to 1140 with the Gloucester Interpolations and the Continuation to 1141*, ed. and trans. P. McGurk (Oxford: Clarendon Press, 1998), 1071, 18–21. As McGurk, 20 n.4, notes, 'JW is quite close to ASC D 1072 E. ASC does not report Edwin and Morkar's fears, Edwin's decision to visit Malcolm, the rebels' intention of wintering on Ely, and the length of William's bridge at Ely; and it does not describe the various fates of the prisoners'.
18 Chibnall, *Orderic Vitalis*, vol. 2, Book IV, 258–9.
19 Ibid., vol. 2, Book IV, 234–5.
20 Ibid., vol. 2, Book IV, 234–5.
21 Ibid., vol. 2, Book IV, 234–5.
22 Ibid., vol. 2, Book IV, 234–5.
23 Ibid., vol. 2, Book IV, 234–5.
24 Ibid., vol. 2, Book IV, 234–5.
25 Ibid., vol. 2, Book IV, 236–7.
26 Ibid., vol. 2, Book IV, 236–7.
27 Ibid., vol. 2, Book IV, 236–7.
28 Ibid., vol. 2, Book IV, 236–7.
29 Ibid., vol. 2, Book IV, 236–7.
30 *MS E*, ed. Irvine, 1071. *MS D*, ed. Cubbin, 1072, gives a slightly different version: '7 hi ealle þa eodon þan kyninge on hand: þæt wæs Ægelwine biscop 7 Morkere eorl 7 ealle þa þe mid heom wæron, buton Herewerde anum 7 ealle þa þe mid him ætfleon mihton, 7 he hi ahtlice ut alædde' (and then they all went to the king's hand, that was Bishop Æthelwine and Earl Morcar and all those who were with them, except for Hereward alone, and all those who were able to flee with him, and he led them out bravely).
31 After Morcar's surrender at Ely, 'se cyng genam scipa 7 wæpna 7 sceattas manega, 7 þa men he ateah swa swa he wolde', *MS E*, ed. Irvine, 1071 (the king seized ships and weapons and a great deal of money, and the men he dealt with exactly as he wished). MS D gives fundamentally the same account.
32 Reynolds, 'Eadric Silvaticus', 104.
33 *MS E*, ed. Irvine, p. xc.
34 Ibid., p. xcvii; see further pp. xci–ci and W. T. Mellows, ed., *The Chronicle of Hugh Candidus, A Monk of Peterborough* (Oxford: Oxford University Press, 1949), pp. xxvi–xxvii and 77–82.
35 *MS E*, ed. Irvine, 1070.
36 Ibid., 1070.
37 Home, *Peterborough Version*, 45–6.
38 *MS E*, ed. Irvine, 1070.
39 Ibid., 1070.
40 Reynolds, 'Eadric Silvaticus', 104.
41 John Hudson, ed. and trans., *Historia Ecclesie Abbendonensis: The History of the*

Church of Abingdon, Oxford Medieval Texts, 2 vols. (Oxford: Clarendon Press, 2007 and 2002), vol. I, 224–45.
42 Jane Sayers and Leslie Watkiss, ed. and trans., *Thomas of Marlborough: History of the Abbey of Evesham*, Oxford Medieval Texts (Oxford: Clarendon Press, 2003), 166–7.
43 William of Malmesbury, *Gesta Regum Anglorum: The History of the English Kings*, vol. I, ed. and trans. by R. A. B. Mynors, and completed by R. M. Thomson and M. Winterbottom (Oxford: Clarendon Press, 1998), 468–9. William of Malmesbury, *Gesta Regum Anglorum: The History of the English Kings*, vol. II, *General Introduction and Commentary*, by R. M. Thomson in collaboration with M. Winterbottom (Oxford: Clarendon Press, 1999).
44 Gaimar, *L'Estoire des Engleis*, ed. A. Bell (Anglo-Norman Text Soc., xiv–xvi, 1960), ll. 5457–61, 5547–8; 'Gesta Herewardi' in Gaimar, *L'Estorie des Engles*, ed. T. D. Hardy and C. T. Martin (2 vols., Rolls Series, 1888–9), i. 372, 392–3; Michael Swanton, trans., *Three Lives of the Last Englishmen* (New York: Garland, 1984), 45–88.
45 Reynolds, 'Eadric Silvaticus', 104.
46 Chibnall, *Orderic Vitalis*, vol. 2, Book IV, 228–9.
47 *Ibid.*, vol. 2, Book IV, 230–1.
48 *Ibid.*, vol. 2, Book IV, 230–1.
49 *Ibid.*, vol. 2, Book IV, 230–1.
50 *Ibid.*, vol. 2, Book IV, 232–3.
51 *Ibid.*, vol. 2, Book IV, 232–3.
52 *Ibid.*, vol. 2, Book IV, 232–3.
53 *Ibid.*, vol. 2, Book IV, 232–3.
54 MS E, ed. Irvine, 1087: 'On þisum geare wæs þis land swiðe astirad 7 mid mycele swicdome afylled, swa þet þa riceste frencisce men þe weron innan þisan lande wolden swican heora hlaforde þam cynge 7 woldon habban his broðer to cynge Rodbeard þe wæs eorl on Normandige' (in this year, this land was greatly stirred up and filled with great treason, so that the mightiest French men who were in this land wished to commit treason against their lord the King, and wished to have his brother Robert as king, who was an earl in Normandy).
55 *Ibid.*, 1087.
56 McGurk, *Chronicle of John of Worcester*, 52–3.
57 MS E, ed. Irvine, 1094.
58 *Ibid.*, 1094.
59 *Ibid.*, 1094.
60 McGurk, *Chronicle of John of Worcester*, 72–3.
61 *Ibid.*, 72–3.
62 *Ibid.*, 72–3.
63 *Ibid.*, 72–3.
64 MS E, ed. Irvine, 1095.
65 *Ibid.*, 1095.

66 *Ibid.*, 1095.
67 *MS E*, ed. Irvine, 1095.
68 McGurk, *Chronicle of John of Worcester*, 78–9.
69 *Ibid.*, 78–9.
70 *MS E*, ed. Irvine, 1096.
71 *Ibid.*, 1096.
72 McGurk, *Chronicle of John of Worcester*, 84–5. As McGurk, 84–5 n.1, notes, there is some confusion between the accounts of ASC and JW, likely based on a 'hasty reading' of ASC, and due to this and the fact that Welsh sources only record one campaign, 'it is probable therefore that William campaigned only once in Wales in 1097'.
73 *MS E*, ed. Irvine, 1097.
74 *Ibid.*, 1097: 'Ða wylisce men syððon hi fram þam cynge gebugon, heom manege ealdras of heom sylfan gecuron, sum þæra wæs Caduugaun gehaten þe heora weorðast wæs, se wæs Griffines broðer sunu cynges' (the Welsh men afterwards turned from their king, and chose many chiefs from among themselves, one of them was named Cadwgan who was the worthiest of them, he was the son of King Gruffudd's brother).
75 *MS E*, ed. Irvine, 1097.
76 Chibnall, *Orderic Vitalis*, vol. 2, Book IV, 258–9. Orderic writes, 'Huc usque Guillelmus Pictauinus historiam suam texuit; in qua Guillelmi gesta Crispi Salustii stilum imitatus subtiliter et eloquenter enucleauit' (William of Poitiers has brought his history up to this point, eloquently describing the deeds of King William in a clever imitation of the style of Sallust).
77 *Ibid.*, vol. 2, Book IV, 260–1.
78 *Ibid.*, vol. 2, Book IV, 260–1.
79 *Ibid.*, vol. 2, Book IV, 260–1.
80 *Ibid.*, vol. 2, Book IV, 260–1.
81 *Ibid.*, vol. 2, Book IV, 260–1.
82 *Ibid.*, vol. 2, Book IV, 262–3.

7

Conclusion: Harold Godwinson, the last Anglo-Saxon in the Welsh borderlands

The Welsh borderlands were a distinctive territory where two peoples came together throughout the Anglo-Saxon period. This conclusion looks just past the Norman arrival in England to the continued depiction of this region as a cultural nexus – both of English and Welsh, and of Anglo-Saxon and Anglo-Norman England – in the *Vita Haroldi*. This understudied thirteenth-century text is, as Stephen Matthews has argued, a work of 'secular hagiography'[1] which claims that Harold was not killed at the Battle of Hastings, but survived for many years afterwards disguised as a hermit in the Welsh borderlands.

The distinctive *Life of Harold Godwinson* is a fitting microcosm of this book because, even after the Norman Conquest, it depicts the Welsh borderlands as a singular place where Anglo-Saxons and Welsh lived side by side. The text underscores the reputation of this region as a place of blurred identities. Harold flees there specifically to live in anonymity and remake himself from king to penitent, and this legend of his survival continues the depiction of the borderlands as a cultural nexus of English and Welsh. Harold's *Vita* also illustrates the perceived violence of this territory[2] and continues the transition, discussed in Chapter Six, of associating the lawlessness of this region with the Welsh in particular in the period after the Norman arrival. The *Vita Haroldi*, written almost a century and a half after the Battle of Hastings, reflects the continued trauma of the Norman presence in England in its longing for the myth of English survival. Yet in this curious text – while the Welsh borderlands are a cultural nexus between Anglo-Saxon and Anglo-Norman England, the last place where English identity survives after the Norman arrival – Harold, the last Anglo-Saxon, can survive only in a place where Anglo-Saxon identity is preserved alongside Welsh. The *Vita Haroldi* embodies the Welsh borderlands as a distinct region where two peoples came together, even when seen from a post-Conquest perspective. It is an area where two peoples meet, but they are not always the same two peoples: Angles and Welsh, north Welsh and south Welsh, Angles and Saxons, Saxons and Welsh, Normans and Welsh, Saxons and Normans, even perhaps borderers and the rest.

The Latin *Life of Harold Godwinson* survives in only one manuscript, London, British Library, Harley MS 3776, folios 1r–25v, where it is the first of several items in a Waltham Abbey composite.[3] The extant text was copied by someone with links to Waltham up to a century after the original *Vita* was first written, which was around the year 1205, to judge by its author's claims.[4] Stephen Matthews has recently argued that the original *Vita* was written not at Waltham but at Chester, which would explain many of the internal contradictions in the surviving copy.[5] As it stands, the *Vita* is a patchwork of written and oral traditions from a range of sources, a transitional text which sits at the intersection of multiple periods and genres. The *Life of Harold Godwinson* is an unsteady blend of hagiography and pseudo-history that was composed in defence of a defeated (and often maligned) Anglo-Saxon king at a point well into the Anglo-Norman period. It is a rare written testament to, in Laura Ashe's apt description, 'the flowering of an astonishing, pseudohistorical myth, denied or doubted in almost all surviving writings, and yet clearly ineradicable as oral legend',[6] a myth which is also well attested in Scandinavian tradition,[7] namely, that England's last king survived the Norman Conquest.

The *Vita Haroldi* combines a range of textual influences. It is a portrait of an Anglo-Saxon saintly king, coloured by contemporary Anglo-Norman romance and hagiography,[8] whose survival parallels the British myth of Arthur, the most famous of those legendary medieval kings – such as Charlemagne, Olaf Tryggvason and Frederick Barbarossa – whose deaths were rumoured to be uncertain.[9] As Ashe concludes, 'while King Harold is systematically damned by, diminished in, or excluded from the mainstream of post-Conquest English historiography, he holds a place on the margins, in the Anglo-Danish and the Anglo-Welsh literary and geographical borderlands'.[10] That it is specifically the Welsh borderlands where Harold can exist in this ambiguous state – dead yet alive, king disguised as hermit, the last Anglo-Saxon in an Anglo-Norman England from which he stands completely apart – underscores the continuity with which this region was understood as a place of blurred identities from the Anglo-Saxon to Anglo-Norman periods. Even after the Norman Conquest, the borderlands are perceived as the place where Anglo-Saxons and Welsh were brought together.[11]

Conclusion: Harold, the last Anglo-Saxon

Harold's experiences in the Welsh borderlands form the bookends to his *Vita*. At the beginning of the text, his earlier campaigns in Wales are characterised as a defining event of his military career. The *Vita*'s author writes 'Viribus autem corporis quantum prestiterit quam acer et strenuus animis armisque innotuerit: subacta immo ad internicionem per Haroldum pene deleta: Wallia est experta' (but how Harold excelled in strength of body, and how famous he became for shrewdness of mind and vigour in arms, was proved by the way he subdued Wales – and nearly destroyed it to extermination).[12] His military success was defined by his rout of Wales early on in his career. Yet the place that Harold attacked at the beginning of his life became his last refuge at the end of it. In the *Vita Haroldi*, Harold is not killed at Hastings but is found half-dead on the battlefield and taken secretly to Winchester, where he is healed by an Arab woman and hidden in a cellar for two years. Once he recovers, he travels to the continent and seeks support from the Danes and the Saxons in Germany to overthrow the Normans. When none is forthcoming, Harold has a spiritual epiphany, lives as a penitent, goes on pilgrimage and spends ten years as a hermit in Dover. Yet the site of his hermitage is too close to Hastings, which causes him to spend too much time in a state of despair at the loss of the battle and the downfall of his people. For that reason, Harold chooses to leave Dover and live out the remainder of his life in anonymity in the Welsh borderlands, only moving to the relative security of a hermit's cell in Chester right before his death.[13]

The later chapters of the *Vita Haroldi* underscore the reputation of the Welsh borderlands as a nexus of multiple identities. Chapter 14 of the *Vita*, in which Harold's time in this region is first discussed, connects the borderlands to identity slippage in its description of 'Quod in confinio Wallensium postmodum Haroldus pluribus in locis tempore multo degens paciencer eorum frequencius tulerit assultus; faciem velans panno et nomen nomine alio ne aliquatenus agnosceretur; et quod tandem ad eius veneratio-nem conversa est immanitas persecutorum' (how Harold afterwards spent a long time in various places on the borders of the Welsh, bore their repeated assaults in patience, hiding his face with a cloth, and changing his name for another lest he should by some means be recognised; how at length the cruelty of his persecutors was changed into veneration for him).[14] The borderlands are where Harold can exist in anonymity, changing his name and face. Yet at the same time, he also alters his character, shifting from the persecutor of the Welsh into their spiritual saviour and precipitating a like turn in their behaviour from cruelty to devoted veneration. But while Harold alters his appearance and persona, the nature of the borderlands itself remains the same as it was in the Anglo-Saxon period. Even after the arrival of the Normans, this region is seen as the place in Britain where Welsh and English are able to dwell together.

The Welsh borderlands are depicted as a site of multiple identities in the *Vita Haroldi*, and as the region that Harold deliberately seeks out as the place to spend his last years. The nature of this place itself is characterised as central to his shifting identity: 'Recolens vero quia et Ualensibus licet ob iustam ut tunc temporis videbatur gentis sue defensionem extitisset quandoque infestus; cupit iam Christianus perferre cum Paulo; quod egerat quondam Haroldus cum Saolo' (living, then, among the Welsh, although he had been at one time an object of hatred to them, on account of what seemed at the time a just defence of his own race, he now desires, as Christian, to suffer with Paul what he had, as Harold, done with Saul).[15] Harold's time in the borderlands is conceptualised as a shift in identity from Saul to Paul, from persecutor to penitent. It is only this place that allows him to make this change, reflecting the nature of the borderlands as a site of multiple identities.

In the secular hagiography of his *Vita*, the suffering he experiences while living among the Welsh is a key part of this transition. After Harold leaves Dover, 'Pertendit igitur Cancie valefaciens usque in partes Wallie multoque ibi diversis in locis moratus tempore: manebat cum illis et orabat pro illis quem illi non se iam oppugnantem; sed pro se pugnantem indesineter impugnabat gratis' (bidding farewell, then, to Kent, he proceeds to Wales, and staying there in various places a long time, he lived with the Welsh and prayed for them, although they, without provocation, ceased not to assault him, who was now not fighting against them, but for them).[16] The Welsh borderlands, with its reputation for violence, is understood as the best place for Harold to undergo a penance befitting the violence he himself wrought in his earlier years. Yet as the narrative of the *Vita* progresses, it becomes clear that it is the ambiguity of Harold's identity – his ability to walk about freely while most of England believes him to be a dead man – which most distinctly defines his time in the Welsh borderlands.

The *Vita* emphasises the effort that Harold takes to keep his identity hidden, describing how

> Accessurus vero ut premissum est in terram sibi ante cognitam ne quavis occasione a quolibet agnitus; virtutis meritum precio vanitatis dum laus oblata iure in eo laudanda prosequitur venditaret faciem suam et nomen proprium omnibus abscondebat; processurus in publicum: velamen panniculi iugiter vultui pretendebat.

(As he was going into a land, as we have stated before, where he was once known, he concealed both his features and his name, wearing always in public the veil of a little piece of cloth before his face, lest, if he were recognised by any, the offer of their adoration to the merits of his virtues might lead him to become vain.)[17]

Yet even though he was once known in this territory, Harold's reason for choosing the Welsh borderlands as the place to live out the rest of his life is that this region offers him the ability to hide in plain sight.[18] Harold 'Sciebat Wallenses: ignotos habere suspicacioni; in religione probatos veneracioni; ideoque illorum aspernari contubernia; istorum admirari' (knew that the Welsh held the unknown in suspicion, but those who were approved in religion in veneration, and that therefore they despised the companionship of the one, and admired that of the other).[19] Because he knows that the borderlands will afford him the ability to do so, after his arrival he disguises himself: 'Qui enim nominis appellacione universis cicatricum vero suarum inspeccione quibusdam innotuerat: vultum simul et vocabulum occultabat' (he, indeed, disguised both his face and his name, because his name was known to all, and his face to many).[20] Throughout the *Vita*, the borderlands are unquestionably a region where one can live in hiding under a different identity.

Harold's decision to live in the Welsh borderlands reflects the continued perspective that this region was a space where Anglo-Saxons and Welsh remained living together after the arrival of the Normans in Britain. As an interesting side note, this legend of Harold's survival raises the question of whether or not it was assumed that he would have known how to speak Welsh, in order to carry out his disguise as a religious hermit in this territory. Llinos Beverley Smith has observed, for example, that 'in the late fourteenth century the parishioners of the parish of Garway [in Herefordshire, a mile from the Welsh border] maintained that their parish priest was unable adequately to minister to their needs "for he knew no Welsh and many of them had no knowledge of English"'.[21] For Harold to interact with the Welsh as an acceptable religious figure and not a stranger to be distrusted, would he have needed the ability to preach to them in their own language? What does this tell us about the types of communities that were imagined to be in the Welsh borderlands in the late eleventh century? Yet regardless of whether or not the legend of the *Vita Haroldi* assumes Harold to be conversant in Welsh, this text depicts the borderlands as a place where Harold can be anonymous. At the same time, his presence there after the Norman Conquest means that it is still a region where identities mix, and English and Welsh come together.

In its hagiographical emphasis on the penance Harold suffers among the Welsh, the *Vita* glosses over some curious implications raised by its narrative. There is, first of all, an unquestioned assumption that anonymity goes unchallenged in the borderlands. Despite the stated mistrust of the Welsh toward strangers, no one appears to challenge Harold to give his real name or identity. Moreover, Harold is in actuality not really anonymous. Rather, he actively signals the fact that he is hiding something about himself. He does not alter his name or appearance, but instead adopts the obvious pseudonym of 'Christian' and wears a veil that calls attention to its role as a disguise. As a point of contrast, in the roughly contemporary *Gesta Herewardi*, when the outlaw Hereward wants to sneak into the camp of the Normans who are besieging him at Ely, he changes his clothes, cuts his hair and beard, disguises himself as a potter, and pretends he is a peasant who can't understand French.[22] Harold's 'disguise', on the other hand, only calls further attention to the fact that he has something to hide.

So too does his refusal to fully distance himself from his prior identity. While in Chester, at the very end of his life, 'Ibidem quoque manes a visitantibus se; et que edificacionis erant ab eo reportantibus; frequenter requisitus an bello ubi rex Haroldus occubuisse ferebatur interfuisset: respondebat; "Interfui plane"' (as he abode there, when he was frequently asked by those who came to visit him, and who reported what edification they gained from him, whether he was present at the war when King Harold was said to have been killed, he replied, 'I was certainly there').[23] His response to further questions about his true identity is even more coy: 'Suspicantibus vero nonnullis ne forte ipse esset Haroldus: et curiosius quoat licuit inde sciscitantibus aliquociens ita de se loquebatur; "Quando apud Hastingas dimicatum est: nullus Haroldo me carior habebatur"' (to some who suspected that perhaps he might be Harold himself, and who questioned him more closely than was right, he would sometimes thus speak of himself, 'When the Battle of Hastings was fought, there was no one more dear to Harold than myself').[24] In his responses, Harold chooses to cultivate deliberate ambiguity instead of active denial. Yet no one he meets during his years in the borderlands appears concerned with his elliptical answers. Existing in open hiding appears unremarkable to those who inhabit this region, reflecting its reputation as a place of multiple identities.

Harold chooses to live among the Welsh as a form of penance for the earlier portion of his life. The *Vita* records that 'Paciendi namque fervens amore quasi parum reputans quicquid ipse sibi carnifex asperitatis intulisset corpori et inedie effere gentis libenter adivit contubernium; a qua etsi quominus crucifigendum, variis tamen modis se noverat affligendum'

Conclusion: Harold, the last Anglo-Saxon

(burning with a love of suffering, as if he thought of too little account all the hardship and fastings he brought on his own body, himself his own torturer, he chose to enter into companionship with a wild race, at whose hands he knew he should be subjected to many afflictions, if not indeed crucifixion itself).[25] His torments are many, and the *Vita Haroldi* does not cast the Welsh in a positive light:

> Nec secus quam sperabat et optabat: ab infidis ferinisque homunculis pertulit; verberibus namque sevissimis a latrunculis eorum sepius vehementer attritus quibus etiam possent dampnis afficiebatur. Fraudabant eum viatico; veste spoliabant utque peccunias quas non habebat exhiberet nimiis et exquisitis eum cruciatibus et iniuriis contorquebant.
>
> (He suffered, in truth, from these treacherous, savage, and despicable men, only what he looked for and expected, for he was often violently beaten with very cruel stripes at the hands of robbers, from whom also he suffered every possible injury. They pilfered his provisions, and robbed him of his clothes; and to induce him to bring forth money, of which he had none, they tortured him with excessive and exquisite torments and ill-treatment.)[26]

These descriptions of Harold's many torments reflect the same pattern articulated in Chapter Six, in which the wildness and lawlessness of the borderlands became shifted, at the end of the eleventh century, to the Welsh alone. For Harold, after the arrival of the Normans in Britain, the Welsh are the embodiment of violence and danger in this region. Yet despite the fact that, in the legend of the *Vita Haroldi*, the Welsh are depicted as a people so violent that living among them can serve as a fitting penance for Harold, his extended presence in the Welsh borderlands in the final years of his life reveals that, even after the changes brought about by the Battle of Hastings, this territory was still viewed as a region of mixed identities where English and Welsh lived together.

The *Vita Haroldi*, by its author's own account, was written at least 140 years after the events of the Norman Conquest.[27] Yet the trauma of this period does not appear to have been forgotten by the *Vita*'s author and many others in England. The *Vita* contains numerous references to eyewitness accounts, stories told to men still living, and oral narratives passed down through generations that together reflect the continued impact of the Norman presence in England, as does its core longing for the myth of English survival. Harold is the last Anglo-Saxon in Anglo-Norman England; in his *Vita*, the Welsh borderlands are the last place where this English identity can survive. Yet at the same time, the *Vita Haroldi* depicts something more complicated than English identity alone having survived the Norman Conquest. The Welsh borderlands persisted as a cultural nexus where Anglo-Saxons and Welsh came together even when the Norman Conquest had eradicated so much else of Anglo-Saxon culture in the decades after 1066.

A strong anti-Norman rhetoric runs throughout the *Vita Haroldi*. The text makes its sympathies clear from its opening sentences, beginning with a strong defence of Harold's legitimacy to the throne, that 'Illustrissimi vere quia regis legitimi Haroldi iam rite ac legitime coronati gesta recensere, nichil aliud est quam divine serenitatis simul et clemencie quasi speculum quoddam lucidissimum piis mentibus exhibere' (to review the actions of the most illustrious and rightfully appointed King Harold, at this time duly and lawfully crowned, is nothing else than to display to pious minds a most brilliant reflection of a divine serenity and meekness).[28] Throughout the *Vita*, its author takes pains to defend Harold against his critics while criticising the oppressiveness of Norman rule. For example, by the time that Harold has recovered from his wounds at the Battle of Hastings, 'Iam victoris sui iugo regni tocius nobilitas vulgusque colla submiserant; iam proceres pene cuncti aut perempti aut patria pulsi; avitos honores alienigenis parciendos ac possidendos dimiserant' (already had the nobles of his kingdom, as well as the people, bowed their necks to the yoke of the conqueror; already had nearly all his chiefs either perished or been driven from the country, leaving their ancestral honours to be divided and possessed by strangers).[29]

The *Vita Haroldi* likewise takes every opportunity to underscore the continued opposition of the English to Norman rule. Its author describes how the English cried out, as one people, 'Absit inquiunt absit ut serviamus Normannis! Absit ut fastus Normanici iugo barbarico; nobilitatis Anglice urbana libertas nullatenus substernatur!' (Heaven forbid, say they, that we should serve the Normans! Heaven forbid that the liberty of our city and of our English nobility should ever be subservient to the barbarian yoke of Norman pride!).[30] Even 140 years after the Battle of Hastings when the *Vita Haroldi* was written, and up to another century after that when it was recopied and preserved at Waltham, the consequences of the Conquest seem to have still been quite bitterly felt.

The *Vita Haroldi* makes clear that the impact of the Norman presence in England was not just a physical one, but that it was also felt to have to have affected the written records of the period at some fundamental level. For the author of the *Vita Haroldi*, making claims for truth that he felt were maligned at every turn, the Norman impact was still perceptible in the competing traditions about Harold's right to the throne, the events of his

Conclusion: Harold, the last Anglo-Saxon

death and, in turn, the narrative of English history itself. The author of the *Vita* directly addresses the contradictory stories about Harold's death and the difficulties of arguing for the truth of his account. He writes,

> Interim vero lectori nostro humiliter suggerendum existimo ne ista uteque a nostra pravitate digesta ducat spernenda; quia aliter atque aliter plerosque forsan meminit de hac ipsa; et dixisse et scripsisse materia. Manifestum enim est quia non solum plebei relatores immo et illustrissimi rethores non modo diversa sed penitus contraria senserunt; et scripserunt super hiis que facta seu fata Haroldi contingunt.

> (Meanwhile, I think I ought in all humility to suggest to the reader that he should not think he ought to despise our history from its evident insignificance, because, perchance, he remembers that many persons have spoken and written on this same subject in one place or another; for it is plain that not only ordinary historians, but also most renowned orators, have thought and written not only differently, but quite the opposite to each other concerning the words of Harold.)[31]

This plea for the truth of his own account ends with the remarkably personal statement that 'non quidem de omnibus dico dabit Dominus simpliciter gradienti intelligere que scribo; sentire que sencio' (I do not speak of all these things; but the Lord will give to him who walks in simplicity the power to understand what I write, to think what I think).[32] For this author, the Norman presence in England had not only immediate political consequences, but also long-term historical ones. The fallout from the Battle of Hastings created a loss of control over the narrative of England's history.

The lingering impact of this loss makes the location of Harold's final years even more remarkable. The *Vita Haroldi* is a transitional text which follows the last Anglo-Saxon into an Anglo-Norman world. At its heart stands a longing for the myth of English survival. Its narrative casts the Welsh borderlands as the last place where this English identity can persist. Yet what survives, in this text, is something more than English identity alone. The Welsh borderlands endure, and their depiction in the *Vita Haroldi* is a microcosm of how this region has been portrayed throughout this book in texts from the Anglo-Saxon period. The Welsh borderlands are a cultural nexus where two peoples, Welsh and Anglo-Saxon, come together. In the *Vita Haroldi*, this region also stands at the intersection of Anglo-Saxon and Anglo-Norman England. Several generations after Hastings, the *Vita Haroldi* illustrates a sense of loss that the English now shared with the Welsh and it shows the continuing impact of the Norman Conquest. In a region where Welsh and Anglo-Saxons had lived in close proximity for hundreds of years, their shared culture had been destroyed by the hostility of the Normans towards the Welsh.

The Welsh borderlands in the *Vita Haroldi* serve as the last refuge of a past identity, a place where the last Anglo-Saxon king can hide in plain sight. The preservation of Englishness in this region of cultural nexus over a century after the Battle of Hastings reflects the strength of the society that flourished there for so many centuries. After the arrival of the Normans had altered so much in England, the Welsh borderlands remained as a last embodiment of Anglo-Saxon England. The region reflected Britain as it had been, a space where two peoples came together.

Notes

1 Stephen Matthews, 'The content and construction of the *Vita Haroldi*', in *King Harold II and the Bayeux Tapestry*, ed. Gale R. Owen-Crocker, Publications of the Manchester Centre for Anglo-Saxon Studies 3 (Woodbridge, Suffolk: Boydell, 2005), 65–73 at 65.
2 For later cultural representations of the March of Wales see e.g. Ralph Hanna, 'The matter of Fulk: romance and history in the Marches', *Journal of English and Germanic Philology* (2011): 337–58; Frederick C. Suppe, 'The cultural significance of decapitation in high medieval Wales and the Marches', *Bulletin of the Board of Celtic Studies* 36 (1989): 147–60; Rees Davies, *The Revolt of Owain Glyn Dŵr* (Oxford: Oxford University Press, 1995); and Ordelle G. Hill, *Looking Westward: Poetry, Landscape, and Politics in 'Sir Gawain and the Green Knight'* (Newark: University of Delaware Press, 2009).
3 The other items are an account of the discovery of the Holy Cross, a list of relics donated by Harold, and accounts of miracles performed before the shrine of the Cross (all in Latin); Michael Swanton, trans. and intro., *Three Lives of the Last Englishmen*, Garland Library of Medieval Literature 10 (New York: Garland, 1984), p. xxv. The *Vita Haroldi* is excerpted in Francisque Michel, *Chroniques Anglo-Normandes*, 3 vols. (Rouen: Edouard Frère, 1836–40); the most recent edition is that of Walter de Gray Birch, *Vita Haroldi: The Romance of the Life of Harold, King of England* (London: Elliot Stock, 1885), from which all quotations and translations are taken, cited by page number (translations slightly modernised).
4 Swanton, *Three Lives*, p. xxvi.
5 Matthews, 'Content and construction', 73.
6 Laura Ashe, 'Harold Godwinson', in *Heroes and Anti-Heroes in Medieval Romance*, ed. Neil Cartlidge (Cambridge: D.S. Brewer, 2012), 59–80 at 73.
7 See Gillian Fellows-Jensen, 'The myth of Harold II's survival in the Scandinavian sources', in *King Harold II and the Bayeux Tapestry*, 53–64, and Christine Fell,

'English history and Norman legend in the Icelandic saga of Edward the Confessor', *Anglo-Saxon England* 6 (1977): 223–36.
8   Ashe, 'Harold Godwinson', 76.
9   See Marc Cohen, 'From Throndheim to Waltham to Chester: Viking and post-Viking attitudes in the survival legends of Olaf Tryggvason and Harold Godwinson', in *The Middle Ages in the North-West*, ed. Tom Scott and Pat Starkey (Oxford: Leopard's Head Press, 1995), 143–53.
10 Ashe, 'Harold Godwinson', 75.
11 For background to the Norman Conquest, see N. J. Higham, *The Death of Anglo-Saxon England* (Stroud: Sutton, 1997).
12 de Gray Birch, *Vita Haroldi*, ch. II, 17 and 117.
13 See Alan Thacker, 'The cult of King Harold at Chester', in *Middle Ages in the North-West*, ed. Scott and Starkie, 155–76. Ashe, 'Harold Godwinson', 74, notes: 'medieval Chester was regarded by its own chroniclers as a land apart, neither English nor Welsh; it had probably been Harold's base for his greatest victories in the region; it rebelled in 1069–70 and suffered punitive destruction as a consequence; and its twelfth-century earls asserted their independence from the king at every opportunity'.
14 de Gray Birch, *Vita Haroldi*, ch. XIV, 71 and 174.
15 *Ibid.*, ch. XIV, 71 and 174.
16 *Ibid.*, ch. XIV, 71 and 174.
17 *Ibid.*, ch. XIV, 71 and 174–5.
18 The very intriguing idea that Harold is disguising himself as a leper has been suggested to me by Andrew Rabin, Paul Russell and Elaine Treharne. While veils in particular do not seem to have been required dress for lepers in medieval England and there was 'no special "uniform" or distinctive item of clothing designed to set lepers in general apart from healthy members of the English public', most lepers who lived in leper hospitals appear to have worn a *de facto* uniform of cloaks with large hoods designed to cover the mouth and prevent contagion through breath, which Harold's disguise is certainly aligned with; Carole Rawcliffe, *Leprosy in Medieval England* (Woodbridge, Suffolk: Boydell, 2006), 265, and see further Saul Nathaniel Brody, *The Disease of the Soul: Leprosy in Medieval Literature* (Ithaca NY: Cornell University Press, 1974).
19 de Gray Birch, *Vita Haroldi*, ch. XX, 91–2 and 196.
20 *Ibid.*, ch. XIV, 72 and 175.
21 Llinos Beverley Smith, 'The Welsh and English languages in late-medieval Wales', in *Multilingualism in Later Medieval Britain*, ed. D. A. Trotter (Cambridge: D.S. Brewer, 2000), 7–21 at 12.
22 For text, see Gesta Herwardi incliti exulis et militis, in *Lestoire des Engles solum la translacion maistre Geffrei Gaimar*, ed. T. D. Hardy and C. T. Martin, 2 vols., Rolls Series (London: Longmans, 1888), vol. II, 339–404; for translation, see Swanton, *Three Lives*, 45–88.
23 de Gray Birch, *Vita Haroldi*, ch. XV, 78 and 181.

24 *Ibid.*, ch. XV, 78 and 181; cf. the 'leper at the ford' scene of the Tristan and Isolde cycle for this motif.
25 *Ibid.*, ch. XIV, 73 and 176–7.
26 *Ibid.*, ch. XIV, 73–4 and 177.
27 *Ibid.*, ch. IX, 51 and 152.
28 *Ibid.*, ch. I, 12 and 112.
29 *Ibid.*, ch. V, 35 and 136.
30 *Ibid.*, ch. X, 54 and 155.
31 *Ibid.*, ch. XVI, 79 and 183.
32 *Ibid.*, ch. XVI, 81 and 186.

Bibliography

Primary sources

Abbo of Fleury, *Passio Sancti Eadmundi*, ed. Michael Winterbottom, *Three Lives of English Saints*. Toronto: PIMS, 1972.

Ancient Laws and Institutes of Wales, ed. and trans. Aneurin Owen. London: Public Records Commissioners, 1841.

The Anglo-Saxon Chronicle, trans. Michael Swanton. New York: Routledge, 1998.

The Anglo-Saxon Chronicle: A Collaborative Edition, gen. eds David N. Dumville and Simon Keynes. Cambridge: D.S. Brewer, 1983–.

The Anglo-Saxon Chronicle: A Collaborative Edition, Volume 3, MS A, ed. Janet M. Bately. Cambridge: D.S. Brewer, 1986.

The Anglo-Saxon Chronicle: A Collaborative Edition, Volume 4: MS B, ed. Simon Taylor. Cambridge: D.S. Brewer, 1983.

The Anglo-Saxon Chronicle: A Collaborative Edition, Volume 5: MS C, ed. Katherine O'Brien O'Keeffe. Cambridge: D.S. Brewer, 2001.

The Anglo-Saxon Chronicle: A Collaborative Edition, Volume 6: MS D, ed. G.P. Cubbin. Cambridge: D.S. Brewer, 1996.

The Anglo-Saxon Chronicle: A Collaborative Edition, Volume 7: MS E, ed. Susan Irvine. Cambridge: D.S. Brewer, 2004.

The Anglo-Saxon Chronicle: A Collaborative Edition, Volume 8: MS F, ed. Peter S. Baker. Cambridge: D.S. Brewer, 2000.

The Anglo-Saxon Chronicle: A Collaborative Edition, Volume 10: The Abingdon Chronicle, AC 956–1066 (MS C, with Reference to BDE), ed. Patrick W. Conner. Cambridge: D.S. Brewer, 1996.

Annales Cambriae, A.D. 682–954: Texts A–C in Parallel, ed. and trans. David N. Dumville. Cambridge: Department of Anglo-Saxon, Norse and Celtic, 2002.

Annales Cambriae, ed. J. Williams ab Ithel. Rolls Series. London: Longman, Green, Longman and Roberts, 1860.

'The *Annales Cambriae* and the Old Welsh Genealogies from Harleian MS. 3859', E. Phillimore. *Y Cymmrodor* 9 (1888): 141–83.

Bibliography

'The Annals of Tigernach: The Third Fragment, A.D. 489–766', ed. and trans. Whitley Stokes, *Revue Celtique* 17 (1896): 119–263.

'The Annals of Tigernach: The Fourth Fragment, A.D. 973–1088', ed. and trans. Whitley Stokes, *Revue Celtique* 17 (1896): 337–420.

Armes Prydein: The Prophecy of Britain, ed. Sir Ifor Williams with English trans. by Rachel Bromwich. Mediaeval and Modern Welsh Series, vol. 6. Dublin: Dublin Institute for Advanced Studies, School of Celtic Studies, 2006.

Alfred the Great: Asser's Life of King Alfred and Other Contemporary Sources, trans. Simon Keynes and Michael Lapidge. London: Penguin, 1983.

Asser's Life of King Alfred, Together with the Annals of Saint Neots, ed. William Henry Stevenson. Oxford: Clarendon Press, 1959.

Bartrum, Peter. *Early Welsh Genealogical Tracts*. Cardiff: University of Wales Press, 1966.

Beda: Storia Degli Inglesi (Historia ecclesiastica gentis Anglorum), ed. Michael Lapidge with Italian trans. by Paolo Chiesa. 2 vols: vol. I (books I–II) and vol. II (books III–V). Milan: Fondazione Lorenzo Valla, 2008 and 2010.

Bede's Ecclesiastical History of the English People, ed. and trans. Bertram Colgrave and R.A.B. Mynors. Oxford: Clarendon Press, 1969; repr. 2007.

Brenhinedd y Saeson or The Kings of the Saxons, ed. and trans. Thomas Jones. Cardiff: University of Wales Press, 1971.

Brut y Tywysogyon, Peniarth MS 20, ed. Thomas Jones. Cardiff: University of Wales Press, 1941.

Brut y Tywysogyon, or, The Chronicle of the Princes: Peniarth MS 20 Version, trans. Thomas Jones. Board of Celtic Studies, University of Wales, History and Law Series 11. Cardiff: University of Wales Press, 1952.

Brut y Tywysogyon or The Chronicle of the Princes, Red Book of Hergest Version, ed. and trans. Thomas Jones. Cardiff: University of Wales Press, 1955.

Cockayne, T.O. *Leechdoms, Wortcunning and Starcraft of Early England*. Rolls Series 35, 3 vols. London: Longmans, 1864–6; repr. Wiesbaden: Kraus, 1965.

Codex Exoniensis: A Collection of Anglo-Saxon Poetry, ed. Benjamin Thorpe. London: Society of Antiquaries of London, 1842.

Cyfrethiau Hywel Dda yn ôl Llawysgrif Coleg yr Iesu LVII Rhydychen, ed. Melville Richards. 2nd edn. Cardiff: University of Wales Press, 1990.

Eadmeri Historia Novorum in Anglia, ed. Martin Rule. Rolls Series 81. London: Longman, 1884.

Eadmer's History of Recent Events in England, trans. Geoffrey Bosanquet. London: Cresset Press, 1964.

The Exeter Anthology of Old English Poetry: An Edition of Exeter Dean and Chapter MS 3501, ed. Bernard J. Muir. 2 vols. Exeter Medieval English Texts and Studies. Exeter: University of Exeter Press, 1994.

The Exeter Book, ed. Elliot Van Kirk Dobbie and George Phillip Krapp. Anglo-Saxon Poetic Records 3. New York: Columbia University Press, 1936.

Felix's Life of Saint Guthlac, ed. and trans. Bertram Colgrave. Cambridge: Cambridge University Press, 1956; repr. 1985.

Geffrei Gaimar, *L'Estoire des Engleis*, ed. A. Bell. Anglo-Norman Text Society xiv–xvi. Oxford: Basil Blackwell, 1960.

Geoffrey of Monmouth. *The History of the Kings of Britain: An Edition and Translation of De gestis Britonum (Historia Regum Britanniae)*, ed. Michael D. Reeve and trans. Neil Wright. Arthurian Studies LXIX. Woodbridge, Suffolk: Boydell, 2007.

The Old English Riddles of the Exeter Book, ed. Craig Williamson. Chapel Hill NC: University of North Carolina Press, 1977.

Giraldi Cambrensis opera, Vol. VI, Itinerarium Kambriae et Descriptio Kambriae, ed. James F. Dimock. Rolls Series. London: Longmans, 1868.

Gerald of Wales: The Journey through Wales and the Description of Wales, trans. Lewis Thorpe. New York: Penguin, 1978.

Gesta Herwardi incliti exulis et militis, in *Lestoire des Engles solum la translacion maistre Geffrei Gaimar*, ed. T.D. Hardy and C.T. Martin. 2 vols. Rolls Series. London: Longmans, 1888.

Gildas: The Ruin of Britain and Other Works, ed. and trans. Michael Winterbottom. Arthurian Period Sources 7. Chichester: Phillimore, 1978.

Gruffydd, R. Geraint. 'Canu Cadwallon ap Cadfan', in *Astudiaethau ar yr Hengerdd*, ed. Rachel Bromwich and R. Brinley Jones. Cardiff: University of Wales Press, 1978, pp. 25–43.

Gruffydd, R. Geraint. 'Marwnad Cynddylan', in *Bardos: Penodau ar y Traddodiad Barddol Cymreig a Cheltaidd*, ed. R. Geraint Gruffydd. Caerdydd: Gwasg Prifysgol Cymru, 1982.

The Guthlac Poems of the Exeter Book. ed. Jane Roberts. Oxford: Oxford University Press, 1979.

Gwaith Cynddelw Brydydd Mawr, vol. I, ed. N.A. Jones and A.P. Owen. Cardiff: University of Wales Press, 1991.

Hessels, J.H. *A Late Eighth-Century Latin–Anglo-Saxon Glossary (Leiden MS. Voss. Qo Lat. No. 69)*. Cambridge: Cambridge University Press, 1906.

Historia Ecclesie Abbendonensis: The History of the Church of Abingdon, ed. and trans. John Hudson. Oxford Medieval Texts. 2 vols. Oxford: Clarendon Press, 2007 and 2002.

Hugh Candidus, *The Chronicle of Hugh Candidus, A Monk of Peterborough*, ed. W.T. Mellows. Oxford: Oxford University Press, 1949.

Isaac, Graham R. 'Trawsganu Kynan Garwyn mab Brochuael: a Tenth-Century Political Poem', *Zeitschrift für celtische Philologie* 51 (1999): 173–85.

James, Christine. *Machlud Cyfraith Hywel: golygiad o BL Add. 22356*. Cambridge: Seminar Cyfraith Hywel, 2013. Hosted online by the University of Wales at www.cyfraith-hywel.org.uk/en/machlud-cyf-hyw.php, accessed 22 March 2016.

John of Worcester, *The Chronicle of John of Worcester, Volume II: The Annals from 450 to 1066*, ed. R.R. Darlington and P. McGurk, and trans. Jennifer Bray and P. McGurk. Oxford: Clarendon Press, 1995.

John of Worcester, *The Chronicle of John of Worcester, Volume III: The Annals from 1067* to 1140 with the Gloucester Interpolations and the Continuation to 1141, ed. and trans. P. McGurk. Oxford: Clarendon Press, 1998.

Koch, John T. *Cunedda, Cynan, Cadwallon, Cynddylan: Four Welsh Poems and Britain 383–655*. Aberystwyth: University of Wales Centre for Advanced Welsh and Celtic Studies, 2013.

Lapidge, Michael. *The Cult of St Swithun*. Winchester Studies 4.11. Oxford: Clarendon Press, 2003.

Liebermann, Felix. *Die Gesetze der Angelsachsen*. 3 vols. Halle: Niemeyer, 1903–16.

Meritt, H.D. *Old English Glosses: A Collection*. MLA General Series 16. New York: MLA, 1945.

Michel, Francisque. *Chroniques Anglo-Normandes*. 3 vols. Rouen: Edouard Frère, 1836–40.

Nennius: British History and the Welsh Annals, ed. and trans. John Morris. London: Phillimore, 1980.

Orderic Vitalis, *The Ecclesiastical History of Orderic Vitalis*, ed. and trans. Marjorie Chibnall. 6 vols. Oxford: Clarendon Press, 1969–80.

The Paris Psalter and the Metres of Boethius, ed. George Phillip Krapp. Anglo-Saxon Poetic Records 5. New York: Columbia University Press, 1932.

PASE (Prosopography of Anglo-Saxon England) database: online at www.pase.ac.uk, accessed 22 March 2016.

Pheifer, J.D. *Old English Glosses in the Epinal–Erfurt Glossary*. Oxford: Clarendon Press, 1974.

Reginald of Durham, *Life of St Oswald*, ed. Thomas Arnold. *Symeonis Monachi Opera Omnia*, 2 vols., Rolls Series. London: Longman, 1885.

Rowland, Jenny. *Early Welsh Saga Poetry*. Cambridge: D.S. Brewer, 1990.

Stryker, W.G. 'The Latin–Old English Glossary in MS. Cotton Cleopatra A.III'. Unpublished doctoral dissertation. Stanford University, 1951.

Swanton, Michael, trans. *Three Lives of the Last Englishmen*. Garland Library of Medieval Literature 10. New York: Garland, 1984.

Taliesin, *The Poems of Taliesin*, ed. Ifor Williams and trans. J.E. Caerwyn Williams. Dublin: The Dublin Institute for Advanced Studies, 1968.

Thomas of Marlborough: History of the Abbey of Evesham, ed. and trans. Jane Sayers and Leslie Watkiss. Oxford Medieval Texts. Oxford: Clarendon Press, 2003.

Trioedd Ynys Prydein, ed. Rachel Bromwich. 3rd edn. Cardiff: University of Wales Press, 2006.

Vita Haroldi: The Romance of the Life of Harold, King of England, ed. and trans. Walter de Gray Birch. London: Elliot Stock, 1885.

The Vita Wulfstani of William of Malmesbury, ed. R.R. Darlington. London: Royal Historical Society, 1928.

Wade-Evans, Arthur W., *Welsh Medieval Law*. Oxford: Clarendon Press, 1909; repr. Aalen: Scientia Verlag, 1979.

Bibliography

Walter Map, *De Nugis Curialium*, ed. and trans. M.R. James and revised by C.N.L. Brooke and R.A.B. Mynors. Oxford: Clarendon Press, 1983; repr. 2002.

William of Malmesbury, *Gesta Regum Anglorum: The History of the English Kings*, vol. I, ed. and trans. R.A.B. Mynors, completed by R.M. Thomson and M. Winterbottom. Oxford: Clarendon Press, 1998.

William of Malmesbury, *Gesta Regum Anglorum: The History of the English Kings*, vol. II, General Introduction and Commentary, by R.M. Thomson in collaboration with M. Winterbottom. Oxford: Clarendon Press, 1999.

William of Malmesbury's Life of St Wulfstan, Bishop of Worcester, trans. J.H.F. Peile. Oxford: Blackwell, 1934.

William of Poitiers, *The Gesta Guillelmi of William of Poitiers*, ed. and trans. R.H.C. Davis and Marjorie Chibnall. Oxford: Clarendon Press, 1998.

Williams, Ifor, *Canu Llywarch Hen*, 3ydd argrff. Caerdydd: Gwasg Prifysgol Cymru, 1970.

Williams, Ifor, 'Marwnad Cynddylan', *Bulletin of the Board of Celtic Studies* 6 (1932): 134–41.

Secondary sources

Abdou, Angela. 'Speech and Power in Old English Conversion Narratives', *Florilegium* 17 (2000): 195–212.

Abulafia, David and Nora Berend, eds, *Medieval Frontiers: Concepts and Practices*. Aldershot: Ashgate, 2002.

Abulafia, David. 'Introduction: Seven Types of Ambiguity, c. 1100–c. 1500', in *Medieval Frontiers: Concepts and Practices*, ed. David Abulafia and Nora Berend, Aldershot: Ashgate, 2002, pp. 1–34.

Alexander, Louis M. 'The Legal Status of the Native Britons in Late Seventh-Century Wessex as Reflected by the Law Code of Ine', *Haskins Society Journal* 7 (1995): 31–8.

Anzaldúa, Gloria. *Borderlands/La Frontera: The New Mestiza*. San Francisco: Aunt Lutte Books, 1987.

Ashe, Laura. 'Harold Godwinson', in *Heroes and Anti-Heroes in Medieval Romance*, ed. Neil Cartlidge. Cambridge: D.S. Brewer, 2012, pp. 59–80.

Banham, Debby. 'Anglo-Saxon Attitudes: In Search of the Origins of English Racism', *European Review of History* 1 (1994): 143–56.

Barrow, Geoffrey. 'Frontier and Settlement: Which Influenced Which? England and Scotland, 1100–1300', in *Medieval Frontier Societies*, ed. Robert Bartlett and Angus MacKay. Oxford: Clarendon Press, 1989, pp. 3–21.

Bartlett, Robert. *The Making of Europe: Conquest, Colonization and Cultural Change, 950–1350*. Princeton NJ: Princeton University Press, 1993.

Bartlett, Robert. 'Medieval and Modern Concepts of Race and Ethnicity', *Journal of Medieval and Early Modern Studies* 31 (2001): 39–56.

Bibliography

Bartlett, Robert and Angus MacKay, eds. *Medieval Frontier Societies*. Oxford: Clarendon Press, 1989.

Bassett, Steven. *The Wootton Wawen Project: Interim Report No. 4*. Birmingham: University of Birmingham School of History, 1986.

Bassett, Steven, ed. *The Origins of Anglo-Saxon Kingdoms*. London: Leicester University Press, 1989.

Bassett, Steven. 'How the West was Won: The Anglo-Saxon Takeover of the West Midlands', *Anglo-Saxon Studies in Archaeology and History* 11 (2000): 107–18.

Bately, Janet. *The Anglo-Saxon Chronicle: Texts and Textual Relationships*. Reading: Reading Medieval Studies Monograph, 1991.

Battles, Dominique. *Cultural Difference and Material Culture in Middle English Romance: Normans and Saxons*. Routledge Studies in Medieval Literature and Culture. New York: Routledge, 2013.

Baud, Michiel and Willem van Schendel, 'Toward a Comparative History of Borderlands', *Journal of World History* 8 (1997): 211–42.

Baum, P. 'Judas' Sunday Rest', *Modern Language Review* 18 (1923): 168–82.

Baxter, Stephen. 'MS C of the Anglo-Saxon Chronicle and the Politics of Mid-Eleventh-Century England', *English Historical Review* 122 (2007): 1189–1227.

Baxter, Stephen. *The Earls of Mercia: Lordship and Power in Late Anglo-Saxon England*. Oxford: Oxford University Press, 2007.

Bentham, James. *The History and Antiquities of the Conventual and Cathedral Church of Ely*. Cambridge: Cambridge University Press, 1771.

Berend, Nora. 'Preface', in *Medieval Frontiers: Concepts and Practices*, ed. David Abulafia and Nora Berend, Aldershot: Ashgate, 2002, pp. x–xv.

Bhabha, Homi K. *The Location of Culture*. London: Routledge, 1994.

Biggs, Frederick M. 'The Politics of Succession in *Beowulf* and Anglo-Saxon England', *Speculum* 80 (2005): 709–41.

Biggs, Frederick M. 'Edgar's Path to the Throne', in *Edgar, King of the English 959–975*, ed. Donald Scragg. Woodbridge, Suffolk: Boydell, 2008, pp. 124–39.

Bitterli, Dieter. *Say What I Am Called: The Old English Riddles of the Exeter Book and the Anglo-Latin Riddle Tradition*. Toronto Anglo-Saxon Series 2. Toronto: University of Toronto Press, 2009.

Blair, John, ed. *Waterways and Canal-Building in Medieval England*. Oxford: Oxford University Press, 2007.

Bolton, Whitney French. 'The Middle English and Latin Poems of Saint Guthlac'. Unpublished doctoral dissertation. Princeton University, 1954.

Bredehoft, Thomas. *Textual Histories: Readings in the Anglo-Saxon Chronicle*. Toronto: University of Toronto Press, 2001.

Brett, Martin and David A. Woodman, eds. *The Long Twelfth Century View of the Anglo-Saxon Past*. Surrey: Ashgate, 2015.

Brody, Saul Nathaniel. *The Disease of the Soul: Leprosy in Medieval Literature*. Ithaca NY: Cornell University Press, 1974.

Bromberg, Eric I. 'Wales and the Mediaeval Slave Trade', *Speculum* 17 (1942): 263–9.

Bibliography

Bromwich, Rachel and R. Brinley Jones, eds. *Astudiaethau ar yr Hengeredd*. Cardiff: University of Wales Press, 1978.

Brooke, Stopford A. *The History of Early English Literature*. New York: Macmillan, 1892.

Brooks, Nicholas. 'The Formation of the Mercian Kingdom', in *The Origins of Anglo-Saxon Kingdoms*, ed. Steven Bassett. London: Leicester University Press, 1989, pp. 159–70.

Brooks, Nicholas. 'English Identity from Bede to the Millenium', The Henry Loyn Memorial Lecture, *Haskins Society Journal* 14 (2005): 33–51.

Brown, Michael. 'Lords and Communities: Political Society in the Thirteenth Century', in James Muldoon, ed., *The North Atlantic Frontier of Medieval Europe*. Surrey: Ashgate, 2009, pp. 123–47.

Brown, Michelle P. and Carol A. Farr, eds. *Mercia: An Anglo-Saxon Kingdom in Europe*. Studies in the Early History of Europe. London: Continuum, 2001.

Brown, R. Allen. *The Normans and the Norman Conquest*. Woodbridge, Suffolk: Boydell, 1968; repr. 2000.

Calder, Daniel G. '*Guthlac A* and *Guthlac B*: Some Discriminations', in *Anglo-Saxon Poetry: Essays in Appreciation for John C. McGalliard*, ed. Lewis E. Nicholson and Dolores W. Freese. Notre Dame IN: Notre Dame University Press, 1975, pp. 65–80.

Cameron, Angus, Ashley Crandell Amos, Antonette diPaolo Healey et al., *Dictionary of Old English: A to G Online* (Toronto, 1986–), online at www.doe.utoronto.ca/, accessed 22 March 2016.

Campbell, James. 'The Late Anglo-Saxon State: A Maximum View', *Proceedings of the British Academy* 87 (1994): 39–65.

Campbell, James. *The Anglo-Saxon State*. London: Hambledon, 2000.

Carr, A.D. *Medieval Anglesey*. Llangefni: Anglesey Antiquarian Society, 1982.

Chadwick, H.M. and Nora K. Chadwick, *The Growth of Literature*. Cambridge: Cambridge University Press, 1932.

Chadwick, Nora K., ed. *Celt and Saxon: Studies in the Early British Border*. Cambridge: Cambridge University Press, 1963.

Chadwick, Nora K. 'The Conversion of Northumbria: A Comparison of Sources', in *Celt and Saxon: Studies in the Early British Border*, ed. Nora K. Chadwick. Cambridge: Cambridge University Press, 1963, pp. 138–66.

Chaney, William A. *The Cult of Kingship in Anglo-Saxon England: The Transition from Paganism to Christianity*. Manchester: Manchester University Press, 1970.

Charles, B.G. *Old Norse Relations With Wales*. Cardiff: University of Wales Press, 1934.

Charles-Edwards, T.M. *The Welsh Laws*. Writers of Wales Series. Cardiff: University of Wales Press, 1989.

Charles-Edwards, T.M. 'The Arthur of History', in *The Arthur of the Welsh*, ed. Rachel Bromwich, A.O.H. Jarman and Brynley F. Roberts. Cardiff: University of Wales Press, 1991, pp. 15–32.

Charles-Edwards, T.M. *Early Irish and Welsh Kinship*. Oxford: Clarendon Press, 1993.

Charles-Edwards, T.M. 'Language and Society among the Insular Celts, AD 400–1000', in *The Celtic World*, ed. M.J. Green. London: Routledge, 1995, pp. 711–13.

Charles-Edwards, T.M. 'Anglo-Saxon Kinship Revisited', in *The Anglo-Saxons from the Migration Period to the Eighth Century*, ed. John Hines. Woodbridge, Suffolk: Boydell, 1997, pp. 171–204.

Charles-Edwards, T.M. 'Wales and Mercia, 613–918', in *Mercia: An Anglo-Saxon Kingdom in Europe*, ed. Michelle P. Brown and Carol A. Farr. Studies in the Early History of Europe. London: Continuum, 2001, pp. 89–105.

Charles-Edwards, T.M. 'The Three Columns of Law: A Comparative Perspective', in T.M. Charles-Edwards and Paul Russell, eds. *Tair Colofn Cyfraith*. Bangor: Cymdeithas Hanes Cyfraith Cymru, 2005, pp. 26–59.

Charles-Edwards, T.M. *Wales and the Britons, 350–1064*. Oxford: Oxford University Press, 2013.

Charles-Edwards, T. M. and Paul Russell, 'The Hendregadredd Manuscript and the Orthography and Phonology of Welsh in the Early Fourteenth Century,' *National Library of Wales Journal* 28 (1993/4): 419–62.

Charles-Edwards, T.M. and Paul Russell, eds. *Tair Colofn Cyfraith: The Three Columns of Law in Medieval Wales: Homicide, Theft and Fire*. Cymdeithas Hanes Cyfraith Cymru 5. Bangor: Cymdeithas Hanes Cyfraith Cymru, 2005.

Cherniss, Michael D. *Ingeld and Christ: Heroic Concepts and Values in Old English Christian Poetry*. The Hague: Mouton, 1972.

Clark, Stephanie. 'A More Permanent Homeland: Land Tenure in *Guthlac A*', *Anglo-Saxon England* 40 (2011): 75–102.

Clarke, Catherine A.M. *Literary Landscapes and the Idea of England, 700–1400*. Cambridge: Boydell & Brewer, 2006.

Clarke, Catherine A.M. 'The Allegory of Landscape: Land Reclamation and Defence at Glastonbury Abbey', in *On Allegory: Some Medieval Aspects and Approaches from Chaucer to Shakespeare*, ed. M. Carr, K.P. Clarke and M. Nievergelt. Newcastle upon Tyne: Cambridge Scholars, 2008, pp. 87–103.

Cohen, Jeffrey Jerome, ed. *The Postcolonial Middle Ages*. New York: Palgrave Macmillan, 2000.

Cohen, Jeffrey Jerome. *Medieval Identity Machines*. Medieval Cultures 35. Minneapolis: University of Minnesota Press, 2003.

Cohen, Jeffrey Jerome. *Hybridity, Identity and Monstrosity in Medieval Britain*. New York: Palgrave Macmillan, 2006.

Cohen, Marc. 'From Throndheim to Waltham to Chester: Viking and post-Viking attitudes in the survival legends of Olaf Tryggvason and Harold Godwinson', in *The Middle Ages in the North West*, ed. Tom Scott and Pat Starkey. Oxford: Leopard's Head Press, 1995, pp. 143–53.

Colman, Fran. *The Grammar of Names in Anglo-Saxon England: The Linguistics and Culture of the Old English Onomasticon*. Oxford: Oxford University Press, 2014.

Bibliography

Conybeare, John William Edward. *A History of Cambridgeshire*. London: Elliot Stock, 1897.

Cornell, Cynthia Edelstein. 'Sources of the Old English Guthlac Poems'. Unpublished doctoral dissertation. University of Missouri-Columbia, 1976.

Crossley-Holland, Kevin, trans., *The Exeter Book Riddles*. Revised edition. Harmondsworth, Middlesex: Penguin Classics, 1993.

Curta, Florin, ed. *Borders, Barriers, and Ethnogenesis: Frontiers in Late Antiquity and the Middle Ages*. Turnhout: Brepols, 2005.

Curta, Florin. 'Introduction'. In *Borders, Barriers, and Ethnogenesis: Frontiers in Late Antiquity and the Middle Ages*, ed. Florin Curta. Turnhout: Brepols, 2005, pp. 1–9.

Darby, H.C. 'The Fenland Frontier in Anglo-Saxon England', *Antiquity* 8 (1934): 185–201.

Darby, H.C. 'The March of Wales in 1086', *Transactions of the Institute of British Geographers* 11 (1986): 259–78.

Davidson, Hilda Ellis. 'The Training of Warriors', in *Weapons and Warfare in Anglo-Saxon England*, ed. Sonia Chadwick Hawkes. Oxford: Oxford University Committee for Archaeology, 1989, pp. 11–23.

Davies, Michael and Sean. *The Last King of Wales: Gruffudd ap Llywelyn c. 1013–1063*. Stroud: History Press, 2012.

Davies, Rees. 'The Law of the March', *Welsh History Review* 5 (1970): 1–30.

Davies, Rees *Lordship and Society in the March of Wales, 1282–1400*. Oxford: Clarendon Press, 1978.

Davies, Rees 'The Status of Women and the Practice of Marriage in Late-Medieval Wales', in Dafydd Jenkins and Morfydd E. Owen, eds, *The Welsh Law of Women: Studies Presented to Professor Daniel A. Binchy on his Eightieth Birthday*. Cardiff: University of Wales Press, 1980, pp. 93–114.

Davies, Rees. 'Frontier Arrangements in Fragmented Societies: Ireland and Wales', in *Medieval Frontier Societies*, ed. Robert Bartlett and Angus MacKay. Oxford: Clarendon Press, 1989, pp. 77–100.

Davies, Rees. *Conquest, Coexistence, and Change: Wales, 1063–1415*. Oxford: Clarendon Press, 1987; repr. as *The Age of Conquest: Wales, 1063–1415*. Oxford: Oxford University Press 1991.

Davies, Rees *The Revolt of Owain Glyn Dŵr*. Oxford: Oxford University Press, 1995.

Davies, Wendy. 'Annals and the Origin of Mercia', in *Mercian Studies*, ed. Ann Dornier. Leicester: Leicester University Press, 1977, pp. 17–30.

Davies, Wendy. *Wales in the Early Middle Ages*. Studies in the Early History of Britain. Leicester: Leicester University Press, 1982.

Davies, Wendy. *Patterns of Power in Early Wales*. Oxford: Clarendon Press, 1990.

Davis, Kathleen. 'National Writing in the Ninth Century: A Reminder for Postcolonial Thinkers about the Nation', *Journal of Medieval and Early Modern Studies* 28 (1998): 611–37.

de Grazia, Margreta. 'The Modern Divide: From Either Side', *Journal of Medieval and Early Modern Studies* 37 (2007): 453–67.

Bibliography

D'Evelyn, Charlotte and Anna J. Mill, eds. *The South English Legendary*. 3 vols. EETS 235, 236 and 244. London: Oxford University Press, 1956–9.

Dietrich, F. 'Die Räthsel des Exeterbuchs. Würdigung, Lösung und Herstellung', *Zeitschrift für deutsches Altertum* 11 (1859): 448–90.

Dornier, Ann, ed. *Mercian Studies*. Leicester: Leicester University Press, 1977.

Duffy, Seán. 'Ostmen, Irish and Welsh in the Eleventh Century', *Peritia* 9 (1995): 379–96.

Dumville, David N. 'Some Aspects of the Chronology of the *Historia Brittonum*', *Bulletin of the Board of Celtic Studies* 25 (1972): 439–45.

Dumville, David N. '"Nennius" and the *Historia Brittonum*', *Studia Celtica* 10/11 (1975–6): 78–95.

Dumville, David N. 'Sub-Roman Britain: History and Legend', *History* 62 (1977): 173–92.

Dumville, David N. *The Historia Brittonum, Volume 3: The Vatican Recension*. Cambridge: D.S. Brewer, 1985.

Dumville, David N. 'The Historical Value of the *Historia Brittonum*', *Arthurian Literature* 6 (1986): 1–26.

Dumville, David N. *Wessex and England from Alfred to Edgar*. Woodbridge, Suffolk: Boydell, 1992.

Dyer, Christopher. *Everyday Life in Medieval England*. London: Continuum International, 1994; repr. 2000.

Edmonds, Fiona. 'Barrier or Unifying Feature? Defining the Nature of Early Medieval Water Transport in the North-West', in John Blair, ed., *Waterways and Canal-Building in Medieval England*. Oxford: Oxford University Press, 2007, pp. 21–36.

Etchingham, Colman. 'North Wales, Ireland and the Isles: The Insular Viking Zone', *Peritia* 15 (2001): 145–87.

Evans, Stephen S. *The Lords of Battle: Image and Reality of the* Comitatus *in Dark-Age Britain*. Woodbridge, Suffolk: Boydell, 1997.

Fanning, Steven. 'Bede, *Imperium*, and the Bretwaldas', *Speculum* 66 (1991): 1–26.

Faull, Margaret Lindsay. 'The Semantic Development of Old English *Wealh*', *Leeds Studies in English* NS 8 (1975): 20–44.

Fell, Christine. 'English history and Norman legend in the Icelandic saga of Edward the Confessor', *Anglo-Saxon England* 6 (1977): 223–36.

Fellows-Jensen, Gillian. 'The Myth of Harold II's Survival in the Scandinavian Sources', in *King Harold II and the Bayeux Tapestry*, ed. Gale R. Owen-Crocker. Manchester Centre for Anglo-Saxon Studies 3. Woodbridge, Suffolk: Boydell, 2005, pp. 53–64.

Finberg, H.P.R. *Lucerna: Studies of Some Problems in the Early History of England*. London: Macmillan, 1964.

Fisher, D.J.V. 'The Anti-Monastic Reaction in the Reign of Edward the Martyr', *Cambridge Historical Journal* 10 (1952): 254–70.

Foot, Sarah. 'The Making of *Angelcynn*: English Identity Before the Norman Conquest', *Transactions of the Royal Historical Society* 6 (1996): 25–49.

Foot, Sarah. *Æthelstan: The First King of England.* New Haven CT: Yale University Press, 2011.
Ford, W.J. 'Settlement Patterns in the Central Region of the Warwickshire Avon', in *Medieval Settlement, Continuity and Change,* ed. P.H. Sawyer. London: Edward Arnold, 1976, pp. 274–94.
Fordham, Michael. 'Peacekeeping and Order on the Anglo-Welsh Frontier in the Early Tenth Century', *Midland History* 32 (2007): 1–18.
Forstmann, Hans. *Untersuchungen Zur Guthlac-Legende.* Bonner Beiträge aur Anglistik 12 (1902): 1–40.
Fox, Sir Cyril. *Offa's Dyke.* London: British Academy, 1955.
Freeman, Edward Augustus. *The History of the Norman Conquest of England.* 6 vols. London: Macmillan, 1873–9.
Fulk, R.D. *A History of Old English Meter.* Philadelphia: University of Pennsylvania Press, 1992.
Gameson, Richard 'The Origin of the Exeter Book of Old English Poetry', *Anglo-Saxon England* 25 (1996): 135–85.
Gaunt, Simon. 'Can the Middle Ages be Postcolonial?' *Comparative Literature* 61 (2009): 160–76.
Gelling, Margaret. *The West Midlands in the Early Middle Ages.* Leicester: Leicester University Press, 1992.
Gillingham, John. *The English in the Twelfth Century: Imperialism, National Identity and Political Values.* Woodbridge, Suffolk: Boydell, 2000.
Gillingham, John. 'The Beginnings of English Imperialism', in James Muldoon, ed., *The North Atlantic Frontier of Medieval Europe.* Farnham: Ashgate, 2009, pp. 71–88.
Gneuss, Helmut. 'Guide to the Editing and Preparation of Texts for the *Dictionary of Old English*', in *The Editing of Old English: Papers from the 1990 Manchester Conference,* ed. Donald G. Scragg and Paul E. Szarmach. Cambridge: D.S. Brewer, 1994.
Goffart, Walter. *The Narrators of Barbarian History (A.D. 550–800): Jordanes, Gregory of Tours, Bede, and Paul the Deacon.* Princeton NJ: Princeton University Press, 1988.
Goodall, I.H. 'Locks and Keys', in *Object and Economy in Medieval Winchester,* ed. Martin Biddle Winchester Studies 7.ii. Oxford: Clarendon Press, 1990.
Goodman, Anthony. 'Religion and Warfare in the Anglo-Scottish Marches', in *Medieval Frontier Societies,* ed. Robert Bartlett and Angus MacKay. Oxford: Clarendon Press, 1989, pp. 245–66.
Gougaud, L. 'La croyance au répit périodique des damnés dans les légendes irlandaises', *Mélanges bretons et celtiques offerts á M. J. Loth,* ed. H. Champion. Paris: H. Champion, 1927, pp. 63–72.
Gransden, Antonia. *Historical Writing in England I: c. 550 to c. 1307.* New York: Routledge, 1974; repr. 1996, 2000.
Gray, Arthur. 'On the Late Survival of a Celtic Population in East Anglia', *Proceedings of the Cambridge Antiquarian Society* 15 (1911): 42–52.
Grein, C.W.M. 'Kleine Mittheilungen', *Germania* 10 (1865): 305–10.

Grein, C.W.M. *Sprachschatz der angelsächsischen Dichter*. In collaboration with F. Holthausen, revised by J.J. Köhler. Heidelberg: Carl Winter, 1912.

Grimmer, Martin. 'Britons in Early Wessex: The Evidence of the Law Code of Ine', in N.J. Higham, ed., *Britons in Anglo-Saxon England*. Manchester Centre for Anglo-Saxon Studies 7. Woodbridge, Suffolk: Boydell, 2007, pp. 102–14.

Groos, Arthur. 'The "Elder" Angel in *Guthlac A*', *Anglia* 101 (1983): 141–6.

Görlach, Manfred. *The Textual Tradition of the South English Legendary*. Leeds Texts and Monographs NS 6. Leeds: University of Leeds, 1974.

Hall, Alaric. 'Constructing Anglo-Saxon Sanctity: Tradition, Innovation and Saint Guthlac', in *Images of Sanctity: Essays in Honour of Gary Dickson*, ed. Debra Higgs Strickland. Visualising the Middle Ages 1. Leiden: Brill, 2007, pp. 207–35.

Hanna, Ralph. 'The Matter of Fulk: Romance and History in the Marches', *Journal of English and Germanic Philology* 110 (2011): 337–58.

Harris, Stephen J. *Race and Ethnicity in Anglo-Saxon Literature*. Studies in Medieval History and Culture 24. New York: Routledge, 2003.

Healey, Antonette diPaolo. *The Old English Vision of St. Paul*. Speculum Anniversary Monographs 2. Cambridge MA: Medieval Academy of America, 1978.

Healey, Antonette diPaolo. 'The Search for Meaning', in *The Editing of Old English: Papers from the 1990 Manchester Conference*, ed. Donald G. Scragg and Paul E. Szarmach. Cambridge: D.S. Brewer, 1994.

Henning, J. 'Gefangenenfesseln im slawischen Siedlungsraum und der europäische Sklavenhandel im 6. bis 12. Jahrhundert. Archäologisches zum Bedeutungswandel von "skālbos-sakliba-sclavus"', *Germania* 70.2 (1990): 403–26.

Herschend, Frands. *The Idea of the Good in Late Iron Age Society*. Occasional Papers in Archaeology 15. Uppsala: Department of Archaeology and Ancient History, 1998.

Higham, N.J. 'King Cearl, the Battle of Chester and the Origins of the Mercian "Overkingship"', *Midland History* 17 (1992): 1–15.

Higham, N.J. *The English Conquest: Gildas and Britain in the Fifth Century*. Manchester: Manchester University Press, 1994.

Higham, N.J. *The Convert Kings: Power and Religious Affiliation in Early Anglo-Saxon England*. Manchester: Manchester University Press, 1997.

Higham, N.J. *The Death of Anglo-Saxon England*. Stroud: Sutton, 1997.

Higham, N.J. *(Re-)Reading Bede: The Ecclesiastical History in Context*. New York: Routledge, 2006.

Higham, N.J. ed. *Britons in Anglo-Saxon England*. Manchester Centre for Anglo-Saxon Studies 7. Woodbridge, Suffolk: Boydell, 2007.

Hill, David. *An Atlas of Anglo-Saxon England*. Toronto: University of Toronto Press, 1981.

Hill, David. 'Mercians: The Dwellers on the Boundary', in *Mercia: An Anglo-Saxon Kingdom in Europe*, ed. Michelle P. Brown and Carol A. Farr. Studies in the Early History of Europe. London: Continuum, 2001, pp. 173–82.

Hill, David and Margaret Worthington. *Offa's Dyke: History and Guide*. Stroud: Tempus, 2003.

Hill, Ordelle G. *Looking Westward: Poetry, Landscape, and Politics in 'Sir Gawain and the Green Knight'*. Newark NJ: University of Delaware Press, 2009.

Hill, Thomas D. 'The Middle Way: *Idel-Wuldor* and *Egesa* in the Old English *Guthlac A*', *Review of English Studies* NS 30 (1979): 182–7.

Hill, Thomas D. '*Imago Dei*: Genre, Symbolism, and Anglo-Saxon Hagiography', in *Holy Men and Holy Women: Old English Prose Saints' Lives and Their Contexts*, ed. Paul E. Szarmach. Albany NY: SUNY Press, 1996, pp. 35–50.

Hilton, R.R. *A Medieval Society: The West Midlands at the End of the Thirteenth Century*. London: Weidenfeld & Nicholson, 1966.

Hines, John. *Voices in the Past: English Literature and Archaeology*. Cambridge: Boydell & Brewer, 2004.

Holden, Brock. *Lords of the Central Marches: English Aristocracy and Frontier Society, 1087–1265*. Oxford: Oxford University Press, 2008.

Holm, Poul. 'The Slave Trade of Dublin, Ninth to Twelfth Centuries', *Peritia* 5 (1986): 317–45.

Holthausen, F. 'Zur Textkritik altenglischer Dichtungen', *Englische Studien* 37 (1907): 198–211.

Holthausen, F. 'Zu altenglischen Denkmälern', *Englische Studien* 51 (1917): 180–8.

Home, Malasree. *The Peterborough Version of the Anglo-Saxon Chronicle: Rewriting Post-Conquest History*. Woodbridge, Suffolk: Boydell, 2015.

Hooke, Della. 'Reconstructing Anglo-Saxon Landscapes in Warwickshire'. *Transactions of the Birmingham and Warwickshire Archaeological Society* 100 (1996): 99–116.

Hooke, Della. *The Landscape of Anglo-Saxon England*. Leicester: Leicester University Press, 1998.

Hooke, Della. 'Mercia: Landscape and Environment', in *Mercia: An Anglo-Saxon Kingdom in Europe*, ed. Michelle P. Brown and Carol A. Farr. Studies in the Early History of Europe. London: Continuum, 2001, pp. 160–72.

Hooke, Della. 'Uses of Waterways in Anglo-Saxon England', in John Blair, ed., *Waterways and Canal-Building in Medieval England*. Oxford: Oxford University Press, 2007, pp. 37–54.

Horstmann, Carl. *The Early South-English Legendary, or Lives of Saints*. EETS OS 87. London: N. Trübner, 1887.

Hough, Carole. 'Cattle-Tracking in the Fonthill Letter', *English Historical Review* 115 (2000): 864–92.

Howe, Nicholas. *Writing the Map of Anglo-Saxon England: Essays in Cultural Geography*. New Haven CT: Yale University Press, 2008.

Hudson, John. *The Formation of the English Common Law: Law and Society in England from the Norman Conquest to Magna Carta*. New York: Longman Press, 1996.

Hughes, Kathleen. *Celtic Britain in the Early Middle Ages*. Woodbridge, Suffolk: Boydell, 1980.

Hughes, Kathleen. 'The A-text of *Annales Cambriae*' in her *Celtic Britain in the Early Middle Ages*. Woodbridge, Suffolk: Boydell, 1980.

Hughes, Kathleen. 'The Welsh Latin Chronicles: *Annales Cambriae* and Related Texts' in her *Celtic Britain in the Early Middle Ages*. Woodbridge, Suffolk: Boydell, 1980.

Hughes, P.G. *Wales and the Drovers*. London: Foyle's Welsh Co., 1943; 2nd edn, Carmarthen, Dyfed, Wales: Golden Grove Editions, 1988.

Hyams, Paul R. *Rancor and Reconciliation in Medieval England*. Ithaca NY: Cornell University Press, 2003.

Ingham, Patricia Clare. *Sovereign Fantasies: Arthurian Romance and the Making of Britain*. Philadelphia: University of Pennsylvania Press, 2001.

Insley, Charles. 'Collapse, Reconfiguration or Renegotiation? The Strange End of the Mercian Kingdom, 850–924', *Reti Medievali Rivista* 17.2 (2016): 1–19.

Isaac, Graham R., review of John T. Koch, *The 'Gododdin' of Aneirin: Text and Context from Dark-Age Britain*. Cardiff: University of Wales Press, 1997. In *Llên Cymru* 22 (1999): 138–60.

Isaac, Graham R. 'Readings in the History and Transmission of the *Gododdin*', *Cambrian Medieval Celtic Studies* 37 (1999): 55–78.

Jackson, Kenneth. 'On the Northern British Section in Nennius', in *Celt and Saxon: Studies in the Early British Border*, ed. Nora K. Chadwick. Cambridge: Cambridge University Press, 1963, pp. 20–62.

Jenkins, Dafydd. 'Crime and Tort and the Three Columns of Law', trans. T.M. Charles-Edwards. In *Tair Colofn Cyfraith: The Three Columns of Law in Medieval Wales: Homicide, Theft and Fire*, ed. T.M. Charles-Edwards and Paul Russell. Cymdeithas Hanes Cyfraith Cymru 5. Bangor: Cymdeithas Hanes Cyfraith Cymru, 2005, pp. 1–25.

Jenkins, Dafydd and Morfydd E. Owen, eds. *The Welsh Law of Women: Studies Presented to Professor Daniel A. Binchy on his Eightieth Birthday*. Cardiff: University of Wales Press, 1980.

Jenkins, Geraint H. *A Concise History of Wales*. Cambridge: Cambridge University Press, 2007.

Johnson, David F. 'Spiritual Combat and the Land of Canaan in *Guthlac A*', in *Intertexts: Studies in Anglo-Saxon Culture Presented to Paul E. Szarmach*, ed. Virginia Blanton and Helene Scheck. Tempe AZ: ACMRS, 2008, pp. 307–17.

Jones, Christopher A. 'Envisioning the *Cenobium* in the Old English *Guthlac A*', *Mediaeval Studies* 57 (1995), 259–91.

Jones, Graham. 'Guthlac', in John T. Koch, *Celtic Culture: A Historical Encyclopedia*. 5 vols. Santa Barbara CA: ABC-CLIO, 2006.

Jones, L., review of J. Williams ab Ithel, *Annales Cambriae*, Rolls Series. London: Longman, 1860; in *Archaeologia Cambrensis* (1861).

Jones, Timothy S. *Outlawry in Medieval Literature*. New York: Palgrave Macmillan, 2010.

Kabir, Ananya Jahanara. *Paradise, Death and Doomsday in Anglo-Saxon Literature*. Cambridge Studies in Anglo-Saxon England 32. Cambridge: Cambridge University Press, 2001.

Bibliography

Katajala, Kimmo and Maria Lähteenmäki, eds. *Imagined, Negotiated, Remembered: Constructing European Borders and Borderlands*. Münster: LIT Verlag, 2012.

Keary, C.F. *Catalogue of English Coins in the British Museum: Anglo-Saxon Series*. London: William Clowes & Sons, 1887.

Kennedy, Ruth and Simon Meecham-Jones, eds. *Authority and Subjugation in Writing of Medieval Wales*. New York: Palgrave Macmillan, 2008.

Keynes, Simon. 'The Historical Context of the Battle of Maldon', in *The Battle of Maldon*, ed. Donald Scragg. Oxford: Basil Blackwell, 1991, pp. 81–113.

Kirby, D.P. 'Hywel Dda: Anglophil?', *Welsh History Review* 8 (1976): 1–13.

Kirby, D.P. *The Earliest English Kings*. Revised edn. London: Routledge, 2000.

Klusáková, Luďa and Steven G. Ellis, eds. *Frontiers and Identities: Exploring the Research Area*. Pisa: Edizioni Plus/Pisa University Press, 2006.

Klusáková, Luďa and Steven G. Ellis, 'Terms and Concepts: "Frontier" and "Identity" in Academic and Popular Usage', in *Frontiers and Identities: Exploring the Research Area*, ed. Luďa Klusáková and Steven G. Ellis (Pisa: Edizioni Plus/Pisa University Press, 2006), pp. 1–15.

Kobos, Chester. 'The Structure and Background of Guthlac A'. Unpublished doctoral dissertation. Fordham University, 1972.

Koch, John T. *Celtic Culture: A Historical Encyclopedia*. 5 vols. Santa Barbara CA: ABC-CLIO, 2006.

Kokkonen, Jukka. 'Border Peace Agreements: Local Attempts to Regulate Early Modern Border Conflicts', in *Imagined, Negotiated, Remembered: Constructing European Borders and Borderlands*, ed. Kimmo Katajala and Maria Lähteenmäki. Münster: LIT Verlag, 2012, pp. 47–66.

Kurtz, Benjamin P. 'From St. Antony to St. Guthlac: A Study in Biography', *University of California Publications in Modern Philology* 12 (1925–6): 103–46.

Lampert-Weissig, Lisa. *Medieval Literature and Postcolonial Studies*. Edinburgh: Edinburgh University Press, 2010.

Lapidge, Michael. 'On the Emendation of Old English Texts', in *The Editing of Old English: Papers from the 1990 Manchester Conference*, ed. Donald G. Scragg and Paul E. Szarmach. Cambridge: D.S. Brewer, 1994.

Lavelle, Ryan. *Alfred's Wars: Sources and Interpretations of Anglo-Saxon Warfare in the Viking Age*. Woodbridge, Suffolk: Boydell, 2010.

Lawson, M.K. *Cnut: the Danes in England in the Early Eleventh Century*. New York: Longman, 1993.

Lee, Alvin A. *The Guest-Hall of Eden: Four Essays on the Design of Old English Poetry*. New Haven CT: Yale University Press, 1972.

Lees, Clare A. and Gillian R. Overing, eds. *A Place to Believe In: Locating Medieval Landscapes*. University Park PA: Pennsylvania State University Press, 2006.

Lerer, Seth. *Literacy and Power in Anglo-Saxon Literature*. Regents Studies in Medieval Culture. Lincoln NE: University of Nebraska Press, 1991.

Lewis, C.P. 'Welsh Territories and Welsh Identities in Late Anglo-Saxon England', in *Britons in Anglo-Saxon England*, ed. N.J. Higham. Manchester Centre for Anglo-Saxon Studies 7. Woodbridge, Suffolk: Boydell, 2007, pp. 130–43.

Lieberman, Max. *The March of Wales, 1067–1300: A Borderland of Medieval Britain.* Cardiff: University of Wales Press, 2008.

Lieberman, Max. *The Medieval March of Wales: The Creation and Perception of a Frontier, 1066–1283.* Cambridge: Cambridge University Press, 2010.

Lipp, Frances Randall. 'Guthlac A: an Interpretation', *Mediaeval Studies* 33 (1971): 46–62.

Loyn, H.R. *The Vikings in Britain.* New York: St Martin's Press, 1977; repr. 1994.

Marafioti, Nicole. *The King's Body: Burial and Succession in Late Anglo-Saxon England.* Toronto: University of Toronto Press, 2014.

Matthews, Stephen. 'The Content and Construction of the *Vita Haroldi*', in *King Harold II and the Bayeux Tapestry*, ed. Gale R. Owen-Crocker. Manchester Centre for Anglo-Saxon Studies 3. Woodbridge, Suffolk: Boydell, 2005, pp. 65–73.

Maund, K.L. 'The Welsh Alliances of Earl Ælfgar of Mercia and his Family in the Mid-Eleventh Century', *Anglo-Norman Studies* 11 (1988): 181–90.

Maund, K.L. *Ireland, Wales and England in the Eleventh Century.* Woodbridge, Suffolk: Boydell, 1991.

Maund, K.L. *The Welsh Kings: The Medieval Rulers of Wales.* Stroud: Tempus, 2000.

McAll, Christopher. 'The Normal Paradigms of a Woman's Life in the Irish and Welsh Law Texts', in Dafydd Jenkins and Morfydd E. Owen, eds, *The Welsh Law of Women: Studies Presented to Professor Daniel A. Binchy on his Eightieth Birthday.* Cardiff: University of Wales Press, 1980, pp. 7–22.

Meecham-Jones, Simon. 'Where was Wales? The Erasure of Wales in Medieval English Culture', in *Authority and Subjugation in Writing of Medieval Wales*, ed. Ruth Kennedy and Simon Meecham-Jones. New York: Palgrave Macmillan, 2008, pp. 27–55.

Michelet, Fabienne L. *Creation, Migration, and Conquest: Imaginary Geography and Sense of Space in Old English Literature.* Oxford: Oxford University Press, 2006.

Molyneaux, George. 'The Ordinance Concerning the *Dunsæte* and the Welsh Frontier in the Late Tenth and Eleventh Centuries', *Anglo-Saxon England* 40 (2012): 249–72.

Moore-Colyer, Richard J. *The Welsh Cattle Drovers: Agriculture and the Welsh Cattle Trade Before and During the Nineteenth Century.* Cardiff: University of Wales Press, 1976; 2nd edn. Ashbourne: Landmark, 2002.

Muldoon, James, ed. *The North Atlantic Frontier of Medieval Europe.* Farnham: Ashgate, 2009.

Mytum, Harold. *The Origins of Early Christian Ireland.* London: Routledge, 1992.

Neville, Jennifer. *Representations of the Natural World in Old English Poetry.* Cambridge Studies in Anglo-Saxon England 27. Cambridge: Cambridge University Press, 1999.

Niles, John D. *Old English Enigmatic Poems and the Play of the Texts.* Studies in the Early Middle Ages 13. Turnhout: Brepols, 2006.

Bibliography

Noble, Frank. *Offa's Dyke Reviewed*, ed. Margaret Gelling. BAR British Series 114. Oxford: BAR, 1983.

Norris, Robin. 'The Augustinian Theory of Use and Enjoyment in *Guthlac A* and *B*', *Neuphilologische Mitteilungen* 104 (2003): 159–78.

Oliver, Lisi. *The Body Legal in Barbarian Law*. Toronto: University of Toronto Press, 2011.

Olsen, Alexandra Hennessey. *Guthlac of Croyland: A Study of Heroic Hagiography*. Washington DC: University Press of America, 1981.

O'Brien, Bruce. *God's Peace and the King's Peace: The Laws of Edward the Confessor*. Philadelphia: University of Pennsylvania Press, 1999.

O'Brien O'Keeffe, Katherine. 'Guthlac's Crossings', *Quaestio: Selected Proceedings of the Cambridge Colloquium in Anglo-Saxon, Norse and Celtic* 2 (2001): 1–26.

Padel, Oliver, review of John T. Koch, *The 'Gododdin' of Aneirin: Text and Context from Dark-Age Britain*. Cardiff: University of Wales Press, 1997. In *Cambrian Medieval Celtic Studies* 35 (1998): 45–55.

Padel, Oliver. 'Slavery in Saxon Cornwall: The Bodmin Manumissions'. Kathleen Hughes Memorial Lectures 7. Cambridge: Department of Anglo-Saxon, Norse and Celtic, 2009.

Page, Raymond Ian. *Life in Anglo-Saxon England*. London: Batsford, 1970.

Patterson, Nerys. 'Women as Vassal: Gender Symmetry in Medieval Wales', *Proceedings of the Harvard Celtic Colloquium* 8 (1988): 31–45.

Pelteret, David A.E. 'Slave Raiding and Slave Trading in Early England', *Anglo-Saxon England* 9 (1981): 99–114.

Pelteret, David A.E. 'Slavery in Anglo-Saxon England', in *The Anglo-Saxons: Synthesis and Achievement*, ed. J. Douglas Woods and David A.E. Pelteret. Waterloo, Ontario: Wilfrid Laurier University Press, 1985, pp. 117–33.

Pelteret, David A.E. *Slavery in Early Mediaeval England: From the Reign of Alfred until the Twelfth Century*. Studies in Anglo-Saxon History 7. Woodbridge, Suffolk: Boydell, 1995.

Pollington, Stephen. *The Mead Hall: The Feasting Tradition in Anglo-Saxon England*. Norfolk: Anglo-Saxon Books, 2003.

Powell, F. York. 'Britain under English and Danes', in *Social England*, vol. I, *From the Earliest Times to the Accession of Edward the First*, ed. H.D. Traill. New York: G.P. Putnam's Sons, 1894.

Power, Daniel. 'Introduction: Frontiers: Terms, Concepts and the Historians of Medieval and Early Modern Europe', in *Frontiers in Question: Eurasian Borderlands, 700–1700*, ed. Daniel Power and Naomi Standen. Basingstoke: Macmillan, 1999, pp. 1–12.

Power, Daniel. *The Norman Frontier in the Twelfth and Early Thirteenth Centuries*. Cambridge: Cambridge University Press, 2004.

Power, Daniel and Naomi Standen, eds. *Frontiers in Question: Eurasian Borderlands, 700–1700*. Basingstoke: Macmillan, 1999.

Bibliography

Prestwich, J.O. 'King Æthelhere and the Battle of the Winwæd', *English Historical Review* 83 (1968): 89–95.

Pryce, Huw. 'British or Welsh? National Identity in Twelfth-Century Wales', *English Historical Review* 116 (2001): 775–801.

Rabin, Andrew. 'Capital Punishment and the Anglo-Saxon Judicial Apparatus: A Maximum View?', in *Capital and Corporal Punishment in Anglo-Saxon England*, ed. Jay Paul Gates and Nicole Marafioti. Woodbridge, Suffolk: Boydell, 2014, pp. 181–99.

Rawcliffe, Carole. *Leprosy in Medieval England*. Woodbridge, Suffolk: Boydell, 2006.

Ray, Keith and Ian Bapty. *Offa's Dyke: Landscape and Hegemony in Eighth-Century Britain*. Oxford: Oxbow Books, 2016.

Reichardt, Paul F. '*Guthlac A* and the Landscape of Spiritual Perfection', *Neophilologus* 56 (1974): 331–8.

Reynolds, Andrew. *Anglo-Saxon Deviant Burial Customs*. Oxford: Oxford University Press, 2009.

Reynolds, Susan. 'Eadric Silvaticus and the English Resistance', *Historical Research* 54 (1981): 102–5.

Richards, Melville. 'Gwŷr, gwragedd a gwehelyth', *Transactions of the Honourable Society of Cymmrodorion* (1965): 27–45.

Roberts, Jane. 'An Inventory of Early Guthlac Materials', *Mediaeval Studies* 32 (1970): 193–233.

Roberts, Jane. 'A Metrical Examination of the Poems "Guthlac A" and "Guthlac B"', *Proceedings of the Royal Irish Academy, Section C: Archaeology, Celtic Studies, History, Linguistics, Literature* 71 (1971): 91–137.

Roberts, Jane. 'Guðlac A, B, and C?', *Medium Ævum* 42 (1973): 43–6.

Roberts, Jane. '*Guthlac A*: Sources and Source Hunting', in *Medieval English Studies presented to George Kane*, ed. Edward Donald Kennedy et al. Wolfeboro NH: Brewer, 1988, pp. 1–18.

Roberts, Jane. 'Hagiography and Literature: The Case of Guthlac of Crowland', in *Mercia: An Anglo-Saxon Kingdom in Europe*, ed. Michelle P. Brown and Carol A. Farr. Studies in the Early History of Europe. London: Continuum, 2001, pp. 69–86.

Ross, Anne. *Pagan Celtic Britain: Studies in Iconography and Tradition*. London: Routledge, 1967.

Rulon-Miller, Nina. 'Sexual Humor and Fettered Desire in *Exeter Book* Riddle 12', in *Humor in Anglo-Saxon Literature*, ed. Jonathan Wilcox. Woodbridge, Suffolk: Boydell, 2000, pp. 99–126.

Rumble, A.R. ed. *The Reign of Cnut, King of England, Denmark and Norway*. London: Leicester University Press, 1994.

Russell, Paul. 'Introduction: The Names of Celtic Origin' and 'Personal Names: Celtic Names' (with Peter McClure and David Rollason), in *The Durham Liber Vitae: London, British Library, MS Cotton Domitian A.VII*, vol. II: *Linguistic*

Commentary, ed. David and Lynda Rollason. London: British Library, 2007, pp. 5–8 and 35–43.

Scott, B.G. 'Iron "Slave-collars" from Lagore Crannog, Co. Meath', *Proceedings of the Royal Irish Academy* 78C (1978): 213–30.

Semple, Sarah. 'A Fear of the Past: The Place of the Prehistoric Burial Mound in the Ideology of Middle and Later Anglo-Saxon England', *World Archaeology* 30 (1998): 109–26.

Sharma, Manish. 'A Reconsideration of the Structure of *Guthlac A*: The Extremes of Saintliness', *Journal of English and Germanic Philology* 101 (2002): 185–200.

Sheppard, Alice. *Families of the King: Writing Identity in the Anglo-Saxon Chronicle*. Toronto: University of Toronto Press, 2004.

Shippey, T.A. *Old English Verse*. London: Hutchinson's, 1972.

Shook, Laurence K. 'The Burial Mound in *Guthlac A*', *Modern Philology* 58 (1960): 1–10.

Shook, Laurence K. 'The Prologue of the Old-English "Guthlac A"', *Mediaeval Studies* 23 (1961): 294–304.

Siewers, Alfred K. 'Landscapes of Conversion: Guthlac's Mound and Grendel's Mere as Expressions of Anglo-Saxon Nation Building', *Viator* 34 (2003): 1–39.

Sims-Williams, Patrick. 'The Settlement of England in Bede and the *Chronicle*', *Anglo-Saxon England* 12 (1983): 1–41.

Sims-Williams, Patrick. *Religion and Literature in Western England: 600–800*. Cambridge Studies in Anglo-Saxon England 3. Cambridge: Cambridge University Press, 1990.

Sims-Williams, Patrick, review of Alex Woolf, ed., *Beyond the Gododdin: Dark Age Scotland in Medieval Wales*. St Andrews: University of St Andrews, 2013. In *Cambrian Medieval Celtic Studies* 66 (2013): 85–8.

Skeel, Caroline. 'The Cattle Trade between Wales and England from the Fifteenth to the Nineteenth Centuries', *Transactions of the Royal Historical Society*, Fourth Series 9 (1926): 135–58.

Smith, Joshua Byron. *Walter Map and the Matter of Britain*. Philadelphia: University of Pennsylvania Press, 2017.

Smith, Llinos Beverley. 'The Welsh and English Languages in Late-Medieval Wales,' in *Multilingualism in Later Medieval Britain*, ed. D.A. Trotter. Cambridge: D.S. Brewer, 2000, pp. 7–21.

Smith, Scott Thompson. *Land and Book: Literature and Land Tenure in Anglo-Saxon England*. Toronto: University of Toronto Press, 2012.

Spiegel, Gabrielle M. 'Épater les Médiévistes', *History and Theory* 39 (2000): 243–50.

Spivak, Gayatri Chakravorty. 'Can the Subaltern Speak?', in *Marxism and the Interpretation of Culture*, ed. Cary Nelson and Lawrence Grossberg. Urbana: University of Illinois Press, 1988, pp. 271–313.

Stacey, Robin Chapman. 'Divorce, Medieval Welsh Style', *Speculum* 77 (2002): 1107–27.

Bibliography

Stacey, Robin Chapman. 'Law and Lawbooks in Mediaeval Wales', *History Compass* 8 (2010): 1180–90.
Stancliffe, Clare and Eric Cambridge, eds. *Oswald: Northumbrian King to European Saint*. Stamford: Paul Watkins, 1995.
Stancliffe, Clare. 'Where was Oswald Killed?', in *Oswald: Northumbrian King to European Saint*, ed. Clare Stancliffe and Eric Cambridge. Stamford: Paul Watkins, 1995, pp. 84–96.
Stenton, Frank M. 'The Road System of Medieval England', *Economic History Review* 7 (1936): 1–21.
Stenton, Frank M. *Anglo-Saxon England*. 3rd edn. Oxford: Clarendon Press, 1971; repr. 1975.
Stevick, Robert D. 'The Length of "Guthlac A"', *Viator* 13 (1982): 15–48.
Stodnick, Jacqueline. 'Second-rate Stories? Changing Approaches to the *Anglo-Saxon Chronicle*', *Literature Compass* 3 (2006): 1253–65.
Suppe, Frederick C. 'The Cultural Significance of Decapitation in High Medieval Wales and the Marches', *Bulletin of the Board of Celtic Studies* 36 (1989): 147–60.
Suppe, Frederick C. *Military Institutions on the Welsh Marches: Shropshire, A.D. 1066–1300*. Studies in Celtic History XIV. Woodbridge, Suffolk: Boydell, 1994.
Suppe, Frederick C. 'Who was Rhys Sais? Some Comments on Anglo-Welsh Relations before 1066', *Haskins Society Journal* 7 (1995): 63–73.
Suppe, Frederick C. 'Interpreter Families and Anglo-Welsh Relations in the Shropshire–Powys Marches in the Twelfth Century', *Anglo-Norman Studies: Proceedings of the Battle Conference* 30 (2007): 196–212.
Swan, Mary and Elaine M. Treharne, eds. *Rewriting Old English in the Twelfth Century*. Cambridge: Cambridge University Press, 2000.
Swartz, Dorothy Dilts. 'The Legal Status of Women in Early Medieval Ireland and Wales in Comparison with Western Europe and Mediterranean Societies: Environmental and Social Correlations', *Proceedings of the Harvard Celtic Colloquium* 13 (1993): 107–18.
Szarmach, Paul. 'Introduction', in *The Editing of Old English: Papers from the 1990 Manchester Conference*, ed. Donald G. Scragg and Paul E. Szarmach. Cambridge: D.S. Brewer, 1994.
Tanke, John W. '*Wonfeax wale*: Ideology and Figuration in the Sexual Riddles of the Exeter Book', in *Class and Gender in Early English Literature: Intersections*, ed. Britton J. Harwood and Gillian R. Overing. Bloomington IN: Indiana University Press, 1994, pp. 21–42.
Thacker, Alan. 'The Cult of King Harold at Chester', in *The Middle Ages in the North-West*, ed. Tom Scott and Pat Starkie. Oxford: Leopard's Head Press, 1995, pp. 155–76.
Thacker, Alan. '*Membra Disjecta*: The Division of the Body and the Diffusion of the Cult', in *Oswald: Northumbrian King to European Saint*, ed. Clare Stancliffe and Eric Cambridge. Stamford: Paul Watkins, 1995, pp. 97–127.
Thornton, David E. 'Maredudd ab Owain (d. 999): The Most Famous King of the Welsh', *Cylchgrawn hanes cymru/Welsh History Review* 18 (1996): 567–91.

Bibliography

Thornton, David E. 'Some Welshmen in Domesday Book and Beyond: Aspects of Anglo-Welsh Relations in the Eleventh Century', in *Britons in Anglo-Saxon England*, ed. N.J. Higham. Manchester Centre for Anglo-Saxon Studies 7. Woodbridge, Suffolk: Boydell, 2007, pp. 144–64.

Toller, T. Northcote, ed. *An Anglo-Saxon Dictionary, Based on the Manuscript Collections of the Late Joseph Bosworth*. Oxford: Clarendon Press, 1898.

Toller, T. Northcote. *An Anglo-Saxon Dictionary Supplement*. Oxford: Clarendon Press, 1921.

Trautmann, Moritz. 'Die Auflösungen der altenglischen Rätsel', *Anglia* 5 (1894): 46–51.

Trautmann, Moritz. 'Zu den altenglischen Rätseln', *Anglia* 17 (1895): 396–400.

Treharne, Elaine M. 'A Unique Old English Formula for Excommunication from Cambridge, Corpus Christi College 303', *Anglo-Saxon England* 24 (1995): 185–211.

Treharne, Elaine M. 'The Form and Function of the Twelfth-Century Old English "Dicts of Cato"', *Journal of English and Germanic Philology* 102 (2003): 465–85.

Treharne, Elaine M. *Living Through Conquest: The Politics of Early English, 1020–1220*. Oxford: Oxford University Press, 2012.

Tudor, Victoria. 'Reginald's *Life of St Oswald*', in *Oswald: Northumbrian King to European Saint*, ed. Clare Stancliffe and Eric Cambridge. Stamford: Paul Watkins, 1995, pp. 178–94.

Tupper, Frederick Jr. *The Riddles of the Exeter Book*. Boston: Ginn, 1910.

Tyler, Damian J. 'An Early Mercian Hegemony: Penda and Overkingship in the Seventh Century', *Midland History* 30 (2005): 1–19.

Tyler, Damian J. 'Early Mercia and the Britons', in *Britons in Anglo-Saxon England*, ed. N.J. Higham. Manchester Centre for Anglo-Saxon Studies 7. Woodbridge, Suffolk: Boydell, 2007, pp. 91–101.

Voss, Manfred. 'Strykers Edition des alphabetischen Cleopatraglossars: Corrigenda und Addenda', *Arbeiten aus Anglistik und Amerikanistik* 13 (1988): 123–38.

Walker, David. *Medieval Wales*. Cambridge Medieval Textbooks. Cambridge: Cambridge University Press, 1990; repr. 1999.

Walker, Ian W. *Mercia and the Making of England*. Stroud: Sutton, 2000.

Wallace-Hadrill, J.M. *Bede's Ecclesiastical History of the English People: A Historical Commentary*. Oxford: Clarendon Press, 1988; repr. paperback 1993.

Walters, D.B. 'The European Legal Context of the Welsh Law of Matrimonial Property', in Dafydd Jenkins and Morfydd E. Owen, eds, *The Welsh Law of Women: Studies Presented to Professor Daniel A. Binchy on his Eightieth Birthday*. Cardiff: University of Wales Press, 1980, pp. 115–31.

Walz, John A. 'Notes on the Anglo-Saxon Riddles', *Harvard Studies and Notes* 5 (1896): 261–8.

Ward-Perkins, Bryan. 'Why Did the Anglo-Saxons Not Become More British?', *English Historical Review* 115 (2000): 513–33.

Warren, Michelle R. *History on the Edge: Excalibur and the Borders of Britain, 1100–1300*. Medieval Cultures 22. Minneapolis: University of Minnesota Press, 2000.

Welch, Martin. *Discovering Anglo-Saxon England*. University Park PA: Pennsylvania State University Press, 1992.
Wentersdorf, Karl P. 'Guthlac A: The Battle for the *Beorg*', *Neophilologus* 62 (1978): 135–42.
Williams, Ann. '*Princeps Merciorum*: The Family, Career and Connections of Ælfhere, Ealdorman of Mercia, 956–983', *Anglo-Saxon England* 10 (1982): 143–72.
Williams, Ann. 'England in the Eleventh Century', in *A Companion to the Anglo-Norman World*, ed. Christopher Harper-Bill and Elisabeth Van Houts. Woodbridge, Suffolk: Boydell, 2003, pp. 1–18.
Williams, Ifor. 'A Reference to the Nennian Bellum Cocboy', *Bulletin of the Board of Celtic Studies* 3 (1926/7): 59–62.
Williams, Ifor. 'Bellum Cantscaul', *Bulletin of the Board of Celtic Studies* 6 (1933): 351–4.
Williams, L.F. Rushbrook. 'The Status of the Welsh in the Laws of Ine', *English Historical Review*, 30 (1915): 271–7.
Wilson, D.R. *Anglo-Saxon Paganism*. London: Routledge, 1992.
Woolf, Alex. 'Caedwalla *Rex Brettonum* and the Passing of the Old North', *Northern History* 41 (2004): 5–24.
Woolf, Alex, ed., *Beyond the Gododdin: Dark Age Scotland in Medieval Wales*. St Andrews: University of St Andrews, 2013.
Woolf, Rosemary. 'Saints' Lives', in *Continuations and Beginnings: Studies in Old English Literature*, ed. Eric Gerald Stanley. London: Nelson, 1966, pp. 37–66.
Wormald, Patrick. 'Bede, the Bretwaldas and the Origins of the Gens Anglorum', in *Ideal and Reality in Frankish and Anglo-Saxon Society: Studies Presented to J.M. Wallace-Hadrill*, ed. Patrick Wormald with Donald Bullough and Roger Collins. Oxford: Blackwell, 1983, pp. 99–129.
Wormald, Patrick. 'A Handlist of Anglo-Saxon Lawsuits', *Anglo-Saxon England* 17 (1988): 247–81.
Wormald, Patrick. '*Engla Lond*: The Making of an Allegiance', *Journal of Historical Sociology* 7 (1994): 1–24.
Wormald, Patrick. *The Making of English Law: King Alfred to the Twelfth Century*. Oxford: Blackwell, 1999.
Wright, Charles D. 'The Three Temptations and the Seven Gifts of the Holy Spirit in "Guthlac A", 160b–169', *Traditio* 38 (1982): 341–3.
Wright, Charles D. *The Irish Tradition in Old English Literature*. Cambridge Studies in Anglo-Saxon England 6. Cambridge: Cambridge University Press, 1993; repr. 2006.
Wright, Charles D. 'Shepherd of Hermas' in *Sources of Anglo-Saxon Literary Culture: The Apocrypha*, ed. Frederick M. Biggs. Instrumenta Anglistica Mediaevalia 1. Kalamazoo MI: Medieval Institute Publications, 2007, pp. 63–6.
Wyatt, David. *Slaves and Warriors in Medieval Britain and Ireland, 800–1200*. Leiden: Brill, 2009.

Bibliography

Yorke, Barbara. *Kings and Kingdoms of Early Anglo-Saxon England.* London: Routledge, 1990; repr. 1997.

Yorke, Barbara. 'Fact or Fiction? The Written Evidence for the Fifth and Sixth Centuries AD', *Anglo-Saxon Studies in Archaeology and History* 6 (1993): 45–50.

Yorke, Barbara. 'The Origins of Mercia', in *Mercia: An Anglo-Saxon Kingdom in Europe*, ed. Michelle P. Brown and Carol A. Farr. Studies in the Early History of Europe. London: Continuum, 2001, pp. 13–22.

Zaluckyj, Sarah. *Mercia: The Anglo-Saxon Kingdom of Central England.* Almeley: Logaston Press, 2001. Repr. with new appendix, 2011.

Index

Aberffraw 36
æht 86
Ælfgar, earl of Mercia 115–20, 122–6
   alliance with Gruffudd ap Llywelyn
      115–20
   daughter Edith 126
   death 120
   exile and restoration 115–20
Ælfhere of Mercia 114–15, 133
   alliance with Hywel ap Ieuaf 114–15,
      133
Ælfnoth (sheriff) 119
Ælfwald of East Anglia 54
Ælfweard of Wessex 112
Ælfwynn of Mercia 112
Æsc 6
Æthelbald of Mercia 54
Æthelflæd of Mercia 112
Æthelfrith of Northumbria 33, 37
Æthelhelm 111
Æthelhere of East Anglia 39, 51
Æthelnoth 111
Æthelred, ealdorman of Mercia
     111–12
   alliance with Anarawd ap Rhodri of
     Gwynedd 111–12
   attack on South Wales 111–12
Æthelred, king of Mercia 53–4
Æthelsige of Mercia 114–15
   alliance with Edwin ab Einion ab
     Owain 114–15
   'Edylfi the Saxon' 133
   raid on Deheubarth 114–15

Æthelstan (king) 112–14
   fosterage in Mercia 112
   joint rule 112
   lost panegyric for 112
   Scottish campaign of 113–14
Æthelwine (bishop) 142, 144, 156
Aidan (bishop) 33–4
Alfred the Great 4, 83, 109–10
   Anglo-Saxon Chronicle 109–10
   domboc 4
   Life of King Alfred see Asser
   vernacular translation program
      109–10
Alhflæd 31
Alhfrith 31–3
alltud 4, 19, 90
   see also Welsh law
Amieria 154
Anarawd ap Rhodri of Gwynedd
     111–12
   alliance with Æthelred, ealdorman
     of Mercia 111–12
   attack on South Wales 111–12
angel and demon motif 70
Anglesey 27, 36, 149
Angli 111
Anglo/British conflict 4–7, 12–14,
     59–73, 82–4, 109–10
Anglo-Norman conquest of Wales *see*
   Conquest of Wales
Anglo-Norman romance 6, 138, 160
Anglo-Saxon Chronicle
   and Alfred the Great 109–10

Index

annal for (473) 6
annal for (893) 111
annal for (909) 86
annal for (918) 112
annal for (926) 113
annal for (934) 114
annal for (1046) 115
annal for (1052) 86
annal for (1055) 115–18
annal for (1056) 118–19
annal for (1058) 119–20
annal for (1063) 120–2
annal for (1065) 122–3
annal for (1067) 124–5
annal for (1070) 117, 145–6
annal for (1071) 141–5
Common Stock 109
MS A 6, 86
MS C 115–20
MS D 116–25
MS E *see* Peterborough Chronicle (MS E of *Anglo-Saxon Chronicle*)
Anglo-Saxon conquest/invasion 6–7, 60–2
Anglo-Saxon England
  agricultural labour in 82–108
  animals in *see* animals
  class in 82–108
  ethnic identity in 6–16, 23–39, 53–9, 60–73, 82–108, 110, 139–55, 159–68
  'national' identity in 7, 23–9, 60, 67–70, 110, 159–68
  slavery in 82–108
  warriors in 23–52, 53–9, 70–3, 82–108
Anglo-Saxon law 1–6, 15–16, 85–7
Anglo-Saxon 'national' identity 7, 23–9, 60, 67–70, 110, 159–68
animals 1–6, 63, 82–108, 117–19, 143–53
Anna of East Anglia 34, 39
Annales Cambriae
  annal for (613) 33, 47–9
  annal for (626) 27–8
  annal for (630) 26
  annal for (644) 37
  annal for (656) 40, 51
  annal for (657) 40, 51
  annal for (658) 40, 51
  annal for (893) 111
  annal for (894) 111
  annal for (983) 114
  annal for (992) 114
  annal for (1058) 120
Annals of Tigernach 37, 120
anti-Norman rhetoric 166
apocryphal tradition 62
apostasy 47
Armes Prydein 6
Arthur 41, 160
Asser, *Life of King Alfred* 83–5, 111
  attacks on South Wales in 111
  Offa's Dyke 83–5

Bamburgh 34, 37, 113
Bangor Iscoed, massacre at 33
barrow *see* beorg in *Guthlac A*
Bartholomew 64–5, 70
Battle of Hastings *see* Hastings, Battle of (1066)
Bebbe 34
Bede, *Historia Ecclesiastica Gentis Anglorum* 23–52, 53–5, 68, 84
beorg in *Guthlac A* 60–73
Bernard of Neufmarché 148
Bernicia 30, 33, 35, 41
Bleddyn 121–6, 140–1
Book of Taliesin 36
border/boundary 8–12, 60–3, 68, 72–3, 83–5, 94, 97
borderlands *see* Welsh borderlands
Borderlands/La Frontera: The New Mestiza 8
boundary *see* border/boundary
Brecknock *see* Brycheiniog
Bristol 88, 121, 122
British Christianity 23–52
British influence on Mercian royal family 29–30, 54–5
British population in the Fens 57–8
Britons
  as demons 57–9, 68
  heresy of in Bede 23–39
Brut y Tywysogyon
  annal for (978) 114
  annal for (983) 114
  annal for (992) 114

195

Index

Brycheiniog
  983 raid on 114
  Norman Marcher lords' attack on 154
Buttington (battle at) 111, 113

Cadafael of Gwynedd 40
Cadfan of Gwynedd 27
Cadwallon of Gwynedd
  alliance with Penda of Mercia 23–52
  death of 37, 49
  and Edwin 23–52
  poems in praise of *see Englynion Cadwallon; Moliant Cadwallon*
  and Welsh kingdoms 34–6
Cadwgan, king in southern Wales 154
Campodunum 34
Campus Gaius see Winwæd, Battle of (655)
Canu Heledd 35, 50, 52
Canu Tyssilyaw 38
Caradog ap Gruffudd ap Rhydderch 122
castles 127, 148–53
cattle droving *see* droving of cattle
cattle raiding/theft 1–6, 14, 17, 85–7, 96–7
  laws against 1–6
  tracking stolen cattle 1–6
Cenwealh 29, 31
Ceorl of Mercia 28, 30, 45
Ceredigion 111, 114
Cernyw 49
Charlemagne 160
Chester 9, 25, 33, 36, 112, 113, 125, 127, 143–4, 154, 160–1, 164
  924 revolt 112
  Battle of (615/16) 33, 36
  rebellion after Norman Conquest 125, 127, 143–4
  Vita Haroldi and 160–1, 164
Clydog ap Cadell 112
Clynnog Fawr 113–14
Coenred of Mercia 57–8
Cogwy, Battle of *see* Maserfelth, Battle of (624)
colonisation 11, 60, 70
comitatus 41, 69
compensation 5, 86
  see also galanas; wergild

Conquest of Wales 3, 7–8, 11, 15–16, 50, 55–6, 60–3, 73, 96–7, 148–55, 159–70
Constantine, king of Scots 113
conversion of the Anglo-Saxons 23–52
Cornovii 49
Cornwall 49, 98
Council of Westminster (1102) 86
Count Brian 127
Crowland (Croyland) 53–81
cultural estuary/nexus 11–13, 29–39, 53–9, 159–68
Cundwalh 29
Cwenburh of Mercia 28
Cydweli 113, 114, 133
Cyfraith Hywel see Welsh law
  poem in praise of *see Trawsganu Kynan Garwyn mab Brochfael*
Cynan Garwyn of Powys 34, 36, 48–9
Cynddelw of Powys 38
Cynddylan of Powys 37–8, 42
Cyneburh 31
Cynewise 39

'dark Welsh' 82–108
de mari usque ad mare 83–5
decapitation 36–9, 50, 120–2
  archaeological evidence 36, 38
  of Eanfrith of Bernicia 37
  of Edwin of Northumbria 36–7
  of Gruffudd ap Llewelyn 120–2
  of Oswald of Northumbria 37–8
  of Penda of Mercia 38–9
Deheubarth 113–14, 133–4
Deira 9, 25, 30, 41
demons 53–81
  appearance as Britons *see* Britons
  disguise 57–8, 159–70
Domesday Book 22, 130
Doncaster 24, 39
Dover 161–2
droving of cattle 94–7
Dublin 120
Dun 18
Dunsæte Agreement 1–6, 94–6
Dunsæte (territory) 1–6
Durham *Liber Vitae* 30
Dyfed 113–14, 131, 133

196

Index

Eadfrith 24–6, 28
Eadred (king) 114
Eadric 'the wild'/'cild' 124–5, 136
Eadwig (king) 114
Eadwine, earl of Mercia 122–8, 140–5
Ealdgyth *see* Edith, daughter of Ælfgar, earl of Mercia
Ealdred of Bamburgh 113
Eanflæd 46
Eanfrith of Bernicia 36–7, 49
East Angles 34, 39, 54, 58, 68
Eawa 37
Ecgfrith 39
Ecgric of East Anglia 34
Edgar (king) 114
Edith, daughter of Ælfgar, earl of Mercia 126
Edmund, king of East Anglia 38
Edward the Confessor 121–5
Edward the Elder 86, 112, 131
Edwardian conquest of Wales *see* Conquest of Wales
Edwin, earl of Mercia *see* Eadwine, earl of Mercia
Edwin ab Einion ab Owain 114–15
  alliance with Æthelsige of Mercia 114–15
  raid on Deheubarth 114–15
Edwin of Northumbria 23–9, 35, 36–7
  baptism by Rhun ap Urien 27–8
  conversion in Bede 26–8
  death and decapitation 36–7
  exile and youth 27–8
  fosterage in court of Cadfan of Gwynedd 27
  marriage to Cwenburh of Mercia 28
  territorial expansion 23–9
  Welsh traditions about 35–7
'Edylfi the Saxon' *see* Æthelsige of Mercia
Einion ab Owain 114–15, 133
Eliseg, king of Powys/Pillar of Eliseg 83
Ely 126–8, 142–6
English army, fighting tactics of 117–19, 144, 150–3
English identity 110, 159–70
  'maximalist' and 'minimalist' view 110
  as response to Vikings 110
  see also Anglo-Saxon 'national' identity
English resistance to Norman Conquest 122–9, 138–55, 159–68
englynion 35, 37, 42, 50
Englynion Cadwallon 35–6
Eobba 37
ethnogenesis 28
Eutropius, *Historiae Romanae Breviarum* 84
Exeter Book
  Guthlac A 59–73
  Guthlac B 59–60
  Riddle 12 85, 88, 94, 101
  Riddle 52 82–108
  Riddle 72 82–108
eþele and *eþelriehte* 61–3, 78

famine 151
Felix, *Vita Sancti Guthlaci* 53–81
Fens
  British population in *see* British population in the Fens
  in Guthlac's *Life* 53–81
  outlaws in 70–3
  as site of rebellion after Norman Conquest 141–2, 147
feter/fetters 85, 88, 91, 101–2
Fín (Irish princess) 46
Finan (bishop) 34
flail 91–2, 104–5
Florence of Worcester *see* John of Worcester, *Chronicle* (*Chronicon ex chronicis*)
forest 139, 141, 146–7, 150
Frederick Barbarossa 160
frið/friðmal 17
frontier 4–6, 8–10, 56–9, 68, 84
  barrier v. zone of cultural exchange 9–10
  frontier law 4–6
  frontier of settlement v. political frontier 10
  Offa's Dyke 84

Gaius' Field *see* Winwæd, Battle of (655)
galanas 5, 86

Index

Garway 163
genge 117, 134, 145
gens Anglorum 28
Geoffrey of Monmouth, *Historia Regum Britanniae* 27
gerædnes 1, 17
Gerald of Wales, *Description of Wales* 134
Gerbod the Fleming 154
Germanic paganism 31, 33, 38, 50
Gesta Herewardi 146, 164
Gildas, *De Excidio et Conquestu Britanniae* 84, 87
Gloria Anzaldúa 8
Gloucester 118, 121
Godwinsons 115–16, 120, 122–3
  see also Harold Godwinson; Sweyn Godwinson; Tostig Godwinson
Gofara Braint 37
Gower 114, 133
Gruffudd ap Llewelyn 115–26
  alliance with Ælfgar, earl of Mercia 115–22
  alliance with Sweyn Godwinson 115
  death and decapitation of 120–2
  marriage to Edith, daughter of Ælfgar 126
Gueith Meicen see Hatfield Chase, Battle of (633)
guerrilla warfare 139, 145, 153
Guthlac A 59–73
  beorg in 59–73
  compared to *Guthlac B* 59–60
  dating of 67–70
  demons in 59–73
  landscape of 59–73
  missing folio of 68
  relationship to Felix, *Vita Sancti Guthlaci* 60, 68, 72
Guthlac B 59–60
Guthlac of Crowland 53–81
  ability to understand Welsh 53–9
  etymology of name 55
  exile among British 53–9
  in Felix, *Vita Sancti Guthlaci* 53–9
  in *Guthlac A* 59–73
  hermitage 59–73
  leader of multi-ethnic warband 53–9, 70–3

Mercian genealogy 53–5
  in *South English Legendary* 73
  temptation into outlawry 70–3
gwalch 46, 74
Gwent 2, 113–14
Gwynedd 4, 8–9, 23–9, 34–43, 111–15, 125

Hadrian's Wall 84
Hæthfelth see Hatfield Chase, Battle of (633)
Harold Godwinson 86, 118–22, 126, 146, 159–70
  Anglo-Saxon Chronicle 86, 118–22
  Battle of Hastings 146
  campaigns against Wales 118–22, 161
  Chester 160–4
  Dover 161–2
  hermitage 159–68
  legendary survival after Hastings 159–70
  legitimacy of rule 166
  oral legend 160, 165
  Scandinavian tradition 160
  Vita Haroldi 159–70
  Waltham 160, 166
  Welsh borderlands 159–70
Hastings, Battle of (1066) 117, 122–9, 138–55, 159–68
Hatfield Chase, Battle of (633) 24–9, 32–6, 41
head cults 36–9, 50
Hebrides 120
Hengest 6
here 117
Hereford/Herefordshire 2, 116–19, 124–51, 148–53, 163
Hereward 'the wake' 117, 144–6, 164
  Gesta Herewardi 164
  rebellion against Norman Conquest 144–6
hermit *see* Harold Godwinson; Guthlac of Crowland
Hexham 143
Hiberno-Scandinavians 89
Historia Brittonum 26–8, 37, 40–1, 46, 84
  baptism of Edwin by Rhun ap Urien 27–8
  Battle of Hatfield Chase (*Gueith Meicen*, 633) 26

Index

Battle of Maserfelth (*Maes Cogwy*, 624) 37
Battle of Winwæd (*Campus Gaius*, 655) 40–1
   campaign at Iudeu 40–1
   Hadrian's Wall 84
   Oswiu's wives 46
Historia Ecclesiastica see Bede, *Historia Ecclesiastica Gentis Anglorum*
Historia Ecclesie Abbendonensis 146
History of the Abbey of Evesham 146
Homi K. Bhabha 11
horses 1, 86, 101, 117–19, 143–4, 150–2
   use of in battle 117–19, 143–4, 150–2
hostages 39, 54, 114–15, 120–1
Hugh, earl in Shropshire 149–51
Hugh of Avranches 154
Hugh Candidus, *Chronicle* 145
hybridity 11
Hywel ap Ieuaf 114, 133
   alliance with Ælfhere of Mercia 114
Hywel Dda (Hywel ap Cadell) 99, 112–14

Icel of Mercia 55
Idwal ap Anarawd of Gwynedd 112–14
Ine's laws 4–6
Ireland 31, 89, 116–17
   and Ælfgar of Mercia and Gruffudd ap Llywelyn 116–17
   and mercenary armies 116–17
   and slave trade 89
   and succession 31
   and Wales 31, 89, 116–17
Isle of Wight 47, 153
Iudeu 40

John of Worcester, *Chronicle* (*Chronicon ex chronicis*)
   annal for (926) 132
   annal for (1067) 124–5
   annal for (1071) 155–6
   annal for (1087) 148–50
   annal for (1094) 149
   annal for (1095) 151
   annal for (1097) 152
joint kingship 30–1, 132

Kynan Garwyn *see* Cynan Garwyn of Powys

Lady Godiva 126
lagemanni 2
lahmen 2–3
landscape 10, 59–73, 83–4, 92–7, 138–55
Law of the March of Wales *see* Marcher Law
Leeds 25, 39
Leofgar (bishop) 118–19, 122
Leofric, earl of Mercia 116, 122–4
Leominster, abbess of 115
leprosy 169–70
Life of Harold Godwinson see Vita Haroldi
Lindisfarne 37
locus amoenus 64–7

mab Pyd *see* Penda of Mercia
Maes Cogwy see Maserfelth, Battle of (624)
Maeshyfaidd 114
Magnus Haraldsson 120
Magonsætan 29
manuscripts
   Cambridge, Corpus Christi College (MS 383) 2
   London, British Library, Harley (MS 3776) 160
   see also Anglo-Saxon Chronicle
March of Wales 4–6, 8, 14–16, 50, 55–6, 73, 84, 94–7, 115–29, 138–55, 168
   and Anglo-Norman literature 6, 138, 168
   and cattle raiding 14, 94–7
   and decapitation 36–9, 50, 121
   and hybrid English/Welsh customs 4–6, 14–16
   lawlessness of 6, 55–6, 96–7, 139–44, 148–55
   laws of *see* Marcher Law
   mercenaries 55–6, 71
   military culture 55–6, 96–7, 115–22, 138–55
   outlaws 110, 115–29, 138–55
   parallels to Anglo-Saxon period 4–6, 8, 15–16, 55–6, 73, 94–7, 138–55
marche 8
Marcher Law 4–6, 15–16
Maredudd, king in southern Wales 154
Maredudd ab Owain (d. 999) 114–15

Index

marshes 141, 147, 153
  see also Fens
Marwnad Cadwallon see *Englynion Cadwallon*
Marwnad Cynddylan 42, 51–2
Maserfelth, Battle of (624) 25, 37, 42, 49
mearc 82, 85, 92–6, 106–7
Meicen see Hatfield Chase, Battle of (633)
Menevia 114, 133
mercenaries 55–6, 71, 115–22
Mercia
  in the 7th century 23–52
  in the 8th century 53–81
  in the 9th century 82–108
  in the 10th century 109–22
  in the 11th century 122–9, 138–47
  paganism of 23–52
Mercian earls see Ælfgar; Eadwine; Leofric; Morcar
Mercian hegemony/supremacy 68–9
Mercian royal family 29–31, 53–9
  British name elements in 29–30, 54–5
Merewalh 29
Middle Angles 31, 54, 59
Middle English romance 73, 128–9, 138–9
Mierce/Merci 68–9
Moliant Cadwallon 35, 42, 48
Monmouth 2
monstrosity 11
Montgomery 150–1
Morcar, earl of Mercia 122–8, 140–6, 153
Morgan of Gwent 114
multi-ethnic warband 53–9

nine-day time limits 5
Norðleoda laga 4
Norman Conquest 15–16, 96–7, 122–9, 138–55, 159–68
  resistance to see English resistance to Norman Conquest
  see also Harold Godwinson
Norman Conquest of Wales see Conquest of Wales
Norman earls/Marcher lords 8, 15–16, 96–7, 148, 153–5
North Wales 4, 8, 44, 109, 111–12, 115–16, 140, 149, 160

Northumbria 3, 23–43, 122–3, 147
Norway 119–20

Oethelwald of Deira 33, 39, 41
Offa, king of Mercia 69, 74, 82–5
Offa's Dyke 9, 82–5, 95–7
  archaeological studies of 82–5
  Asser, description 'from sea to sea' 82–5
  frontier zone 82–5
Olaf Tryggvason 160
oral legend 69, 160, 165
Orderic Vitalis, *Ecclesiastical History* 125–9, 138–55
Ordinance Concerning the Dunsæte see Dunsæte Agreement
Orkneys 120
Orosius, *Historiae contra Paganos* 84
Osfrith 26, 28
Oswald of Northumbria 26–7, 33, 36–8, 39, 47
  death and decapitation of 33, 36–8, 50
Oswestry 25, 37, 42, 49
Oswiu 31, 33, 37–42, 46
  and death of Penda 38–42
  wives of 46
outlaws 70–3, 115–29, 138–55, 164
  in Anglo-Norman England 122–9, 138–55
  in Anglo-Saxon England 70–3, 115–22
  in Fens 70–3, 138–47
  in *Life* of Guthlac 70–3
  in Wales 148–55
  in Welsh borderlands 115–29, 138–44
Owain of Gwent 113
oxen 85–97

Peada of Mercia 31–2
Penda of Mercia 23–52
  alliances with Welsh 23–52
  death of 38–43
  length of reign 31, 44
  name (British influence) 29–30
  religious tolerance 31–2
  sister 31
penn 29
Penwald 74

Index

Penwalh of Mercia 29, 54–5, 74
  British name of 54–5
Peterborough (looted by Hereward) 117–18, 146
Peterborough Chronicle (MS E of Anglo-Saxon Chronicle) 86, 116–17, 120, 138–55
  annal for (1052) 86
  annal for (1055) 116–17
  annal for (1063) 120
  annal for (1070) 117, 145–6
  annal for (1071) 141–2, 144–5
  annal for (1087) 148
  annal for (1094) 149
  annal for (1095) 150–1
  annal for (1096) 151–2
  annal for (1097) 152–3
Pillar of Eliseg 83, 98
Portskewett 113, 122
postcolonial theory 7, 11, 60, 67
Powys 4, 8–9, 23–52, 83–5, 115
Psalms (72:8) 84
pseudo-history 35, 160
psychomachia 71
Pybba 30, 37, 42, 52

Quadripartitus 2

rædboran 1–3
raiding 33, 82–108, 111–18, 122–5, 143–53
  and Vikings 85–9
Ralph, earl of Hereford 116–19
Ralph Mortimer 148
rebellion 122–9, 138–58
  see also English resistance to Norman Conquest
Red Book of Hergest 35, 132
Reginald of Durham, *Life of St Oswald* 27, 45
Repton 54, 57
respite of the damned 61–3
Rhiwallon 121–5
Rhuddlan 121
Rhun ap Urien 27–8, 46
Rhys, king in southern Wales 154
Rhys Sais 74, 130
Richard, son of Scrob 125
Rieinmellt 46
Robert of Malpas 154

Robert of Rhuddlan 154
Roger de Lacy 148
Roger, earl of Shrewsbury 148
Roman Christianity 23–52

sais 54
Saxones 111
Scottish frontier 8, 20
Scriptores Historiae Augustae 84
Selyf ap Cynan 36, 48, 49
Shrewsbury 125–7, 136, 143–4, 148, 151, 154
Shropshire 37, 49, 124, 148–9
Sigeberht 34
silvatici 124, 144–7
Siward Bearn 142
Siward (earl) 116
slavery 82–108, 118
  laws concerning 85–90
  raiding 82–108
  Viking role in 87–90
Snowdon 151
social class 82–108
South English Legendary version of Guthlac's life 73, 80–1
South Wales 36, 111–15, 120, 149, 160
St Æthelberht's minster 117
St Alban 38
St Anthony 58, 71
St Guthlac *see* Guthlac of Crowland
St Swithun 88
St Tysilio 38
Stirling 40
subaltern 7, 11
succession 30–1
Sunday rest *see* respite of the damned
Sweyn II of Denmark 145
Sweyn Godwinson 115

taxation 124, 149, 151
Tees (river) 143, 147
Tostig Godwinson 120–3
Trawsganu Kynan Garwyn mab Brochfael 36, 47–8
tumulus 61

Vikings 38, 69, 85–90, 110–11
violence to noncombatants 29–39, 53–9, 85–90, 96–7, 115–22

201

Index

Vita Haroldi 159–70
Vita Sancti Guthlaci see Felix, *Vita Sancti Guthlaci*
Vita Wulfstani 88

-*walh* element in name see *wealh*
Walter of Lacy 153
Walter Map, *De Nugis Curialium* 136
Waltham Abbey 160, 166
wang 65–7
warbands 53–9
   see also raiding
Warin the Bald 154
warranty 3
Wealas 85, 87, 94
wealh 3–5, 29–30, 46, 54–5, 87–8, 100
   meaning of 87–8, 100
   name-element 29–30, 46, 54–5
Welsh borderlands
   culture of/daily life in 1–6, 15–16, 29–39, 53–9
   definition of 6–12
   languages spoken in 1–6, 29–39, 53–9, 163
   military culture of 23–52, 53–9, 82–108, 109–29, 138–55
   religion of 23–43
Welsh identity 68
Welsh law 1–6, 85–90
   alltud 4, 19, 90
   animals in 85–90
   galanas 5, 86
   rights of women in 91
   see also Marcher Law

'Welsh penumbra' 11
Welsh triads 27
Went (river) 39
wergild 3–5
   of Britons 4
   Welsh equivalent of see *galanas*
Wessex/West Saxons 2–4, 110–14
West Welsh 113, 149
White Book of Rhydderch 35
wilderness 10, 62–9, 139–55
William the Conqueror 126–8, 136, 142–7, 150–5
William of Malmesbury, *Gesta Regum Anglorum* 88, 112, 146
   924 revolt at Chester 112
   Æthelstan fostered in Mercia 112
   lost panegyric for Æthelstan 112
William fitzOsbern 127, 153–4
William of Poitiers, *Gesta Guillelmi* 126, 153
Winchester 161
winter 92, 95, 121, 127, 143–4, 151
Winwæd, Battle of (655) 25, 38–43
witan 1–3
women, property rights of 1, 91
wonfah Wale 85, 91, 94
woods see forest
Wye (river) 2, 95

yoke 88–9, 91
York 9, 25, 36, 123, 137, 141, 147
Yorkshire 24, 123
Ystrad Tywi 111

EU authorised representative for GPSR:
Easy Access System Europe, Mustamäe tee 50,
10621 Tallinn, Estonia
gpsr.requests@easproject.com

www.ingramcontent.com/pod-product-compliance
Ingram Content Group UK Ltd.
Pitfield, Milton Keynes, MK11 3LW, UK
UKHW021840140426
5217IPUK00022B/1537